MAX BEERBOHM'S LETTERS TO
REGGIE TURNER

MAX BEERBOHM'S
LETTERS TO REGGIE TURNER

BY MAX BEERBOHM

edited by
Rupert Hart-Davis

J. B. LIPPINCOTT COMPANY
Philadelphia and New York
1965

The passage on pages 13-14 is quoted from *And Even Now* by Max Beerbohm. Copyright, 1921, by E. P. Dutton & Co., Inc. Renewal, 1949, by Max Beerbohm. Reprinted by permission of the publishers.

The quotations on pages 56 and 250 are from *Seven Men* and *Mainly on the Air* respectively, published in the U.S.A. by Alfred A. Knopf, and are reprinted by permission of the publisher.

This work is published in England under the title
Letters to Reggie Turner

Letters copyright © 1964 by Eva Reichmann
Editorial matter copyright © 1964 by Rupert Hart-Davis
Printed in the United States of America
Library of Congress Catalog Card Number: 65-15124

CONTENTS

ILLUSTRATIONS

INTRODUCTION

(1)

Max Beerbohm was born at 57 Palace Gardens Terrace, Kensington, on 24 August 1872. His father, Julius Edward Beerbohm, born at Memel in 1810, had settled in London during the 1830s. For many years he was a successful corn-merchant and he founded two commercial newspapers. He was a cultivated man of great charm and spoke seven languages. In 1849 he married Constantia Draper, by whom he had four children: Ernest Frederick William (b. 1851); Herbert Draper (b. 1852 and later famous as Herbert Beerbohm Tree); Julius (b. 1854): and Constance Marie (Con, b. 1856).

In 1858 Mrs Beerbohm died, and some time later her widower married her sister Eliza Draper (b. 1831). By her he had another five children: Matilda Helen (b. 1863); twin daughters in 1865, Gertrude and Marie Agnes (Aggie); Dora Margaretta (b. 1868); and finally Max.

Soon after his birth the family moved to Clanricarde Gardens, Bayswater, and from 1881 to 1885 Max attended a school run by Mr Wilkinson in nearby Orme Square. From 1885 to 1890 he was at Charterhouse, where he made little mark, apart from publishing his first drawings in the school paper, and in October 1890 he went up to Merton College, Oxford, to read Classics. For his first year he lived in Mob Quad, and thereafter in rooms at 19 Merton Street.

(2)

Reggie Turner's parentage is still obscure. He believed that he had been born on 2 June 1869, but I can find no birth-certificate in confirmation. Many people assumed that he was an illegitimate son of the newspaper proprietor Edward Levy (1833–1916), who later changed his name to Lawson, was made a baronet in 1892, and in 1903 became the first Lord Burnham. Following this persistent rumour, and lacking any contradictory evidence, I so described him in the first printing of *The Letters of Oscar Wilde* (1962), but I have since come to think otherwise.

The common gossip about Reggie's parentage has been summed

up by Hesketh Pearson, on the authority of Lord Alfred Douglas, as follows:

He was the illegitimate son of a well-known and wealthy news-paper proprietor, who had two children by a Frenchwoman, Frank Lawson and Reginald Turner, as well as other children by other women. His method was to allow £100 a year for the keep of each of his offspring up to the age of twelve, when, after an interview, he would settle a considerable sum on those he liked. On the whole he was a good 'natural' father, for even the children he did not like were given a fair start in life. In due time Frank Lawson came up for inspection, passed with flying colours, and was enriched; but Reginald Turner was not so lucky, his father dying before he could qualify for the donation. However, Frank was a generous fellow, and an income of five or six hundred pounds a year was passed on to Reginald, who inherited a lot more at the death of his elder brother.[1]

Douglas was seldom a reliable witness, but he never quarrelled with Reggie, and there seems little reason why he should have invented such a story. Except for the statement that the two boys were sons of the same mother (which Douglas himself contradicted by referring to them as half-brothers[2]) I am inclined to accept the story as basically true, and if one so accepts it, Reggie's father can hardly have been the first Lord Burnham, who lived until 1916, when Reggie was supposedly forty-seven.

I am now convinced that Reggie was in fact the son of Lord Burnham's uncle, Lionel Lawson (originally Levy), who was born in 1824 and died in 1879, when Reggie was supposedly ten. Lionel inherited a large fortune from his father Moses Lionel Levy, and increased it by building a prosperous printing-ink factory in France. When his elder brother, Joseph Moses Levy (father of the future Lord Burnham), took over the *Daily Telegraph* from its founder, Colonel Arthur Burroughes Sleigh, in 1855, Lionel put up half the necessary capital. In 1867 he built the Queen's Theatre in Long Acre, and in 1867–68 the Gaiety Theatre in the Strand. He was described in obituary notices as a gay and generous bachelor, with a flat in the Boulevard des Italiens, another in the roof of the Gaiety,

[1] *The Life of Oscar Wilde* (1946), pp. 266–7.
[2] *Autobiography* (1929), p. 73.

8

and some connection with Brighton. In his will, which is dated 4 August 1875, he wrote:

> I appoint my nephew Edward Levy and George Faudel Phillips[1] of Newgate Street Executors and Trustees of my Will and Guardians of Reginald Turner and Frank Simpson hereinafter named.

Then, after bequests to his brother and sisters, he instructs his executors:

> To pay to Fannie Simpson of Peterborough an annuity of £500 for her life. To pay to Reginald Turner who is at school at Hova Villas Brighton an annuity of £100 per annum for his life.
>
> I confirm all settlements made by me at any time, particularly the settlement made by me on my daughter Louise on her marriage with Sir George R. Prescott, Baronet.

The residue of his estate is to be divided into five parts, of which four go to his nephews and nieces, and:

> One part free of legacy succession duty to Frank Simpson who was lately at school at Hova Villas Brighton aforesaid and he is to take the name of Lawson.

This he did. Frank Lawson and Reggie always treated each other as brothers, and when Frank married in 1886 he gave Lionel Lawson as his father's name. When he died in 1920 he left Reggie £20,000 and half the residue of his estate, which totalled £200,479.[2] The other half he left to Louise Prescott. She died in 1922, aged sixty-eight. The identity of her mother is unknown, but she always described herself in *Who's Who* as "daughter of Lionel Lawson," and it is possible that, despite his reputation as a gay bachelor, her father was in fact married to her mother; his open recognition of her as his daughter in his will rather suggests this.

The implications of Lionel Lawson's will seem to me inescapable.

[1] Who had married Edward Levy's sister Helen in 1867. See also note, p. 228.
[2] When the last of Frank's children died in December 1930 Reggie referred to him as his "half-nephew" in a letter to Mrs Frank Harris, and to Max he wrote: "That accounts for the last of any sort and kind of relations I have ever had." All three of Lord Burnham's children were still alive.

Both Frank and Reggie were his illegitimate sons, but Frank, having passed his twelfth birthday (he was born in 1864 or 1865), came into a fifth of the estate, whereas Reggie, still only ten (or perhaps even nine), was left only the £100 a year of the gossips' story—which incidentally the will largely substantiates. Both boys were sent to the same school, and given the same guardians, and this is surely how Edward Lawson came to be considered Reggie's father.

Moreover, when it began to be rumoured that Reggie's father was a rich man called Lawson who owned some of the *Daily Telegraph*, people naturally assumed him to be the increasingly well-known Edward Lawson rather than the long-dead and forgotten Lionel. For instance, Mr S. N. Behrman, who must have obtained his information from Max, writes (*Conversation with Max*, p. 184): ". . . Turner's father, Lord Burnham. He was the proprietor of the *Daily Telegraph* and a great pioneer in English journalism. He also owned the Gaiety Theatre." Lionel in his day owned considerably more of the *Daily Telegraph* than Lord Burnham, and Lord Burnham never owned the Gaiety Theatre. In his will (1909), in which there is no mention of Reggie, Lord Burnham wrote "whereas I have three children and no more," and then named them. Lionel was admittedly a gay dog, but I have never read or heard any similar suggestion concerning Lord Burnham, except for this mistaken attribution of Reggie's paternity.

The conclusive evidence comes from Reggie himself. In a letter to Violet Schiff dated 8 August 1933 he wrote: "Lord Pirbright's second wife was the sister of a man who married a cousin of mine."

Henry de Worms, Baron Pirbright (1840–1903), married in 1887 as his second wife Sarah, sister of Sir George Faudel-Phillips.

Sir George Faudel-Phillips was married to Helen Levy, daughter of Joseph Moses Levy and sister of the first Lord Burnham. She was thus a niece of Lionel Lawson.

If Reggie's father was Lionel, Helen was indeed his cousin; she would have been his aunt if his father was Lord Burnham. Although cousin is often a loosely used word I can think of no reason why an aunt should be so described.

(3)

If Lionel Lawson was Reggie's father, who was his mother?

From Lionel's will the immediate assumption is that Fannie Simpson was Frank's mother, and that the absence from the will of any other lady who might have been Reggie's mother is explained by her already being dead, estranged or provided for. On the other hand, Fannie Simpson may have been the mother of both the boys, or of neither. And here again gossip takes a hand.

The general belief was that Reggie's mother was a French actress or singer called (probably only on the stage) Miss L. Henrie. When John Hollingshead, the first lessee of the Gaiety Theatre, wrote its history (*Gaiety Chronicles*, 1898) he said that people "no doubt wondered why a capitalist like Mr Lionel Lawson with no particular lady *protégée* connected with the stage . . . should have turned his financial attention to theatrical 'bricks and mortar'." But one cannot help wondering whether he does not protest a little too much, and whether one of Lionel Lawson's objects in building the theatre, with his own flat in the roof, was not precisely what Hollingshead goes out of his way to disclaim. At all events, when the new theatre opened on 21 December 1868 with a triple bill (operetta, comedy-drama and operatic extravaganza) the cast of the third and longest item, *Robert the Devil* by W. S. Gilbert, headed by Alfred Wigan, Madge Robertson (later Kendal) and Nellie Farren, included Miss L. Henrie in the part of Ferdinando.

In the next production, *Columbus*, an opera bouffe by Alfred Thompson (July 1869), she appeared as Don Trabucos, one of Columbus's pupils; and in *A Life Chase*, a new drama by John Oxenford and Horace Wigan (autumn 1869), as Madame Godeau. Finally, in the new triple bill for Christmas 1869 she made two appearances: as Kate Landrail in *Uncle Dick's Darling*, a new drama by H. J. Byron; and as Walworth Road in *Wat Tyler M.P.*, an operatic extravaganza by George Augustus Sala. (The fact that three of these five rôles were masculine suggests a young and boyish appearance.) This bill ran until March 1870, after which Miss L. Henrie disappears from theatrical and all other history.

If she was indeed Reggie's mother, she can scarcely have given birth to him in the midst of all this activity on the stage, but if he was born a year later than he believed, i.e. on 2 June 1870, the dates agree well enough. Miss Henrie could conceivably have acted to within three months of his birth, or have left the Gaiety before the end of the run, and if she went home to France to have her baby, the absence of an English birth-certificate is explained.[1]

It seems safe to assume that Reggie was never sure who his mother was, and S. N. Behrman quotes Max as saying that Reggie "became very curious about his mother's identity, and he was about to engage in research on the subject when he was gently advised by his solicitor not to try to find out anything about her."[2]

(4)

After his early schooling at Hova Villas, Brighton, Reggie moved on in September 1884 to the nearby Hurstpierpoint College at Hassocks, Sussex, which he left in 1886. His next two years are a blank, but in October 1888 he turned up as an undergraduate at Merton College, Oxford. In 1892 he took a Third Class in Modern History, and in 1894 he was called to the Bar (Inner Temple), though he never practised. The rest of his story can be deduced from the letters and notes that follow.

Everyone who knew him agreed that he was a conversational wit of the highest order, some said the equal of Oscar Wilde himself. To Somerset Maugham he "was on the whole the most amusing man I have known . . . Reggie liked an audience, though he was quite content with one of three or four, and then he would take a theme, and embroider upon it with such drollery that he made your sides so ache with laughter that at last you had to beg him to stop."[3]

According to Osbert Sitwell, "the ugliness of his appearance at first took strangers aback, yet it was not unsympathetic and even possessed a certain distinction. It was a hideousness hard to describe, because the features and the whole face were rather formless. Out of a chaos of sallow skin and wrinkles shone two quick but contemplative, amused but rather melancholy, blue eyes, light in colour. His voice was emphatic and attractive, and there was an undoubted charm about him, especially when he talked, for he was

[1] The only other piece of evidence about Miss Henrie is in the second volume of Hollingshead's *My Lifetime* (1895) where she is described as "a sister of Madame Henriquez the concert singer," but she has proved equally elusive.
[2] *Conversation with Max* (1960), pp. 184–5.
[3] *The Vagrant Mood* (1952), p. 209.

a most lively and amusing companion . . . His jokes were often brilliant, his understanding of character most shrewd."[1]

Harold Acton described him as "one of the kindest and wittiest of men. Reggie was small, quietly dressed, with a sallow complexion, thick purplish lips and perpetually blinking eyes. Not prepossessing at a first glimpse, but his features were intensely mobile and this highly expressive mobility counteracted his ugliness and made you forget it. His wit had the lightest butterfly touch and fluttered its wings from what he left unsaid as well as from what he said."[2]

Max himself introduced Reggie as Comus in his essay "Laughter," which was published in *And Even Now*

Many of his acquaintances—friends, too—relatives, even— have lived and died in the belief that he was quite ordinary. Thus is he the more greatly valued by his cronies. Thus do we pride ourselves on possessing some curious right quality to which alone he is responsive. But it would seem that either this asset of ours or its effect on him is intermittent. He can be dull and null enough with us sometimes—a mere asker of questions, or drawer of comparisons between this and that brand of cigarettes, or full expatiator on the merits of some new patent razor. A whole hour and more may be wasted in such humdrum and darkness. And then—something will have happened. There has come a spark in the murk; a flame now, presage of a radiance: Comus has begun. His face is a great part of his equipment. A cast of it might be somewhat akin to the comic mask of the ancients; but no cast could be worthy of it; mobility is the essence of it. It flickers and shifts in accord to the matter of his discourse; it contracts and it expands; is there anything its elastic can't express? Comus would be eloquent even were he dumb. And he is mellifluous. His voice, while he develops an idea or conjures up a scene, takes on a peculiar richness and unction. If he be describing an actual scene, voice and face are adaptable to those of the actual persons therein. But it is not in such mimicry that he excels. As a reporter he has rivals. For the most part, he moves on a higher plane than that of mere fact: he imagines, he creates, giving you not a person, but a type, a synthesis, and not what anywhere has been, but what anywhere might be—what, as one feels, for all the absurdity of it,

[1] *Noble Essences* (1950), pp. 154–5.
[2] *Memoirs of an Aesthete* (1948), p. 64.

13

just would be. He knows his world well, and nothing human is alien to him, but certain skeins of life have a special hold on him, and he on them. In his youth he wished to be a clergyman; and over the clergy of all grades and denominations his genius hovers and swoops and ranges with a special mastery. Lawyers he loves less; yet the legal mind seems to lie almost as wide-open to him as the sacerdotal; and the legal manner in all its phases he can unerringly burlesque. In the minds of journalists, diverse journalists, he is not less thoroughly at home, so that of the wild contingencies imagined by him there is none about which he cannot reel off an oral "leader" or "middle" in the likeliest style, and with as much ease as he can preach a High Church or Low Church sermon on it. Nor are his improvisations limited by prose. If a theme calls for nobler treatment, he becomes an unflagging fountain of ludicrously adequate blank-verse. Or again, he may deliver himself in rhyme. There is no form of utterance that comes amiss to him for interpreting the human comedy, or for broadening the farce into which that comedy is turned by him. Nothing can stop him when once he is in the vein. No appeals move him. He goes from strength to strength while his audience is more and more piteously debilitated.

What a gift to have been endowed with! What a power to wield! And how often I have envied Comus! But this envy of him has never taken root in me. His mind laughs, doubtless, at his own conceptions; but not his body. And if you tell him something that you have been sure will convulse him you are likely to be rewarded with no more than a smile betokening that he sees the point. Incomparable laughter-giver, he is not much a laugher. He is vintner, not toper. I would therefore not change places with him. I am well content to have been his beneficiary during thirty years, and to be so for as many more as may be given us.

It has been said that Reggie was in some way offended by the passage, but this seems unlikely, and when he first read it on 1 January 1921 he wrote to Max:

I was very touched—I need hardly say—at the passage you intimate refers to me. It is a wonderful thing to think that I shall for ever lie snugly hidden in your prose, though I feel prematurely jealous that in future generations some earnest woman tutor will discover that Comus was W. L. Courtney.[1] But there it is, *I* shall know, in my little, little grave, and be very proud. As a matter of fact, though I rarely really laugh, I am capable of an awful laugh, though I don't quite know what excites it when I find it difficult to laugh—though not to enjoy—as merrily as most people often. The last huge laugh I had was when I read the bicycle scene in "Maltby and Braxton,"[2] when I laughed so terribly that I slightly ruptured myself, and the awkward thing is that when I have a bad cough—as I have had lately—I feel the rupture and that reminds me of the vision, and I have sternly to banish it—as St Anthony the ladies—lest I should begin to laugh again. Perhaps God has granted me a small faculty for laughter so that I shan't rupture myself all over.

When Max broadcast on "Speed" from London 19 on April 1936, he said:

> But, as a good listener, I rather sigh for the old leisurely repasts and the habit of lingering long after them to hear more from the lips of such talkers as Oscar Wilde or Henry James, Reginald Turner or Charles Brookfield.

That same evening Reggie wrote from Florence:

> I listened entranced. And then came among those names, very firmly and clearly, hitting me all over, my own! Not by my merit indeed but your faithful affection. To me it was terribly dramatic. I confess that the rest of the broadcast was somewhat blurred by my emotion. . . . It was a sensation I never thought to experience.

Unfortunately Reggie's wit deserted him when he tried to write it down. His letters are gossipy, affectionate, and touching, but only occasionally witty. None of his twelve novels achieved any great success, and he was fond of saying that, whereas most authors' first editions were rare, with him it was the second editions.

But the quality in Reggie that most deeply appealed to his true friends was his ready understanding and unfailing sympathy. Everyone, from Oscar Wilde to Max, wrote more frankly and freely to him than to anyone else. Max was never a copious or a willing letter-writer, and I know no other series of his letters so revealing and affectionate as these.

[1] See note, p. 135.   [2] In Max's *Seven Men.*

Apart from his possessions and money in Italy Reggie left £40,943. Of this he bequeathed £8000 to his Italian servants and their son; £3000 to Max: £6000 to Giuseppe Martino (Pino) Orioli, the Florentine bookseller and publisher; £5500 to his and Orioli's friend Corrado Gerbi; and the residue to Orioli.[1] Doubtless his effects in Italy went to Orioli too, and on 25 July 1939 the majority of his books, drawings and papers were sold at Sotheby's, where they fetched £3145.

Orioli died in Lisbon in 1942, leaving everything to his secretary–companion, and in 1946 Irving Davis, Orioli's former partner, went to Florence to buy the antiquarian portion of his library. Max's friends, Selwyn and Tania Jepson, accompanied him with the object of buying the English section of the library, much of it inherited from Reggie. Among the books and papers they bought were 235 letters from Max to Reggie. These Tania Jepson transcribed, took to Rapallo and offered to Max. He read them with the greatest interest and amusement, but refused to take them, saying that he was only too thankful they should have fallen into her hands. He said he would have no objection to their publication after his death provided that they were purged of anything that might offend or cause pain, and that certain youthful extravagances were removed. He accordingly went through them, marking the passages for excision and providing a few explanatory notes (here prefaced by the words "Max noted").

His wishes have been respected, and 200 of the letters are here printed, in whole or in part; 183 of them from the originals, which are now in the Houghton Library at Harvard, and the other seventeen from Mrs Jepson's transcripts of originals which were later destroyed. Each of these seventeen is indicated in the text by an asterisk after its date. All the excisions, of whatever length, are represented by three dots, except for an occasional postscript which I have removed without trace. Occasionally, to save further excision, I have replaced a name by a misleading initial. I dislike having to print incomplete letters, but here the excised letters and passages are mostly of little interest or importance, and I prefer to accept

[1] If Orioli predeceased him, half was to go to Merton College and half to the City of Florence.

Max's very reasonable conditions rather than relegate the whole correspondence to limbo.

One hundred and two of Reggie's letters to Max have survived, and are also at Harvard. I have quoted from them in the footnotes as much as seemed necessary or interesting.

(6)

Max's handwriting is almost always legible, and his spelling good. I have silently corrected slips and have not hesitated to repunctuate in aid of the reader or the sense. In his early letters Max, like Oscar Wilde, often used a short dash to represent every punctuation-mark: later he became more exact and careful.

Each address from which Max wrote is given in full the first time it occurs, and thereafter abbreviated to the essential minimum. No distinction has been made between printed and written addresses. For convenience the address is always printed on the right, and the date, in standardised form, on the left. Abbreviations in the text have been lengthened, and figures of small numbers written out in words. The printing of titles has been standardised: those of poems, stories and articles are printed in Roman type between quotation marks; those of books, plays and periodicals in italics. All foreign words are printed in italics. All dates not written by Max are enclosed within square brackets: doubtful ones are preceded by a query.

At one time or another Max drew caricatures of almost everyone who is mentioned in this book, but to avoid overcrowding the footnotes I have referred only to the drawings that are directly relevant to the letters. Full details will be included in the complete catalogue of Max's caricatures on which I am now engaged.

(7)

In preparing this edition my greatest debt is to Mrs Eva Reichmann, Max's sister-in-law and the owner of the copyright in all his letters, caricatures and writings. She inherited me as editor of these letters from her beloved sister Elisabeth Beerbohm, and she has treated me with the utmost generosity, trust, encouragement and forbearance.

My debt to Mrs Tania Jepson is also immense. She transcribed all Max's letters with great skill and care, and helped me to check all their dates and envelopes. Further than that, she transcribed all Reggie's surviving letters to Max, and only those unfortunates who have attempted to decipher Reggie's execrable hand will appreciate her astonishing success.

The whole undertaking has been carried out with the permission and help of the Harvard College Library, and I am deeply indebted to Mr W. H. Bond and the staff of the Houghton Library for much kindness and expert help.

For permission to publish copyright material I am grateful to the following: Mr Harold Acton and Messrs Methuen & Co. Ltd for a passage from *Memoirs of An Aesthete*; Miss Dorothy Collins for an extract from Mrs G. K. Chesterton's diary; Messrs William Heinemann Ltd for quotations from *And Even Now, Mainly On The Air, Seven Men* and *Zuleika Dobson*; Mr John James for a letter by Henry James; Mr W. Somerset Maugham and Messrs William Heinemann Ltd for an extract from *The Vagrant Mood*; Mrs Hesketh Pearson and Messrs Methuen & Co. Ltd for a passage from *The Life of Oscar Wilde;* Sir Osbert Sitwell and Messrs Macmillan for a quotation from *Noble Essences.*

For providing me with three of my best illustrations I am indebted to Mr Alvin Langdon Coburn, Mr Carl Van Vechten and Mr Brian Daley, the Secretary of the Myrmidon Club at Merton, who also allowed me to examine and quote from the club's minute-book.

The Warden and Fellows of Merton have given me unlimited access to the collection in the Max Beerbohm Room in the College, and have allowed me to reprint a silhouette and quote from letters. I owe much to them, and in particular to Dr Roger Highfield, who has taken immense pains to identify past members of the College and has helped me in countless ways. So too has Mr P. S. Morrish of the College Library.

For much information in the footnotes I am once again deeply indebted to that genius of research, Mr Ernest Mehew. His flair is equalled only by his assiduity and his kindness. I should have been in a poor way without him.

Messrs Raymond Mander and Joe Mitchenson have generously supplied me with much theatrical information, and for a variety of help I salute with gratitude Mr Harold Acton; Mr Nicolas Barker; Mr Wilfrid Blunt; Mr John Benson, Secretary of the Eighty Club; Mr Coss Bilson, Secretary of the National Liberal Club;

Mrs Lysandros Caftanzoglu; Miss Jane Cain; Lord David Cecil; Mrs Marguerite Cockerell; Mr S. C. Cockerell; Mr E. V. Corbett of the Central Library, Wandsworth; Miss Grace Cranston; Mr J. S. Davey of the National Central Library; Mrs Molly Estridge; Mr Dwye Evans; Mr George Freedley of the Theatre Collection, New York Public Library; Mr Roger Fulford; Miss Freda Gaye; the Reverend Mother and Sister Grizel Margaret, S.S.S.M., of St Saviour's Priory; Mr Stuart Hibberd; Mr Anthony Hobson; Mr Laurence Irving; Mr F. R. Kaye of Messrs Ladbroke & Co Ltd; Mr Collie Knox; Professor Dan H. Laurence; Mr Christopher Medley; Mr Percy Muir; Sir Ralph Murray; Mr Simon Nowell-Smith; Mrs J. M. Patterson of the Royal Society of Literature; Mrs Mary Price; Sir Sydney Roberts; the Countess of Rosse; Mrs Norah Smallwood; Professor Arnold Toynbee; Miss Margaret Toynbee; Major R. J. Treyer-Evans, Bursar of Hurstpierpoint College; Mr R. Walters of the Oxford Union Society; Mrs Katharine Grant Watson; Mr Bart Weiner; Professor Stanley Weintraub; Professor Roberto Weiss; and Mr H. D. Ziman.

The book has been read in proof, and its notes much improved, by Professor Richard Ellmann, Mrs Jepson, Mr Henry Maas, Mr Mehew, Mrs Reichmann and Mr Robin Wright.

August 1964   RUPERT HART-DAVIS

Thursday [20 August 1891]   *Hôtel des Pays Bas, Spa*

My dear Turner,

I suppose that you and Madame[1] have got my letter safely. There is not much more to tell you. Spa is a very dull place—quite a little purgatory—Hell, if Hell had mineral springs. However I shall be carried to Abraham's bosom—in the form of Ostend—by next Monday perhaps. My mother and one of my sisters leave for Switzerland before then.

Now that I have been rejected by the Cercle des Etrangers of the Casino there is extremely little to do. A few nights ago I went with my people to an evening fête in the open air near Spa. The grounds were lighted with many lamps: near the entrance the words *Aux Dames* were brilliantly depicted in green lamps, which was rather awkward for delicate-minded English people. The evening was glacially cold. Napoleon crossing the Alps was cosy by comparison. (Smart, that.)

Have you read Willard's article in the *P.M. Budget*? Jones is said to have absolutely no dramatic instinct, and from what I have seen of him he is a very weak-minded person, so I don't wonder at his wishing to be in an autocratic position of his own. Shocking taste of Willard to say that about Jones's H's.[2]

I found your advertisement in the *Daily Telegraph* yesterday and have pasted it on the other side of this sheet with a picture. Dear old fellow, I am *awfully* glad. And how quiet you were about it all the time at Rouen. By marrying Miss Powell you will of course have the entrée of the Corporals' Combination Room of the Second Dragoon Guards. Calculating rogue!

Greet for me Lemanion, who, though zealous in the faith, did seem unto me in wit lacking. Greet Peria, who was in all ministration

---

[1] Madame d'Oliviera, in whose house Reggie was lodging at Bois Guillaume, near Rouen.
[2] "In Defence of Actor Managers," an article by the actor Edmund Smith Willard (1853–1915) appeared in the *Pall Mall Budget* on 13 August 1891. In it he criticised the playwright Henry Arthur Jones for announcing the taking of a London theatre for the production of his new play.

unto me most gracious.[1] Strengthen the brethren of Oxonia, unto whomsoever thou shalt first send message. Who are, I take cognisance, scattered.

Farewell. Sorry, but I took you for the Ephesians.

Love to Madame.[2]

[*Late June 1892*]   *19 Hyde Park Place*

Many thanks, my dear Turner, for your delightful and long letter —many pleas for forgiveness also for want of initiative on my own part. . . . In my way I have been enjoying myself quite egregiously well—not bored once. I went to the *Pantomime Rehearsal*,[3] and thought the dancing very pretty indeed and Miss Terriss quite charming, but the play itself! What a play! I give you my word I did not once laugh throughout the whole evening. I thought it too dull, too flat, too stupid and conventional for words. Perhaps I am singular in this as in all other respects. I went also to the Gaiety, where Letty Lind now acts Cinder-Ellen most nicely.[4] . . .

Isn't it killing also about Oscar's *Salome* being interdicted by the Lord Chamberlain.[5] I have designed a great picture in which King Bull makes a great feast and when they have feasted the daughter of Mrs Grundy dances before them and pleases the King—insomuch that he promises her whatsoever she shall desire. After consultation with her mother she demands that "they bring unto her by and by the head of Oscar the Poëtast on a charger." The picture—which will be

[1] Peria was almost certainly a servant at Bois Guillaume, and Lemanion another acquaintance there.

[2] The last page of the letter is reproduced opposite.

[3] *A Pantomime Rehearsal*, a burlesque by Cecil Clay, first produced at Terry's Theatre on 6 June 1891, had reopened at the Court on 29 February 1892, with Ellaline Terriss in the cast. It ran there till 15 October.

[4] *Cinder-Ellen Up Too Late*, a burlesque by A. C. Torr and W. T. Vincent, with music by Meyer Lutz, had been first produced at the Gaiety Theatre on 24 December 1891. The title-rôle, created by Kate James, had now been taken over by Letty Lind.

[5] *Salome* was in rehearsal at the Palace Theatre, with Sarah Bernhardt in the title-rôle, when towards the end of June the Lord Chamberlain refused to license the production, on the ground that it contained biblical characters.

OXFORD.—ZÆO.—Exclusively engaged.

Merton Chapel — Canon Freeling officiating

The pasted-on advertisement appeared on the front page of the *Daily Telegraph* on 17, 18, 19 and 20 August 1891 as part of the publicity of the Oxford Music Hall. At the top of the bill was Zæo, a beautiful female gymnast, who had caused a sensation at the Royal Aquarium, Westminster, in 1890. Two clergymen on the Theatres and Music Halls Committee of the newly (1888) established London County Council protested at the poster advertising Zæo, "which disgraced the walls of the metropolis" and which they described as a "most gross and wanton insult to the delicacy of London's moral feeling." They were ruled out of order, but the episode gave Zæo much free publicity, and by the time she reached the Oxford Music Hall in May 1891 she was being advertised on the largest posters ever seen in London, 45 ft × 13 ft 4 inches.

George Nowell Freeling (c. 1830–92) was a Fellow of Merton from 1852 and Chaplain from 1869.

MAX   REGGIE

THE MYRMIDON CLUB MERTON COLLEGE

called *The Modern Salome*—represents Lord Lathom[1] holding the charger. . . .

Your affectionate friend   MAX BEERBOHM

Friday [Early July 1892]   *19 Hyde Park Place*
My dear Turner,

     I do not exactly know what course Oscar will take: but inasmuch as French naturalisation entails a period of service in the French army, I fancy that his house in Tite Street will not be in the hands of an agent.[2]

     I shall not be able to visit Rouen "before your *viva*" as I have promised to stay on my way with some friends at Fontainebleau. I shall however be at Rouen simultaneously with you—July 24 I suppose. . . .

     I am afraid I should have no use for the "standing desk." As to the screen, I should like it immensely: it is very good of you.

     Unless—a very possible contingency—my plans change I shall not be up for your *viva* at Oxford. . . .

     I am going to bring a copy of *Richard Feverel*[3] with me to Rouen: which, I insist, you shall read but *not* in the W.C.

     I saw Henry Irving Junior in Brook Street today: also a photograph of him in the Burlington Arcade.[4] . . .

Yours   MAX

P.S. I take great interest in the General Election: do you?[5] I am going to take you in hand as soon as I come to Rouen.

[1] Edward Bootle-Wilbraham, first Earl of Lathom (1837–98), was Lord Chamberlain 1892–95.
[2] As a result of the banning of *Salome* Wilde had threatened to move to France and take up French citizenship.
[3] *The Ordeal of Richard Feverel*, by George Meredith (1859).
[4] Henry Brodribb Irving, actor and criminologist (1870–1919), had been an undergraduate at New College, where Max breakfasted with him (see "H. B. Irving as a Young Man" in *Mainly on the Air*, 1957).
[5] Lord Salisbury's Conservative Government had resigned. Parliament was dissolved on 29 June, and as a result of the ensuing General Election Gladstone was returned to power as Liberal Prime Minister for the fourth and last time.

Saturday [*July 1892*]*   *19 Hyde Park Place*

My dear Turner . . .

I have done nothing much lately except dabbling in the Law Courts and the Music Halls. I am in rather good spirits today seeing that Newnes of the *Strand Magazine*[1] has accepted twenty drawings of mine called "Club Types": what he will pay I know not: they are well worth £1000 in my opinion.[2]

I was so pleased with your excellent ballads: do write some more —also some rondeaux.

By the way the people at Fontainebleau were genuine, but I think I shall not go there at any rate until after Rouen. I want however very much to spend two or three days at Dieppe so as to try my luck *aux petits chevaux*: useless I suppose to ask you to be with me? . . .   Yours MAX

[*Early September 1892*]   *19 Hyde Park Place*

My dear Reg,

Thank you so much for your kind letter. It seems strange that sympathy at a time like this should be of any comfort, but I do find that it is.[3]

I was going to write to you and tell you of my father's death last week, only I thought you had doubtless left Rouen by that time. If I had caught the train that morning, I might just have seen my father living: but I might have been an hour too late and that would have been more painful.

He was buried last Saturday. I do not quite know where I shall go now; my people have let the house which they had taken in Brighton.

Do let me hear from you again. I think it was quite the best thing to give up the Continent and its quarantines for the present.

Ever yours MAX

[1] George Newnes (1851–1910) had founded the *Strand Magazine* in 1891. He was made a Baronet in 1895.
[2] In fact thirty-six of these drawings appeared in the *Strand Magazine*, eighteen in September, nine each in November and December. They were the first of Max's caricatures to be published outside a school magazine.
[3] Max's father, Julius Beerbohm, had died on 30 August 1892, aged eighty-two.

[September 1892][1]   *[London]*

My dear Reg,

It is so good of Mrs Lawson[2] to ask me to stay. I should like it immensely and have just written to her. (They say my hand is getting illegible, by the way; is this so?)

Are you quite well? I have been rather liverish for the last few days. So glad you liked the *Strand*: the fool of an editor or manager does not know what to pay me and wishes to see me personally: no doubt he draws the line at £500.

Yours in great haste because of the post   MAX

[September 1892]   *19 Hyde Park Place*

My dear Reg,

I broke off my letter last night in such a hurry that I must resume its thread. I have just written to the man at the *Strand* office to say that I am leaving town and so cannot see him. If I went, that dreadful Shrimpton scene would be repeated I expect—five shillings, half-a-crown and then splitting the difference.[3] By the way you remember those links you gave me? Well I have had them enamelled (two l's?) and they look charming and nor threats nor entreaties will make me return them. London is really awful—I admit it—just now, but I am going away today and look forward to seeing you next week. I hope that the letters I wrote to you and to Mrs Lawson were in time yesterday for the post.

Oscar is writing a play[4] which my brother will *probably* have, but this is a secret.   Yours   MAX

P.S. I went down to Charterhouse the other day, putting up at an inn in the town. After a solitary dinner I walked up the hill and peered through the windows of my house where boys were sitting

[1] Written on black-edged paper.
[2] Reggie's half-brother Frank Lawson had married in 1886 Mary Comber, widow of Sir Julius Benedict.
[3] Thomas Shrimpton & Son, booksellers and publishers of Broad Street, Oxford, in whose window Max's caricatures had sometimes been displayed.
[4] *A Woman of No Importance.*

at "preparation" with rough hair on long forms giggling covertly—just as when I was among them. I suppose if I went there twenty years hence I should see just the same thing. Isn't school an awful place?

Monday [*10 October 1892*][1]*   [*London*]

My dear Reg,

Many thanks for your letter which arrived after I had sent mine off. . . . Yesterday I paid little Ross[2] a long visit in Kensington and we had a long comfortable chat about "certain forms of crime"[3] and John Gray[4] and St Cyres[5] and modern poetry and other select topics. It seems that he writes a good deal for the *National Observer*, but does not at all like Henley because he uses such frightful language and pays very poorly. We are going to dine together tonight at some place ending in -ino,[6] and do something or other afterwards.

I am rather sorry it is my last night in town and the last night of my long vac: which I have on the whole enjoyed: especially Bois Guillaume and Aboyne. . . . Thanks very much for my battels.[7]

With kind regards to Mr and Mrs Lawson.

Ever yours   MAX

Friday [*?14 October 1892*]   *Merton College, Oxford*

My dear Reg![8]

Forgive a broken pen—the only one in the Club. I am *delighted* at the thought of seeing you again in Oxford and trust *implicitly*

[1] Written on black-edged paper.
[2] Robert Baldwin Ross (1869–1918), literary journalist and art-critic, Oscar Wilde's most faithful friend.
[3] Cf. p. 97, line 7.
[4] 1866–1934. Poet and Roman Catholic priest.
[5] Stafford Harry Northcote, Viscount St Cyres (1869–1926), only son of the second Earl of Iddesleigh. Merton undergraduate 1888–92, Christ Church don 1893. It was in his rooms that Max first met Will Rothenstein (see note, p. 56).
[6] Solferino's in Rupert Street, off Shaftesbury Avenue, which was frequented by the staff of W. E. Henley's *National Observer* (the Henley Regatta, Max called them).
[7] Terminal bills in Oxford colleges.
[8] Max first wrote "Turner" and then replaced it with "Reg!"

that you will not change that kaleidoscope, your mind. I am sending you the Henley books which are rather dilapidated to look at but really most brilliant.

Blackwell's shop sprinkled all over with copies of R le G's book.[1] I spent a long time there yesterday afternoon, unable to think that your form was not flitting to and fro amongst the bookcases. I have got off Collections![2] Isn't it clever of me? Thus: I told How[3] that at the beginning of the Vac I had decided to read a pass and so had not done a stroke of work. At the same time I was willing to stay up for the four years and read for Honours if *he* thought it any good. . . . To-morrow morning then I shall see the Professor and hear the conclusion of the whole matter. Now that I have been so very very near a pass and freedom after the third year I cannot help regretting rather that I did not seize these good things once and for all. But I am young and strong and Europe is before me. . . .

By the way, do you know that the play has been finally accepted by my brother.[4] Please thank Mrs Lawson for her kind letter and for *The Happy Prince*.[5] Have you quite persuaded her that you did not annotate the Giant story?

What a descent from my tiny writing of yore. My affectations are dying for want of an audience: so come unfailingly.

Yours MAX

[*?October 1892*]   *Myrmidon Club*,[6] *Oxford*

My dear Reg,

In a certain house in the best street in Oxford there is a little room papered in blue and white. In this room, between two windows,

---

[1] Richard Le Gallienne's recently published *New Poems*, of which his wife reported a pile of copies in a bookshop on 3 October 1892.
[2] The terminal examination held in each Oxford college.
[3] Walter Wybergh How (1861–1932), Fellow of Merton from 1884, and lecturer in Classics.
[4] *A Woman of No Importance.*
[5] By Oscar Wilde (1888).
[6] According to its minute-book "this club was established in Merton by several members of the College in October 1865. The number of members was originally limited to twelve and its object was 'to explore the rivers

stands a soft, small bed. At this moment it is being smoothed and warmed by the hands of serving-girls. Someone is going to sleep in it when night comes tomorrow and when the day after that is wrapped in night. It is so, is it not? How nice it will be.

Yours MAX

P.S. I have engaged you a bedroom at Adamson's. Hope you'll turn up in good time tomorrow.

[*Postmark 23 November 1892*]*   *Merton College*

My dear Reg,

How sorry I am to have kept you till the other day in suspense about the theatre. The fact was (not the fiction is) I had misread your note and had understood you to say that if I liked to come next Saturday you would be charmed, but as the end of term was so near you thought it would hardly be worth while before the vac.

My people are at Brighton: they leave soon—probably to stay at Tunbridge Wells: which is I believe a healthy place, and surely the Pantiles will inspire in me a masterly *rondeau*. But I shall certainly be in London at some time and then we must grace some theatre together. . . .

And you, are you coming to Oxford again this term? I hope that yes. Oxford simply yawns for you and I want you to see a beautiful new lampshade which I have acquired. It is of green silk made out of the green cloth of the roulette-table. (For I have sat much this term at the receipt of custom and a Goddess has winged the ball in my favour.) . . .

Another freshman—Bush James[1]—was lunching with me the other day. "Where," asked he, "is Turner? I haven't seen him about lately." "Turner?" I said with a vague smile. "Yes," was the reply;

---

and streams of Europe'—which was however subsequently abandoned." Today the club holds terminal dinners, but it no longer enjoys the club-room over the shop of Adamson the tailor in the High Street, from which Max was writing. (See "Groups of Myrmidons" in *More*, 1899.)

[1] George Fitzhugh Bush James (b. 1873) was a Merton undergraduate 1892–94.

"that man who sang *so awfully well* at the S.C.S.[1] wine." I explained that you had taken your degree and had only been up on a visit. He suggested that you ought to go on the stage where you would make your fortune. "It is his great ambition," I said and began to puff you mercilessly: winding up by saying that you were a charming man—up to a certain point, but that one never seemed to get any "forrader" with you. Am I not a friend?

Your affectionate MAX

[*Postmark 19 December 1892*]   *Moreland House, Tunbridge Wells*

My dear Reg,

There you have my address: make the most of it, by writing often and a great deal at a time. I so enjoyed myself in London: how charming the knowledge that one need not be in all night unless one particularly wishes to be: the result naturally being that one turns in at 11.30. Have you had an answer from the Powers at the Haymarket as to the first night?[2] I am quite happy in my way here and am much admired: my buff surtout is *the* sensation of the Pantiles and renews almost the days of Beau Austin and his merrymen—or was it Robin Hood who had merrymen?[3]

I am going to employ my time with a series of Oxford Studies (this is quite true): a kind of types such as Rudolph the Lehmann published in *Punch*:[4] they will be for the most part personal attacks on my friends . . . but not a word to *anybody*: for they will be published very anonymously by Blackwell or somebody and will be of wonderful brilliancy.[5]

[1] *Septem Contra Somnum* (Seven Against Sleep), a Merton club, founded in the 1880s to sit up all night discussing the affairs of this world and the next. It eventually developed into a wine-club and was finally merged with the Myrmidon.

[2] Of *Hypatia* (see next letter).

[3] *Beau Austin*, a Regency play set in Tunbridge Wells, by W. E. Henley and Robert Louis Stevenson, had been produced by Tree at the Haymarket Theatre on 3 November 1890.

[4] Rudolph Chambers Lehmann (1856–1919), author, journalist and oarsman, was on the staff of *Punch*, 1890–1919, and was the father of Rosamond, Beatrix and John Lehmann.

[5] This project came to nothing.

I do hope you will pass easily your exam[1]—do you think I shall do well in Greats? I am sure you have all the ability to get through and a good lot to spare, only you are such an idle chap and *won't work*. Is not that nice of me? Confess you are pleased by it. The only complete art of letter-writing—I am persuaded—is to talk about your interlocutor (or interscriptor or whatever it is) and about nothing else. Lord Chesterfield did this to his nephew, Fénelon did it to Women, and St Paul did it to the Ephesians. And are not their quills standing in the pen-rack of Olympus? Of Cicero and Byron, the egotists, whoever takes account? Yet their letters were masterpieces one and all.

But I am talking over your head: as the elder Bassett[2] said to the undergraduate who was being shaved and protested he could not understand what he was saying.

I went to *In Town* that night when I last saw you and loved it to desperation. Miss Massey had returned and Phyllis Broughton acted *too* charmingly.[3]

My love to you and kind regards to Mrs Lawson: I hope your brother is in better spirits.   Yours MAX

[*Early January 1893*]   *19 Hyde Park Place, or rather Moreland House, Tunbridge Wells*

My dear Reg,

How very nice of Mrs Lawson to ask me. I wrote to thank her yesterday and to say how pleased and charmed I should be to come. Tell me when we meet—or by letter before that—whether you thought *Hypatia* as bad as I did or worse or not so bad.[4] Strange (is

[1] Presumably a legal one, since Reggie had gone down from Oxford in June and was now reading for the Bar in London.
[2] The fashionable Oxford barber of the day.
[3] *In Town*, a musical farce by Adrian Ross and James Leader, with music by Osmond Carr, had opened at the Prince of Wales's Theatre on 15 October 1892, with Arthur Roberts, Florence St John and Phyllis Broughton in leading rôles, and Blanche Massey in a minor part.
[4] *Hypatia*, a poetic drama by Stuart Ogilvie based on Charles Kingsley's novel, was produced by Tree at the Haymarket Theatre on 2 January 1893, with Julia Neilson, Fred Terry, Lewis Waller and Tree himself in the cast. It ran until 15 April.

it not?) that the critics should smile and say "It is well done" like the slave-dealer in *Don Quixote* when, as one would have thought, it was just *the* play on which they would have fallen asplike. One cannot ever tell. I supped with the actor-manager after the performance.

Ogilvie, who is just a cut above Kingsley (was it to you that I said that the other day?), was there and took too much wine and began to ramble about having stroked the Rugby boat and God knows what to the deep embarrassment of his admirers. Was not the blank verse bad? The play has been cut *tremendously* since the first night.

What am I to give you as your Christmas present? Do write and tell me: *anything* between a shilling and two-and-six. Here in Tunbridge there is nothing but what is called Tunbridge-ware, so we will choose something in London.

Yours till then with much looking forward   MAX

Monday [Postmark 23 January 1893]*   *Merton College*

My dear Reg,

Many thanks for your letters; I await the photographs with intensest anxiety. You do not mention the groups. I suppose they also have arrived, is it not so? Oxford is rather dreadful, though rendered tolerable to me (am I not charming?) by the expectation of you. I did so enjoy myself at Hill Street.[1] Are you enjoying yourself? I have begun quite a new *régime* in Oxford. I really must not again make myself ill by constant sedentariness. So this afternoon I have been for a long walk . . . and tomorrow after roller[2] am going round the meadows. . . . You must fall in with my way of life whilst you are here. I feel much better for it. I am so sorry your portrait is not a success. As far as I could tell, I thought it would be rather good—but perhaps I shall like it. . . .

---

[1] 31 Hill Street, Mayfair, the home of the Frank Lawsons, where Reggie was temporarily living.
[2] Roll-call.

Isn't Marie Lloyd charming and sweet in the Pantomime?[1] I think of little besides her—except Marie Loftus and you and so forth.

I wrote last night to Mrs Lawson thanking her for my enjoyment in town.   Yours affectionately MAX

Saturday [25 February 1893]   *Merton College*
My dear Reg,

The book that they have bound in Parma violets and across whose page is the silver voice of the Master made visible—how could it not be lovely?[2] I am enamoured of it. It has charmed my eyes from their sockets and through the voids has sent incense to my brain: my tongue is loosed in its praise. Have you read it? In construction it is very like a Greek play, I think: yet in conception so modern that its publication in any century would seem premature. It is a marvellous play. If Oscar would re-write *all* the Bible, there would be no sceptics. I say it is a marvellous play. It is a lovely present.

But oh did you see (perhaps inspired?) a paragraph in the *Daily Telegraph*, saying that Mr Wilde had distorted the facts of one of the most straightforward of Biblical tales and that his version of it left an unpleasant taste in the mouth? This criticism appeared this morning. What will be done to the writer? Dismissal would be too good for him.[3]

I have been quoting and puffing you loud and long and far and wide in Oxford, insomuch that many have agreed to reconsider you and want to see you here for this purpose. I hope you will perhaps come if only for an instant. . . .

Over my mantelpiece I have put the outside sheet of that song "What do I Care?" It has a fascinating figure of Ada Reeve[4] on it.

[1] *Little Bo-Peep, Little Red Riding Hood, and Hop o' My Thumb,* a pantomime by Sir Augustus Harris and J. Wilton Jones, with music by J. Crook, had opened at Drury Lane on 26 December 1892. The three title-rôles were played by Marie Loftus, Marie Lloyd and Little Tich, with Dan Leno as Daddy Thumb.
[2] The original (French) edition of Wilde's *Salome* was published on 22 February 1893, bound in purple wrappers.
[3] This paragraph appeared in the *Daily Telegraph* of 25 February.
[4] English actress (b. 1874).

Have you heard her sing? You should. So pretty, so clever, and with just that dash of vulgarity which when allied with cleverness and prettiness is as the dash of garlic (a thing not in itself nice) to some exquisite dish.

Write and tell me a great deal about yourself: you so seldom write to me now, and I am rather hurt. . . .

I am so very glad that Mrs Lawson and you enjoyed staying in Oxford, and am your affectionate MAX

[*Postmark 3 March 1893*]   *Merton College*

My dear Reg,

Thanks very much: but I think really I will not join the Sports Club. . . . Now if you were to join the Savile, how nice *that* would be. Think of us there together on a divan composing pointless epigrams on the rest of the members: who will have nothing to do with us or else think of us as the favourites of the Club—really a good literary club in its way and not expensive. Do join![1]

My article on Oscar has been accepted by the *Anglo-American*, a very good paper of recent birth. I have just been curtailing it for them. It is very brilliant, and consists of fulsome praise of the Master and filthy abuse of his disciples: of whom I say that "sitting eternally at the feet of Gamaliel, they learn nothing but the taste of boot-polish."[2] You must read it. Behold, high and sheer into the air rise the walls of the Temple of Fame: against them is a ladder placed and on the first rung of it rests my foot.

All love to you. MAX

[*25 March 1893*]*   *Merton College*

Dear Reg,

A hurried note of horror to find that I have not sent off my reply to Mrs Lawson's invitation, and am just doing so. I quite thought that I had and beg you to convey all apologies to her for being so long in answering.

[1] Max was in fact elected to the Savile Club in 1899, and Reggie in 1900.
[2] This article, entitled "Oscar Wilde by an American," appeared in the *Anglo-American Times* on 25 March 1893, and is now reprinted as Appendix A on p. 285.

Oscar thinks my article (which he has read in proof and which will appear today) "incomparably brilliant," though he is rather hurt at my reference to *Dorian Gray*[1] . . .   Yours MAX

[*Postmark 12 April 1893*]   *19 Hyde Park Place*

My dear Reg,

I can't think *why* I haven't written to you before. I have had so much spare time that I have been unable to do anything: time has lain so heavily on my hands that the pen has fallen from them, but now I hasten to make all amends. . . .

And how are you yourself and when do you come to England?[2] I long to see you again. I have been to Hill Street but was sorry not to find Mrs Lawson in. I suppose she will soon be starting to meet your brother on his way home. I am feeling very fairly happy, have spent a great deal of my time in the Music Halls and Theatres and Courts of Law—especially the last.

Also my O.W. article has appeared and I send you a copy of it. Oscar himself (of whom I have seen a good deal this vac) liked it very much and said he thought it "incomparably clever" which was nice of him, wasn't it? I still admire him immensely, though I do *not* think his play will be a *succès fou*: all the jokes come straight out of *Dorian Gray*: my brother's part is simply a dramatised Henry Wotton.

Have you heard about Gordon Craig's elopement? It must be a sunbeam through the darkened life of Henry the younger, seeing that Ellen Terry, remembering the romantic immoralities of her early days, is furious that her son has married the girl, and Henry the elder is also incensed that Gordon has thrown over his American engagement in favour of a prolonged honeymoon. It seems that the young youth has put by £200 in the Bank of England and that he began married life by ordering from Buszard an enormous cake costing £30. It is rather sad, isn't it? None of his relations will touch a morsel of it.[3]

[1] See p. 291.
[2] This letter is addressed to Bois Guillaume.
[3] Gordon Craig (b. 1872) was married to May Gibson on 27 March 1893. He had previously been acting with Irving at the Lyceum.

Oscar was speaking the other day of old Irving's *Lear*[1] and was furious that all the "wretched little donkeys of critics" had dared to attack him. "Surely," he said, "a gentleman has a right to fail if he chooses." I am sorry to say that Oscar drinks far more than he ought: indeed the first time I saw him, after all that long period of distant adoration and reverence, he was in a hopeless state of intoxication. He has deteriorated very much in appearance: his cheeks being quite a dark purple and fat to a fault. I think he will die of apoplexy on the first night of the play. What a lot I have written about him! His play is to be produced on the Wednesday before I go back to Oxford. . . .

How nice it was your coming up to Oxford last term: I enjoyed your visits very much, though during the last one you were rather unkind and unfriendly and I felt a little hurt. . . . Best love to all.

Your affectionate MAX

[*Postmark 15 April 1893*]   *19 Hyde Park Place*

My dear Reg,

Many thanks for your nice letter which has just arrived. . . . Last night I went to the House and heard Asquith's speech and the scene over Lord Cranborne's remark.[2] Personally I don't care much about the whole business and would rather hear the meanest and most nugatory case in a Court of Law than the most momentous Debate in history. Still, I had a very nice seat and rather enjoyed myself. Poor Gladstone! How he has aged: he positively looks older than Randolph Churchill and so very undistinguished: and how senile! I could not hear a word he said, except when occasionally he cheered Asquith in a quavering, common voice: he reminded me of a figure in a picture of Michaelmas Day in the Almshouses. John Morley was there also, not at all like your imitation of him.[3]

[1] Produced at the Lyceum on 10 November 1892.
[2] On 14 April, during a speech by H. H. Asquith in the debate on the second reading of the Home Rule Bill, Viscount Cranborne interjected "Murderer" when the Member for North-East Cork was mentioned, but quickly apologised.
[3] Gladstone, still Prime Minister, was now eighty-three. Lord Randolph Churchill (in the Conservative Opposition) was forty-four. Asquith was Home Secretary, and John Morley Chief Secretary for Ireland.

Did I tell you about Oscar at the Restaurant in my last note to you? I think not. During the rehearsal, he went to a place with my brother to have some lunch. He ordered a watercress sandwich: which in due course was brought to him: not a thin, diaphanous green thing such as he had meant but a very stout, satisfying article of food. This he ate with assumed disgust (but evident relish) and when he paid the waiter, he said "Tell the cook of this restaurant with the compliments of Mr Oscar Wilde that these are the very worst sandwiches in the whole world and that, when I ask for a watercress sandwich, I do not mean a loaf with a field in the middle of it."

It seems that he speaks French with a shocking accent, which is rather a disillusionment, and that when he visits the *Décadents* he has to repeat once or twice everything he says to them, and sometimes even to write it down for them.[1] They always speak of him as "Scurroveeld"—French for Oscar Wilde!

Your great friend   MAX BEERBOHM

Speaking of plagiarism the other day, Oscar said: "Of course I plagiarise. It is the privilege of the appreciative man. I never read Flaubert's *Tentation de St Antoine* without signing my name at the end of it. *Que voulez-vous?* All the Best Hundred Books bear my signature in this manner."

Friday [21 April 1893]   *19 Hyde Park Place*

My dear Reg,

Thank you for your letter with which I was ever so pleased and which I have duly added to the growing file of your letters in my bureau. They are all arranged in order of literary merit and I spend a good deal of time in reading, shifting, re-shifting, re-reading them. I always place each one, when I have read it, at the bottom and so on to the end.

[1] On the other hand, André Gide declared that Wilde's French accent was almost perfect.

Have you read any of the notices of Oscar's play?[1] The first night was very brilliant in its audience. . . . Balfour and Chamberlain and all the politicians were there. When little Oscar came on to make his bow there was a slight mingling of hoots and hisses, though he looked very sweet in a new white waistcoat and a large bunch of little lilies in his coat. The notices are better than I had expected: the piece is sure of a long, of a very long run, despite all that the critics may say in its favour.

Last night I went again: the Prince also there. He had command of the Royal Box (is it not the irony of fate?) just after it had been allotted to Mrs Langtry.[2] I believe she suggested that they should share it but the Prince was adamant. After the play I supped with Oscar and Alfred Douglas[3] (who is staying with him) and my brother at the Albemarle. Oscar talked a great deal about my article—said that he knew no other undergraduate who could have written it, that I had a marvellous intuition and sense of the phrase, that I must take to literature alone, and that my style was like a silver dagger. I am becoming vainer than ever. He told us one lovely thing. A little journalist who had several times attacked him vulgarly came up to him in the street the other day and cordially accosted him. Oscar stared at him and said after a moment or two "You will pardon me: I remember your name perfectly but I can't recall your face."

After supper I walked as far as Hyde Park Corner when I saw a glare in the sky like some false dawn. A cabman told me it was a fire and drove me to it—right away past Westminster. It was quite lovely, though there was no life lost I am afraid. Still, the timber

[1] *A Woman of No Importance* was produced by Tree at the Haymarket Theatre on 19 April 1893, with Tree, Mrs Tree, Fred Terry, Julia Neilson and Mrs Bernard Beere in the cast. Tree had married Helen Maud Holt (1864–1937) in 1883.
[2] Emily Charlotte Le Breton (1852–1929), who came from Jersey and was considered the most beautiful woman of her generation, married in her teens Edward Langtry, an Irish widower of thirty. He brought her to London, where she quickly became a leading figure in Society, an actress and a friend of the Prince of Wales. Max, in his essay "1880," written in 1894, called her "*cette Cléopatre de son siècle.*"
[3] Lord Alfred Bruce Douglas (1870–1945), third son of the eighth Marquess of Queensberry. He was an undergraduate at Magdalen College, Oxford, 1890–93.

yard was quite burnt and as I walked away the dawn was making the helmets of the firemen ghastly. It was bright daylight when I reached home and the sun shone brightly into my bed. I slept very deeply.[1]

Write to me. How I have rambled and how marvellously!

Yours MAX

Whistler's dictum on *Salome* was "Oscar has scored another brilliant—exposure." . . .

Oscar was furious when I told him that R had lost his child. "Mediocrities," he said, "have no business to have tragedies. I always knew the man would turn out badly." . . .

Everything is charming just now, the weather most lovely. I go back to Oxford—alas!—today.

Sunday [30 April 1893]*   *Merton College*

My dear Reg, . . .

How goes the affair of your rooms? . . . You might come and live in Oxford for a short time—why not? . . .

How the critics attack gentle Oscar: have you, though, read Archer's very very true and just critiques? Walkley also is to the point, but the rest have scarcely tried to write on the play at all.[2] They have simply abused Oscar.

Your loving MAX

[Postmark 7 May 1893]   *Merton College*

My dear Reg, . . .

I have had a rather gay term but my gaiety has been all enjoyed in the company of out-college men—especially that of Denis Browne[3] and Bosey[4] Douglas. The latter is rather charming—a

[1] For Max's continuing delight in fires see "An Infamous Brigade" in *More* (1899).
[2] William Archer's review of *A Woman of No Importance* appeared in the *World* of 26 April; A. B. Walkley's in the *Speaker* of 29 April.
[3] Beauchamp Denis Browne (1871–1910), a kinsman of the Marquess of Sligo, was a Balliol undergraduate 1890–93. He was an honorary attaché at the British Embassy in Rome 1896–99.
[4] Max's spelling of Bosie, Lord Alfred Douglas's nickname.

very pretty reflection of Oscar—and we get on very nicely. Have you seen the new *Spirit Lamp*?[1] Oscar came to see me the other day with Douglas (at whose house he was staying). Leonard Messel was present: he behaved quite quietly and gentlemanly and the visit was quite a success.[2]

I wish, though, you yourself would come very soon: you amuse me so and really, though I fear that other surroundings and occupations have rather weakened your sympathy with me, yet my appreciation and liking for you have not undergone the slightest change. Usually I become quite indifferent to people behind their backs and my friendship is all at the mercy of time and space, so you really ought to try to be kind to me—and not (as on your last visit to Oxford you did somewhat) to "terrify" me.

Last night I was dining with St Cyres: a young French artist was there and the dinner, in his own rooms, very nicely cooked. I had to leave early as (listen!) I am "gated" for a week at ten—for being in after twelve twice last week. I feel it a frightful indignity in my third year. Write to me.   Yours MAX

[*Postmark 13 May 1893*]   *Merton College*

My dear Reg,

I am so glad you liked my letter—indeed I knew you would. If you really want to please a man, tell him you know he has forgotten you: the plan is simple but infallible: and I was much delighted with your reply, not only by reason of its nice spirit, but also as the fulfilment of a prophecy. You need not, by the way, be jealous of Alfred Douglas as he does not peculiarly fascinate me: he is for one thing obviously mad (like all his family I believe) and though he is pretty and clever and nice I never judge my friends from an

[1] An Oxford undergraduate magazine (1892–93), of which the last eight numbers were edited by Lord Alfred Douglas. Vol IV, No 1 (4 May 1893) contained prose and verse by Douglas (including a critical review of Wilde's *Salome*), Lionel Johnson, Robert Ross, Pierre Louÿs and John Addington Symonds.
[2] Leonard Messel (1872–1953), Merton undergraduate 1890–93, became a stockbroker of cultivated tastes and a great collector. Father of Oliver Messel and grandfather of the Earl of Snowdon.

Aesthetic, an Intellectual or an Ethical standpoint: I simply like them or dislike: that is all. You are fortunate enough to have fallen into the former category, and even if tomorrow you became as stupid as Slender or as ugly as Caliban or as horrid as most of my friends, I should like you none the less. Your personality, I conceive, would remain despite the change of your condition.

My people tell me they met you the other day: I am so glad you are able to go out and do hope soon to see you in bonny Oxford. How amusing the debates in the House are! I am becoming a very keen politician, you will be surprised to hear. Last night at the Union—you must not laugh at me—I spoke on a motion that the clauses of the Home Rule Bill were formed inadequately for the needs of Ireland. I spoke sixth and made really rather a success.[1] Beauchamp,[2] the president, has asked me to speak third next Thursday, but it is not yet fixed what the motion shall be, so I am not sure whether or not I shall do so.

Though I spoke so late in the evening there were a good many people there. . . . I thought of you and how amused you would be at me. All this is *really* true: write and advise me whether it is worth while seriously to follow it up. I think I made really quite a success —though rather nervous at first. York Powell[3] was there and came up to me afterwards and said he liked my speech "as much as any he had heard there for a very long time." . . . I should not care to drift into the character of irregular Unionman but I think I may as well speak again now that I have done so once. Forgive all this about myself: do write and tell me what you think.   Ever yours MAX

P.S. I have just heard that the motion next week is to be about Modern Literature. I think it would be a good subject if I could manage it.

[1] The Oxford Union debated the Home Rule Bill on 4 and 12 May 1893, but its records do not mention Max as speaking on this or any other occasion.
[2] William Lygon, Viscount Elmley (1872–1938), succeeded his father as seventh Earl Beauchamp 1891. He was an undergraduate at Christ Church 1890–93, and President of the Oxford Union in the Trinity Term 1893.
[3] Frederick York Powell (1850–1904), author, editor and scholar, was a don at Christ Church 1884–94 and Regius Professor of Modern History at Oxford 1894–1904.

My dear Reg . . .

Write, really and seriously, telling me what you think about the whole idea of the Union?

Can anyone—can *even you?*—remain for one instant in doubt about two nice warm modernly-fitted rooms and three lonely, loathsome, over-old rooms in the Temple. I know a man called Fergusson who lived for two years in the latter—partly with a view to economy, partly to being always on the legal spot. He told me that people living there spend their time in prolonged gloom and discomfort and despair: that they can think of nothing but food decently cooked and decently served, and have a perpetual craving for hot water laid on, which never leaves them even in after-life. I know no such person as a matter of fact, but I am sure that all I have written has a large measure of truth. Of course you must have *two comfortable* rooms: if not I should never come and see you, and what, after all, is a room gained to a friend—and such a friend—lost?

Last night I dined with Denis Browne to meet the Divinity Oscar. Bosey Douglas also was there and Encombe,[1] with whom I have scraped quite a warm friendship; also Kerry[2] and B. Blackwood[3]— quite a peers' dinner: at any rate as regards aristocracy of intellect as represented by me and the Divinity. He was in a very nice mood —young and schweet and most amusing. I have, at the instance of Fischer Williams,[4] done a picture for the Eights number of the Magazine: it is called "The New Culture"[5] and is highly decorative,

[1] John Scott, Viscount Encombe (1870–1900), eldest son of the third Earl of Eldon, was Alfred Douglas's friend and contemporary at Winchester and Magdalen. They shared rooms in the High Street, Oxford.
[2] Henry William Edmund Petty-Fitzmaurice, Earl of Kerry (1872–1936), succeeded his father as sixth Marquess of Lansdowne 1927.
[3] Lord Basil Blackwood (1870–1917, killed in action), third son of the first Marquess of Dufferin and Ava, was a Balliol undergraduate 1891–94. He illustrated Hilaire Belloc's *Bad Child's Book of Beasts* [1896] and four later books.
[4] John Fischer Williams (1870–1947), New College undergraduate 1888–92, Fellow 1892–99. Became a barrister and expert on international law. Knighted 1923.
[5] This full-page drawing, signed H.M.B., was published in the special Eights Week issue of the *Oxford Magazine* on 18 May 1893.

and damaging to the *Spirit Lamp*: for which by the way I am writing my article on "The Incomparable Beauty of Modern Dress."[1]

Do, do come up.   Your loving friend   MAX

P.S. *What* a possession my letters to you are!

[*Postmark 10 July 1893*]   *19 Hyde Park Place*

I am suffering, my dear Reg, from a plethora of brilliancy, so I must write to someone for relief—why not to you? . . .

I walked all the way back from your place[2] to my home the other night; fearfully tired too I was by the time I reached Piccadilly, and by the time I reached Park Lane I simply followed my feet at a weary and seemingly respectful distance, but—oh—I saw the dawn, the lovely dawn of London: what a privilege to live in a city through whose vapours and buildings the sun rises with solemnity and fitting slowness: how different from the country where it pops up over the bare horizon like a yellow jack-in-the-box. How lovely in London is the growing of gray into blue and blue into gray and the hardening of all outlines against the sky. Why do I write all this? I suppose because I am clever but I don't know that it isn't all thrown away.
. . .   Yours ever   MAX

[*Postmark 9 August 1893*]   *19 Hyde Park Place*

My dear Reg,

Yes, I thought you must be ill at the time—you looked distinctly pale and *distrait*. I shall certainly look upon you as another potent argument against Bank Holidays and hope you are all right again now. I have just sent off the interview with the Lady Cecilia:[3] not

---

[1] This essay, signed H. M. Beerbohm, appeared in the June 1893 issue of the *Spirit Lamp*. It was the first of Max's essays to be published over his name.

[2] Reggie had by now taken rooms at 2 Clement's Inn, to which this letter was addressed.

[3] One of Max's nicknames for Cissy (Marie Cecilia) Loftus (1876–1943), daughter of the actress Marie Loftus. She had made her début at the Oxford Music Hall on 15 July 1893, and was already acclaimed as an infant prodigy of mimicry and singing. Max's professed passion for her was at any rate partly assumed for Reggie's amusement.

one word of truth in it from beginning to end. I have represented her as a sweet idiot without a touch of genius, whereas she is nothing of the sort or kind—only a white child whom the gods love for the charm they have given her.

By the way, I have not sent the interview in my own name. Suppose the *Pall Mall* sends to the white child asking if it be genuine —"did Mr Maxwell (the name I give)[1] interview you?" "No, but a Mr Beerbohm (the name I gave) did." Confusion and a cold scene when I call, as I must, upon Harry Cust[2] tomorrow. Of course it would not do to make my début in his eyes as the questioner of a white girl, catching her—so to speak—in my arms as she leaps from the convent-window on to the Boards of the Hall beneath. I begin to feel rather uncomfortable. So glad you really liked the Lady Cecilia. See you tomorrow, yes, at 8 p.m.

Yours MAX

Thursday [*10 August 1893. Postmark 11 August*]
19 Hyde Park Place

My dear Reg,

The yellow blinds of this room save me from the dull glare of heat without. I am paralysed with lassitude all the same and have spent the afternoon in a flannel suit and an S.C.S. tie, watching the candles as they slowly bow their white heads lower and lower—for grief, perhaps, as thinking me dead. Oh I am so very tired. Why is not the white child with me to chaff me out of my languor and bathe my lips in *eau-de-Cologne*, sitting by my sofa and telling me that she does not love Gus Elen[3] a little bit? I have just seen through half-closed eyes the *Pall Mall*—does it contain my interview with her?

[1] The name Maximilian may well have seemed pretentious, or at least teaseworthy, to the young Max, and he sometimes translated it to Maxwell; for instance, when he signed the admission book at Merton (1890), and over his second batch of drawings, "Club Types," in the *Strand Magazine* (1892).
[2] Henry John Cockayne Cust (1861–1917) was editor of the *Pall Mall Gazette* 1892–96.
[3] Comedian and singer of Cockney songs (1862–1940), imitated by Cissy Loftus.

I was too weary to look for it and also too shocked by what it said of her in the latest edition: it seems that she really has got mixed up in some silly litigation and the lawyers have been wrangling and cutting their jests over her little head.[1] What is she doing in this

---

[1] The *Pall Mall Gazette* of 10 August printed this on its front page:

THE FIGHT FOR MISS CISSY LOFTUS
Theatre v. Music-Hall

Readers of our music-hall notes must be well aware of the extra-ordinary success that the fifteen-year old daughter of Miss Marie Loftus has achieved with her imitations of famous singers both at music-halls and theatre. It is now only a little more than three weeks since she made her first appearance on any stage at the Oxford music-hall. Her success was so immense and instantaneous that she was immediately engaged at the Tivoli also, and within a fortnight had received an offer of a three years' engagement at the Gaiety Theatre, which she—or rather her mother—closed with. The Gaiety—represented by Mr George Edwardes —claim that their engagement, being "exclusive," Miss Cissy may no longer perform at either of the music-halls in which she made her initial success, and with which she has earlier engagements. . . .

Mr Farwell, Q.C., with whom was Mr Cave, opened the case for Mr George Edwardes, of the Gaiety. The affair, from the outset, was amusing. First, the Gaiety agreement was put in, and Mr Justice Chitty's comment was to the effect that it was not very well drawn; although the fact that the fair artist of fifteen was getting a similar number of pounds as a weekly salary seemed to the learned judge decidedly agreeable. The judge then pretended to be mixed up between the mother and the daughter, and, indeed, the agreement gave him a good opportunity, for it was signed by the Miss Marie, but made out in favour of Miss Cissy. As, how-ever, Miss Marie was described as a widow, and Miss Cissy is only fifteen, the learned judge decided that they were distinct people. Moreover, Miss Cissy was engaged "to do her mimetic entertainment," and her mother's performance is of a rather different order.

This point took a long time to settle. The next was how the word "exclusively," undoubtedly contained in the agreement, affected its sub-stance. The wording of the clause was "to perform (exclusively) her mimetic entertainment at the Gaiety Theatre." But this was complicated by what the learned counsel referred to as "an ablative absolute," which the still more classical judge declared was a *nominativus pendens*.

The judge remarked that he could "get over the bad grammar," but wasn't going to transpose important words. The whole argument was a most amusing dialogue between judge and counsel, with occasional inter-ruptions from the audience. The fact that the engagement of £5 a week at the Oxford was previous to the one made by the Gaiety seemed to strongly influence the bench in Miss Cissy's favour.

When Mr Farwell had finished his "turn," Mr Cave took up the tale,

galley? I quite sympathise with the Gaiety people in not wishing her to be running about night after night to so many places: it must tire her terribly and I expect it is a *ruse* of Miss Mahrie Loftus to lead her back to the convent. However, the case is decided, it seems, and I never discuss a suit that is not *sub judice*: what is the good? You effect nothing.

Oh God—how I wish myself wholly free and able to lay vast riches at her feet and marry and live with her unhappily ever after. Oscar may be right about the only two tragedies in life[1] but certainly you can fall asleep at the performance of the second or smoke a cigarette in the entr'actes. The first is too harrowing for that. Didn't she look sweet when she came on with the elastic band under her chin? I suppose she didn't sing because the band refused to accompany her—do you think that was the reason? The joke is terribly like Dodo's[2] jokes but the sun has dissolved my own individuality.

Do write to me before I see you tomorrow (Metropole, 7 sharp!) and write all about Cissie. I have got to that stage when I derive keen pleasure from the mere sight of her little name in writing. *She* has only got as far as the Variety stage. Dodo again.

The sun is just setting and my spirit rises. Shall I go to the Tivoli again tonight, I wonder? I can hardly bear to think of her being anywhere at all without my seeing her. I like your portrait of

---

but with indifferent success. He was, in fact, rather dull, and the audience in court looked bored. When he had finished Mr Justice Chitty again commented on the looseness of Mr Didcot's agreement. The word "exclusively," he said, merely applied in the text to the "mimetic entertainment," and had nothing to do with the engagement at the Gaiety. According to the wording of the agreement the plain meaning was that Miss Loftus was to do her special "show" at the Gaiety and nothing else—not nowhere else. Moreover, there was the fact that the performer was already under a five weeks' engagement at the Oxford, and this alone seemed to him decisive. He had therefore no option but to refuse the application of the Gaiety with costs. The curtain then fell.

[1] "In this world there are only two tragedies. One is not getting what one wants, and the other is getting it." (*Lady Windermere's Fan*, Act III.)

[2] The eponymous heroine of E. F. Benson's novel (1893), widely supposed to have been based on Margot Tennant (later Asquith).

Miss Cumberlidge[1]—do you like the portrait in the *Sketch*?[2] I went to sleep last night looking at it and on waking this morning found I had crumpled it up in my hand. What Joseph shall interpret this? I sent out to the newspaper shop for another copy and am awaiting some sequel to what happened. Was it a good omen do you think? Forgive me for boring you with this very needless letter, but I must write about her to someone sympathetic, and I wrote to Parker[3] yesterday.

The Metropole at 7 sharp! No gentleman dines etc.[4]

Yours ever   MAX

. . . I wish Cissie would go into a convent—the Courts and the Halls, what a nursery for a child!

[*Postmark 13 August 1893*]   *19 Hyde Park Place*

My dear Reg,

Are you enjoying yourself very much at Hassocks[5] or have you found what a great mistake you made in leaving town at this time of the year? I know of experience that you do not answer my letters when you are with the Marshalls, but that does not dissuade me from writing and I don't even blame you. If I were staying very near the white child, able to talk to her and laugh with her, I don't think I should answer *your* letters. Probably you feel hurt at this—if you have read it—for you really are a very morbid man, however much you may deny it, my dear Reg. I don't mean so much that you are sensitive—on the contrary I think you rather thick-skinned and

[1] Possibly an imaginary lady, invented by Reggie to match Cissy Loftus.
[2] A photograph of Cissy Loftus, which appeared in the *Sketch* on 9 August (here reproduced opposite p. 48), accompanied by an interview entitled "Maiden Mimicry, a chat with Miss Cissy Loftus."
[3] Eric Parker (1870–1955), a Merton friend of Max and Reggie, later famous as a writer on sport, the countryside and natural history.
[4] "Half-past six! What an hour! It will be like having a meat-tea, or reading an English novel. It must be seven. No gentleman dines before seven." (Oscar Wilde, *The Picture of Dorian Gray*, ch. iv.)
[5] In Sussex, where Reggie was staying with Mr and Mrs Marshall. Their son, Chapman Frederick Dendy Marshall (1872–1945), later the author of standard works on railway history and philately, had been at school with Reggie.

46

things bounce off you with a loud report, whilst in my flesh they stick, silently drawing blood and no one is any the wiser.

How is Miss Cumberlidge? Write and let me know—one word will suffice, "ill" or "well," and the rest of your letter shall be all about Cissie. What a quick and exquisite life hers has been! She has wantoned in the sunlight long enough and I would say to her "My dearest, is it not enough? You have heaped laughter upon the singers in Halls, and in the breast of her who did give you birth you have conjured envy; you have dazzled Demos and laughed in the face of the lawyers. Have you lived? You have lived your life! Get thee to a nunnery." Picture her moving always between the walls of some nunnery—wearing at first the veil of the Novitiate and dying long after either of us and being buried in the parcel of ground where the nuns' graves are—Sister Cecilia. It would be lovelier almost than if we married—unless she were to die in childbirth. I cannot imagine anything lovelier than that. Think of one year's happiness—always at its height: then a great sudden grief that will sanctify the rest of one's life, though it grows less day by day: a grief growing fainter, instead of a joy, as would happen if she had not died. Happy the man whose young wife dies in childbirth! His pain is not degraded by any knowledge of how good the gods have been to him. But generally "Love *is* stronger than death"[1]—that is the great draw-back of married life. I am going to buy a dear little revolver that I have long had my eye on: it is in the window of a gun-shop on the right side of Bond Street as you walk down. Not that I suppose I shall ever use it, but, as I am always saying, the feeling that you may at any moment solve the whole problem of life (simple division by death) is certainly a consolation. Life is a prison without bars— but I begin to realise that it *is* a prison. However, that is talking at large—time enough for suicide later on: at present I think more of Cissy than of anything else. It may not sound paradoxical to say so, but it is very very charming to feel really in love—and for the first time. You have so often been in love before; Lucy Webling, Mabel Hoare, that terrible girl Zoe and many others have caught your affection: why have you never told me, when I was in my dead state, how exquisite it is to be really in love? Perhaps if you had, I should have tried to fall in love with someone and half-succeeded, and so

[1] "Love is strong as death" (*Song of Solomon*, viii, 6).

lost a little of my first happiness now. I am glad you never did tell me or at any rate were not believed.

Life has veered round suddenly for me and I am so glad and feel —oh so good. Never before have I felt any wish to confide in anyone about anything—you are my first confidant; but don't let that lead you to repose any confidences in me: in my present condition I could not understand anyone else's happiness. If you really wish to, write to me all about yourself and I will read your letter another time—but do *please* write to me.   Yours ever MAX

Isn't Cissie absolutely sweet to look upon? And when she comes on to the stage with her eyes down and looks up suddenly as her song begins. Her hair waves when she dances, have you noticed that? It is awful to hear the men in the audience remark upon her performance—criticism of an artist should be the monopoly of her lovers. I love her very much.

[*14 August 1893. Postmark 15 August*]   *19 Hyde Park Place*

My dear Reg,

Many thanks: all that you say about the white girl is very true and, as Miss Horlock[1] would say, so, so helpful. Do write again— you don't know how I really enjoy reading even her name.

I wrote to you only yesterday so that our letters crossed and I must write again, risking your disgust.

Yesterday I felt exceedingly depressed—partly, no doubt, because of your departure in a neat grey suit and the prospect of not seeing you for a long time: partly too because of my liver that the hot weather had upset, and partly because the vitality of a healthy young Englishman is always at its lowest ebb on Sunday and the day that precedes it. But today I feel very different and ready for anything: not that I am fond of Monday as a day, but there is a certain charm in recovering from the prostration of Sunday—the charm of convalescence. What is your favourite day? Tuesdays make me feel very gentlemanly, Wednesdays bring out my cleverness—do not think this is affectation for it really is not—my moods vary always in this way. On Saturdays I am common, have you

[1] Unidentified.

48

No. 28.—Vol. III.   WEDNESDAY, AUGUST 9, 1893.   SIXPENCE.
By Post, 6½d.

Reproduced by kind permission of from the "Lady's Pictorial."

MISS CISSY LOFTUS, THE NEW "STAR" AT THE GAIETY THEATRE.

LINES SUGGESTED BY MISS CISSY LOFTUS.

DRAWN BY MAX BEERBOHM.

noticed that?[1] At all events I feel fairly happy today and shall go *au* Tivoli tonight, I think: also I feel very fond of you. Listen! Yesterday I was holding forth on humour—how rare a thing it was and how sacred. "Reggie Turner and Oscar," I said, "are the only two men who really amuse me."

Write and tell me about yourself and your life. I think you very enviable and wish I had your days to live instead of mine. Much as I have loved my love of the Small Saint[2] I cannot pretend that it leaves me as happy as I have been. She has shewn me what a small distorted career mine has been. After all what have I done since I came to Oxford with power to make myself? What have my pleasures been? To dress carefully, to lie in a canoe in the summer and read minor verse by the fire in the winter, to talk of Oscar, to sit down to dinner looking forward to rising from it drunk, to draw more or less amusing caricatures—a few friends, a few theatres and music-halls and a few cigarettes a day—and there you have my life. Accompanied by a sense of humour, an utter absence of the moral sense and an easy temper, it has been fairly happy I suppose, but now that the moral sense is suddenly, suddenly returning because of the Small Saint, disgust comes with it. I am no longer contented —and she is only the end of the old life to me I am afraid, not the beginning of a new one. I haven't the vitality for that. "As one sows so shall one reap" and the wisest are they who sow well and of those who sow ill they are wisest who avoid harvest altogether. That is what I should love to do if I had the courage. Last night I looked at my hand carefully: according to it I live on, as far as I can judge, to a fairly old age—*ce n'est pas toujours gai, la vie.* However do not think I am writing *de profundis*: I feel far brighter than yesterday: besides I am going to the Tivoli tonight. Are you very much in love with Miss Cumberlidge? Do tell me about it when you write and do write soon for the consolation of your Ariadnean   MAX

P.S. Please keep my letters for the present if you can: they would interest me hereafter and perhaps throw some light upon a character that I find almost unintelligible.

[1] Cf. "that most depressing of all days, Saturday" ("Pretending" in *More*).
[2] Another nickname for Cissy Loftus.

My dear Reg,

Forgive me. I cannot help writing to you again: the lust of letters implects me, and the sad part of it is that, whereas I enjoy confiding in you even at such a distance inasmuch as you were the companion of my happiest days, you probably are utterly out of touch with me and see in me a mere (in the ordinary sense of the word) speck on the mental horizon. However it is more blessed to receive letters than to write them, for if you feel bored you need not even open them—in fact I would rather you did not open mine —they might lose something of their delicate fragrance by exposure, and as for reading them, Posterity will do that with dear little marginal notes (P—r and P—e would always be called P by the delicate editor: what a confusion of malice it would make). In any case you have your reward: you will be known—will you not?—as "the friend of Henry Beerbohm" and "the receiver of those confessions which have come down to us in the 'Letters' and form one of the most luminous and fascinating pieces of self-exposition ever given to the world." Really my letters to you indicate a certain trend of character: they have their value.

Me voici talking self and psychologics whilst you are probably wrapped up in the thought of Miss Cumberlidge: how charming for you to have been away from her for so long and to realise that you had almost forgotten her. Did you give her the *bonbonnière* or whatever it was you had got for her?

The Gaiety season is almost at a close, so that little Mistress Mere[1] will have only the Halls to appear in till October: I wish she would stay there: to her peculiar art the narrow, vapourish quality of the Gaiety must be fatal: and then—oh think of the corrupt and silly audience: think how and for what they will praise her in their own hideous jargon. Only to the gracious mind can her very great charm shew itself really: to me she is a girl, an artist, a child from a convent, an exquisite thing: I call her by delightful names and understand all her beauty. I should love to be with her. Why doesn't she act only for me night after night? You and a few polished admirers

[1] Yet another name for Cissy Loftus. Max called the heroine of *The Happy Hypocrite* (1897) Jenny Mere.

could come too whenever you liked; she should receive no salary but have breakfast and lunch and dinner with me—supper as an occasional treat when she has been sweeter than ever, in which case we should never sup. If she wished it, she should have breakfast in bed sometimes, with iced tea and little pieces of toast shaped like the letters of the alphabet, for she probably cannot spell yet—she left her convent so soon. In the morning she could help me to draw caricatures for the papers. Either she must do this or go back to the convent: even the hooded nuns could recognise her art more clearly than the youths at the Gaiety: the youths at the Gaiety could no more recognise it than the crawling snakes could truly appreciate the voice and beauty of the snake-charmer. Why should the Lady Cecilia charm snakes at the Gaiety? She shall not.

I did not go last night, but tonight I am going to hear her. My aunt died on Sunday evening, of which I am very sorry, and my sister Dora goes to her Sisterhood next Monday.[1] I am sorry of both these events. My aunt was very old and longed to live on: my sister is quite young and is determined to cut herself off from life. Strange, isn't it?

Forgive this letter. I suppose I am one of the loveliest of God's creatures—I am sure that Cissie is quite the loveliest.

Your affectionate MAX

[*Postmark 19 August 1893*]   *19 Hyde Park Place*

Oh my dear Reg, the heat, the heat. I am dead or as one dead and everything is bright crimson—except your nice letter which arrived looking delightfully cool all in black and white.

At my side is a bowl of water with *eau-de-Cologne* in it: this is my only solace. So glad you are happy with the Inamorata: I think she is charming. So was the chorus that you sent me and that should certainly be sung.

I must tell you that I went *au* Tivoli on—was it Tuesday?

[1] Max's youngest sister Dora Margaretta (1868–1940) spent the rest of her life as a Sister of Charity at St Saviour's Priory in the east end of London. Max's obituary notice of her in the *Orient*, the journal of the Order, which she had edited, is here reprinted as Appendix B on p. 293.

Mistress Mere had a rather small voice that night but she was perhaps less resistible than ever she has been and imitated Gus Elen to the point of paradise.

Celli[1] sang a new verse—a political verse:

"Gingerbread and Gladstone they have lost their gilt.
It wasn't in a day or two that our empire was built"

and the rest of it.

Miss Ethel Matthews[2] was there, convulsed with laughter at the wit and wisdom of James Fawn[3] and looking not at all like the type of English beauty that she is. In the next box to her lolled William Terriss[4] with his face artificially bronzed—quite the *gentilhomme campagnard*. Otherwise the house was rather empty: the heat was the reason. Did I say that *eau-de-Cologne* was my only solace? If so, it was a sort of lie, for I have bought two saintlike photographs of the Lady Cecilia taken by Elliott & Fry—I don't know which took which but they are a very great pleasure to me. In the one she is looking up with bowed head and arms folded: evidently she is just saying "No, Sir, she am *Out*." But in the other she is simply her little self: she is smiling briskly with her head slightly on one side. I have seen her look so when someone in the Gallery has insisted on another imitation.

You need not be afraid by the way about my relapsing into "cynicism and cigarettes." I have a firm and inexpugnable faith in everything now—everything that is good—and smoke nothing but cigars, for fear of conjuring up the "twittering ghosts" of my former self.

Apropos of my former self, Oscar was at the last night of the Haymarket:[5] with him Bosie and Robbie[6] and Aubrey Beardsley.[7]

[1] Frank H. Celli, English actor and singer (1841–1904).
[2] English actress (b. 1870).
[3] Singer and music-hall performer (1850–1923). In "The Blight on the Music Halls" in *More*, Max referred to his "homely humour."
[4] Stage-name of William Charles James Lewin (1847–97), handsome romantic actor, popular hero of a series of melodramas at the Adelphi Theatre.
[5] Of *A Woman of No Importance* on 16 August.
[6] Robert Ross.
[7] English artist (1872–98). He worked in an insurance office 1889–92, and his illustrations to *Morte Darthur* were now being published.

The last of these had forgotten to put vine-leaves in his hair, but the other three wore rich clusters—especially poor Robbie. Nor have I ever seen Oscar so fatuous: he called Mrs Beere[1] "Juno-like" and Kemble[2] "Olympian quite" and waved his cigarette round and round his head. Of course I would rather see Oscar free than sober, but still, suddenly meeting him after my simple and lovely little ways of life since the Lady Cecilia first looked out from her convent-window, I felt quite repelled. Robbie is very much in debt, so he tells me. I have just been reading *Salome* again: terribly corrupt but there is much that is beautiful in it, much lovely writing: I almost wonder Oscar doesn't dramatise it.

Yesterday in the sandy heat I went down with my mother to some little village in Hampshire where my aunt was buried. Such a sweet little church-yard in the shade with a low hedge dividing it from the road and children peering through: there was an old sexton too with horn-spectacles and a very young curate from Oxford with a violet stole. Quite an admirable scene in its way. All the time that they were reading the words of the service—"Earth to earth, ashes to ashes"—I tried to fancy that it was my young wife Cecilia, *aetat*: 17, who was being mourned and that the whole scene belonged to the future. Oh how lovely it would be. But I must stop, for I am going to pour a libation to the shade of the late Herr Fahrenheit that his spirit may not vex the world.　　　　Your affectionate　MAX

Oh, I have from the *P.M.G.* extremely sorry, unable to print my interview, owing to strict office-rule against publishing any interview not held by member of regular staff. Silly, isn't it?

P.S. . . . My darling Cissie—as I came away from the Tivoli her tiny shabby carriage was waiting for her and I saw a glimpse of white skirt coming from the darkness of the stage-door.

How can you ask if my love of her is genuine? I think I shall pay another visit to Herne Hill[3] tomorrow afternoon. What would I not give for an excuse—however far-fetched—to call. Perhaps the chimney will be on fire and I can ring and raise an alarm, and be

---

[1] English actress (1856–1915), originally Fanny Mary Whitehead, she married three times, but always acted under her second married name.
[2] Henry Kemble (1848–1907), actor and nephew of Fanny Kemble.
[3] Where the Loftus family lived.

treated henceforth as one of the family Loftus. I suppose those girls we saw with Miss Mahrie Loftus were sisters of the Lady Cecilia—how lovely to change places with one of them and be able to have little quarrels and reconciliations in the back-garden with the desired one.

[*Postmark 21 August 1893*]   *19 Hyde Park Place*

My dear Reg,

Your letter came this morning and brought great pleasure with it —and I was in great need of comfort, for where is the lovely heat that has left us? I was so happy in languor while it was with me: now I seem brought suddenly face to face with the realities of life, whatever they may be. The Lady Cecilia has been the only reality to me of late and I hope that, if I have a blazing fire lit and lie all day on a sofa with a bottle of *eau-de-Cologne*, the illusion will continue. Think of overcoats! How awful it seems. Think of frosty gusts of wind meeting the Lady Cecilia as she comes out of the Tivoli flushed with success. Oh my dear Reg, *à propos* of the flush of success: when I visited the Oxford last Saturday night she sang so sweetly and the audience simply lost itself in a rapture of thunder and applause. You know the grave, expressionless and utterly delightful way in which my little genius usually announces the name of her next imitation—never smiling but pressing her chin slightly into her neck—which is I suppose her idea of a bow and a very sweet idea too. Well, elated with the excessive applause that greeted her, she came forward on this occasion, threw back her head with a winning smile at the Gallery, almost struck an attitude and cried "Miss Letty Lind in *Morocco Bound*!!!"[1] in the highest staccato accents. I trembled for her like an aspen leaf: to me who love her, her manner seemed simply delightful—anything she could do in whatever way must always be perfection for me—but what of the censorious world when it returns to London and sees a perfect girl and perfect artist with the ordinary manners of the boards? Perhaps her

[1] A farcical comedy by Arthur Branscombe and Adrian Ross, with music by F. Osmond Carr, first produced at the Shaftesbury Theatre on 13 April 1893, in which Letty Lind scored a great success with a caricature of the skirt-dance as performed by fashionable amateurs.

little lapse was only for the moment. Her personality is too young and strong to have suffered yet by any contact. Besides the Music Halls are a very nursery of personality, but I do tremble for her when she finally casts in her lot with the Monotony Entertainment of Geo. Edwardes.[1] A three-years engagement must have a wretched effect upon her method, or her want of method rather. How I wish she could have rejected the offer of Geo. and I could have given her an introduction to my brother, Mr Beerbohm Tree of the Haymarket: think of her there as an *ingénue*: how charming for her to have failed there or even succeeded. It is all bosh her ambition to be a "serious" actress after her Gaiety engagement. She could not succeed, after such a narrow experience of art. Oh why doesn't she stay and grow up and foster her gifts—in the Music Halls. Forgive me for meandering so far. I feel so very strongly about the future of Mistress Mere. I went again to Herne Hill on Saturday. She was not *en évidence* but I enjoyed walking on the same suburban gravel that she must tread so often. There are a lot of tennis-courts behind the houses of *les* Loftus and their neighbours. I am sure Mistress Mere plays tennis, with a strong overhand service. How shall I continue to know her? To talk to her?

I suppose anyone else would have stood Frank Celli a drink in the auditorium long ago. Perhaps, though, my little idyll had better rest where it is: honestly it is the *only* good influence I have known.

Miss Cumberlidge—are you really and deeply in love with her? I think your whole romance quite charming and most creditable and potent and envy you immensely.

By the way, your songs will arrive tomorrow, and I hope you will sing them well: perhaps you will just make your *début* at the Music Halls as Mistress Mere returns to them. Do you recall an article on Oxford life written by . . . Wood and Marston, and how they badgered me to draw pictures for it? I had thought no paper on earth could have accepted such nonsense: but the ways of Providence and Newnes his puppet are very marvellous. The *Strand* has

[1] English theatre manager (1852–1915). Ran the Gaiety Theatre from 1886, and largely invented the form of entertainment known as Musical Comedy. In 1893 built Daly's Theatre for the American impresario Augustin Daly, and ran it successfully for years.

accepted it.[1] Marston writes in high glee, adding modestly and rightly that it must have been the drawings that pulled the article through. I know not when the thing appears.   Yours MAX

P.S. Here you have a photograph of me by Gillman: did you like it, I forget? I try to fancy poor Rothenstein[2] is the Lady Cecilia: but he's not. Tell me what it was that you said in your rigmarole about me.

[*Postmark 24 August 1893*]   *19 Hyde Park Place*

My dear Reg,

If I were asked for a definition of Beauty, I am in doubt whether I should define it as Cissie or your present:[3] both have much in

[1] This article, "Oxford at Home," by Harold George, with eight illustrations by Max, appeared in the *Strand Magazine* for January 1895. Harold George was the joint pseudonym of John Harold Marston (b. 1868) and George Ronald Wood (b. 1869), who were both at Merton with Max and Reggie.

[2] William Rothenstein (1872–1945), English artist. In "Enoch Soames" (1916; included in *Seven Men*, 1919) Max wrote:

"In the Summer Term of '93 a bolt from the blue flashed down on Oxford. It drove deep, it hurtlingly embedded itself in the soil. Dons and undergraduates stood around, rather pale, discussing nothing but it. Whence came it, this meteorite? From Paris. Its name? Will Rothenstein. Its aim? To do a series of twenty-four portraits in lithograph. These were to be published from the Bodley Head, London. The matter was urgent. Already the Warden of A, and the Master of B, and the Regius Professor of C, had meekly 'sat.' Dignified and doddering old men, who had never consented to sit to any one, could not withstand this dynamic little stranger. He did not sue: he invited; he did not invite: he commanded. He was twenty-one years old. He wore spectacles that flashed more than any other pair ever seen. He was a wit. He was brimful of ideas. He knew Whistler. He knew Edmond de Goncourt. He knew every one in Paris. He knew them all by heart. He was Paris in Oxford. It was whispered that, as soon as he had polished off his selection of dons, he was going to include a few undergraduates. It was a proud day for me when I—I—was included. I liked Rothenstein not less than I feared him; and there arose between us a friendship that has grown ever warmer, and been more and more valued by me, with every passing year."

[3] A copy of Oscar Wilde's book of essays, *Intentions* (1891), bound in vellum. It was inscribed "To my dear Max: on his 21st birthday, Aug 24th 1893," and on the verso of the title-page Max wrote: "Hell is paved with good Intentions, but heaven is roofed with the best. HMB."

common. How very nice of you to think of my birthday, how very clever to think of the one thing of all others I should love. Thanks immensely. Perhaps Mistress Mere is less lovely than the book, for she is always the same, whilst the book is of an exquisite blue by night and of a heavenly green by day, so that its beauty is twofold: one would say that a hundred chosen peacocks were mounting guard over the page. And do you know it is the only *surprise* present I have had on my birthday ever since I was quite small: of late years I have always either chosen or else been shewn my presents before-hand: when I was quite small I always had lead-soldiers, so that even then the only excitement was as to whether they would be cavalry or infantry, and generally they were infantry. Except for the confusion which *must* arise between it and Cissie, your present is quite perfect, my dear Reg: thanks again immensely. I only got it last night on returning from *les* Tree who are staying a little way out of London—I forget where: the husband was away but the wife was *très sympathique* about Cissie and wishes she could be engaged for the Haymarket: I must try to bring about a meeting between the manager and the artist: how charming her *début* would be in the future.

So glad that you are happy and in love. Why leave next Saturday? Why not stay one or two days longer in Hassocks? Ah, what an antinomian I am! In reading The Book again I have come across Wainewright's description of the influence of Art upon his life: "The noisome mists were purged: my feelings, hot, parched and tarnished, were renovated with fresh bloom, simple, beautiful to the simple-hearted."[1] Do you remember it? I wish I had written it, only in my case it has been not Art but an Artist—a thing infinitely higher—that revealed itself for my saving.

Your affectionate MAX

P.S. *Au* Tivoli tonight. Thanks yet again. We have given up the idea of Devonshire and shall possibly go to Whitby: personally I would far rather not leave town: I am always suggesting Herne Hill to my people: it is very healthy and rural and you can't see the Crystal Palace from it.

[1] In the essay in *Intentions* called "Pen, Pencil, and Poison" Wilde quoted this passage from the writings of Thomas Griffiths Wainewright, artist and poisoner (1794–1852).

My dear Reg,

In greatest haste I ask why have you been so absurd and charming as to give me the very lovely holder of cigarettes: nothing could excuse such sweet excess—not even your memorable letter whose advice I have duly laid to heart: a month ago I should have laughed at the homely advice it contains, but now it is hardly necessary. I am so good already: who could help being good with your presents in his keeping?

In haste again and with promise of fuller letter tomorrow morning.   Your affectionate MAX

[Late August 1893]   *The Tivoli*

My dear Reg,

Ever so many thanks for your delightful letter: how nice to be in dainty Dieppe even without me and with the cursed X who may be a very sweet and clever and good man but as a companion—oh Lor'. However you are by the sea and there are cliffs to tip him over. I should, I know.

I am certain he is plucked for the Indian Civil. From all which remarks you will infer that I am jealous of him, though really I am not. Indeed it were charming to be with you, but you seem from your letter to be still very much in love with Miss Cumberlidge, and, as Cissie is dearer to me than ever, we might clash. What, by the way, means your rather cryptic remark about "things going better than you ever could have hoped"? Have you proposed to her actually, or simply do you mean that you had a lovely time near to her? Write and explain. As for me, though I have written such a charming address at the top of the page, I am far elsewhere—at Totteridge again with *les* Tree and longing to be back again in Town: the heat is still far too great and the provinces are quite yellow with wasps and I am stifled with talk of the Legitimate Drama.

My sister-in-law is very sympathetic about Mistress Mere but does not think her pretty. She must really think her lovely I am sure, for the portraits I have of her are beyond mortal praise. How

I hate being in the provinces: we are, it is true, quite near to London, but Totteridge is terribly rural and the house has a large green garden full of those coloured things—(flowers, I think they are called)—that you can buy at Solomon's.[1] And the result of all this isolation and simplicity of life is that my love of the Lady Cecilia, which in London was so quiet and pure and so fresh, has become fevered. I have become quite restless and long to be married to her and make a fool of myself for her sake—how I don't know. She mimicked Mademoiselle Mealy[2] very cleverly last time I saw her. Tomorrow I shall leave Totteridge I think and go home for a day or two, after which alas my people are going into the provinces for a few weeks. Rothenstein has returned to town—which reminds me that Robbie Ross put me up for the 'Ogarth[3] the other day. Would you like to belong also? I think you said you really would. There has been a terrible man staying here—Nisbet, who is dramatic critic for *The Times*:[4] so fat and vulgar and saturnine: he said that *The Second Mrs Tanqueray*[5] left a nasty taste in the mouth and quite prejudiced me against the idea of becoming a journalist. Thanks again enormously for the lovely presents: they are both very like the Blessed Damozel (her new name) but the cigarette-holder especially is the image of her. It seems from one of the interviews that Eugene Stratton[6] also thinks her marvellous. Think of her circle of admirers: Celli, Elen, Stratton and probably R. G. Knowles the Very Peculiar.[7] I hope she will never love one of them, for of such is the Chamber of

[1] A fashionable florist in Piccadilly.
[2] A supposedly French music-hall artist then appearing at the Empire. On 11 August 1893 the *Music Hall and Theatre Review* wrote: "Mdlle Mealy, besides having a voice of wonderful purity and freshness, has a remarkable fund of humour which she skilfully infuses into the audience."
[3] The Hogarth Club was at 175 Bond Street for the last thirty years of the nineteenth century, and was much frequented by artists and writers.
[4] John Ferguson Nisbet (1851–99) was dramatic critic of *The Times* from 1882 until his death.
[5] By A. W. Pinero. First produced at the St James's Theatre on 27 May 1893, with George Alexander and Mrs Patrick Campbell in the leading rôles.
[6] American Negro impersonator (1861–1918). Very successful in the music-halls, where he popularised "Lily of Laguna" and other songs by Leslie Stuart.
[7] Richard George Knowles (1858–1919), music-hall star who billed himself as "the very peculiar American comedian."

Horrors. Perhaps she and I will marry eventually—who knows? Write and tell me more about Miss Cumberlidge. I am ever so interested.   Your affectionate M

P.S. Be very sympathetic.

Saturday [Early September 1893]   *19 Hyde Park Place*
                                                   [and Broadstairs]

My dear Reg,

   Reality has sent her brokers into my little air-castle: my Cupid's eyes are red with crying. Yesterday I came up from the provinces and dined and went *au* Tivoli where I stood in my accustomed place by the side of the stalls. A good many common music-hallish people were standing in front of me, and as I peered over their heads I discerned standing in the front row—whom do you think? You will never guess. I discerned the back of a small girl with a large brown hat and with straight hair falling round her shoulders and a chaperone at her side. Soon she turned round and I saw that she wore a large childish locket and that her face was the face of the Lady Cecilia. There she was standing shoulder to shoulder with cads and harlots. It was dreadful. She was holding a little kind of levée—a little court of fat Spanish Jews in frock-coats with watered-silk facings and horsy young music-hall artists. As I say, it was dreadful: she seemed very much at her ease and quite "the god-child of the Variety Stage" as her mother proudly called her in one of the interviews: but I think she looked a little abashed—bless her!—when she saw me. I did not trust myself to catch her eye but went upstairs to think it all over. I had soon quite forgiven her and meant to waylay her as she went behind for her "turn" but—alas!—there was some back-door on the staircase of which I did not know and I missed my little chance. I had invented a charming story to account for the non-appearance of the interview.

———

   I broke off yesterday in my letter, my dear Reg, and since writing what you have just read have left dear London once more for the provinces. Totteridge was bad enough, but there I certainly enjoyed having fresh flowers in the garden every morning—though when one thinks of what they must have cost, apart from the expense of their carriage from the London dealers, one cannot but wish the money were spent on some more lasting object: people talk of agricultural depression and so forth, but it is a fact that every tiny humble cottage has an enclosed space around it which is filled every morning with fresh flowers. The expenditure is simply profligate: when I have time I mean to write a pamphlet on the "Luxury in Our Villages." And now I am in a terrible little place called Broadstairs: it is utterly remote and uncivilised—you can't even get the evening papers before two o'clock in the afternoon. And I am sure the place is unhealthy: just opposite our house there is a huge stretch of stagnant greenish water which makes everything damp, and must, I am sure, be very bad indeed for people who live near to it. You cannot fancy how I hate it. But of you, my dear Reg, what? You have not written to me again to tell me about your idyll and I am all attention.

Talking of sympathy I spent all yesterday with Will Rothenstein: we were both of us very brilliant, lunched and dined together and talked long of Mistress Mere. In the evening we went *au* Tivoli and he admired her immensely as an artist should. He was very sympathetic, and she—perhaps she looked lovelier than ever in her pink frock and her yellow shoes. But ah, I had more to suffer. Do you remember R. G. Knowles and his song about Columbus and the particular verse about his discovering Pimlico? She imitated him in this verse to the delight of the audience. I blushed crimson, which was silly perhaps, for I am sure she did not know what it all meant. Still there were the horrid suggestive words and manner reproduced by her little voice and face and gestures with terrible truth. Why did her miserable family allow her to sing it? Strange as it may seem, I can nearly wish she had never displayed her talent and were just an ordinary school-girl going back to her school in a week or two quite unheard of by the vile world and unknown of by me. Perhaps I do not really nearly wish that, but certainly it is awful when a tipsy man—there was such a man last night at the Tivoli—reels from his seat in the stalls waving his hat and crying "Three cheers for Cissie Loftus!" I feel that my air-castle has been built without a draw-bridge when that sort of thing happens. Do you see that she is advertised in the papers as "the mimetic marvel"? Do write me a few words of sympathy.

I am going to read here in beastly Broadstairs. I only arrived this morning and have spent the day on the beach straining my eyes over the sea for a glimpse of the good ship Cholera which, I am certain, will touch at this port before any other.[1]

Love to X. I do not know what Madame's address is: so perhaps I shall send this to Dieppe: you are at the *Grand* Hotel, aren't you? Did you get my last letter which I addressed there? Good God, suppose it were lost.   Your affectionate   MAX

Rothenstein (whom I dearly love) was ecstatic quite over the binding of *Intentions*.

He admires too a series of impressionist caricatures I have done and is very anxious for Lane to publish them.

Rothenstein says the Blesséd Damozel is exactly like the Infanta of Spain. I sometimes call her the Infanta now: it is rather a pretty name.

[*September 1893*]   *not 19 Hyde Park Place*
                                  but 4 Chandos Square, Broadstairs

My dear Reg,

I have written to you twice since you arrived at the Grand Hotel in dear Dieppe, but now that you have gone so suddenly to the north I am not sure whether you will have received these human documents, so I have written a sweet note to the manager imploring him to let you have any letters which may have arrived for you. It would be dreadful for me to feel that two vital links in our chain of letters were lying buried in French sand. My egoism is rather touching, I think: you might tell me if you get the letters—one was from Totteridge, the other from this place. Certainly there is an element of pathos in me. How nice for you to be enjoying yourself with the Rs—but how could you suggest that I might have been captivated by anyone other than Cissie? In comparison to her all

[1] Cholera, which was mildly endemic in various parts of Europe, had recently flared up in the Humber ports, and on 16 September *The Times* reported that the outbreak at Grimsby was even more serious than that at Hull.

other girls look and seem and are hideous: besides even if I ever cease to feel the intensity of my love for her I shall always revere her as my ideal: she will be the Small Saint always.

Broadstairs are very *triste* indeed and I long for London: my only consolation has been Willie Wilde,[1] the brother of Oscar, of whom I have seen a good deal. He is very vulgar and unwashed and inferior, but if I shut my eyes I can imagine his voice to be the voice of Oscar. Who was it that said "Scratch Oscar and you will find Willie"? It is a very pregnant saying: if Oscar had not been such a success in life as he has been he would be the image of Willie. It was Willie, by the way, who was found by his host in the smoking-room filling his pockets with handfuls of cigars—wasn't it dreadful?

In a week I go back—*adsit hora*—to Town: I am rather excited to know whether that poor fly in the amber of modernity, John Lane, will wish to publish my Impressions. Dear Will Rothenstein has been "puffing" me to all sorts of people: I hope you will do likewise—and with much love to the Lady Cecilia I remain

Yours affectionately MAX

Sunday [17 September 1893. Postmark 18 September]
19 Hyde Park Place

My dear Reg,

So many thanks for your letter and Heaven be praised that mine has arrived after its wandering. I begin to think that the post is too prosaic and too unsafe a means of communication for us two: could we not have a few homing-doves as the ministers of our penship?

I have just shaken the sand of Broadstairs from my feet. London is quite suffocating with heat and sodden with rain: the dead leaves lie thick in the parks, every one of them the very incarnation of Cholera. I can hardly breathe but am very happy in the dear town. Have you seen Jones's sonnets in advance of the play?[2] Aren't they

[1] William Charles Kingsbury Wilde (1852–99), Oscar's elder brother, was a journalist, for many years on the *Daily Telegraph*.
[2] Presumably the appearance in a newspaper of the two sonnets which Henry Arthur Jones printed as Prologue to the published version (1898) of *The Tempter*, a four-act blank-verse tragedy, set in the fourteenth century.

ghastly? Bad language is very well for a long play on an improper subject to be acted before an audience of vulgar people: but it is terribly out of its place in a delicate sequence of fourteen lines. The author wanted Herbert to recite it.

I hope you are not really reading. I am not, though I have purchased a tiny blue-paper copy of Plato's *Republic*: it looks very difficult indeed and is all written in a crabbed kind of hieroglyphic which I read with extreme difficulty. I suppose it must be Greek, which I used to learn at Charterhouse but had quite put aside with other childish things. However Greats is drawing on and I really must study the language. I shall take a morbid interest in your exam next month and shall forge you several letters from touting tutors as of yore.

But, oh my dear Reg, last night I spoke to the Infanta. It was at the Tivoli—where she was standing again "in front"—and I asked her if she had forgotten our interview. It appeared from her charming manner—she is developing a manner—that she had not, but feared I must think she had, forgotten the photograph. Do you remember that she promised me one whenever the "interview" appeared? It was rather nice of her not to have forgotten: she asked if it was too late to send one, and then I told her that I already had several and that I should be very proud if she would write her name upon them for me.

I am going to send her three tomorrow with a nice note: won't it be lovely to have them? And then I shall write another note thanking her and hinting at a future interview. By the way, I explained to her with pardonable falseness that I had not liked to take notes in a notebook for fear of boring her: that I had rather a bad memory and so by the next day had forgotten all the exact details she had given me, and so the interview could not be written. She is still very mere but not quite so mere—in the strict sense of the word—as she was four weeks ago. She wore a hideous brown dress and a huge hat and looked, I am afraid, rather pale. She has been ill, you see, for the last week, which is not surprising when one thinks how continuously she has performed and how very young she is. I adore her.

Yours affectionately MAX

My dear Reg,

Have you heard about A? *Has* he written to tell you? Very likely
not, for he thinks you are angry with him about something or other.
Well, he has accepted a mastership (salary £80 with an annual rise
of £20) at a large preparatory school seven miles from his home. He
wrote me a charming letter and only announced this in parenthesis:
so I suppose he feels his position rather acutely, poor devil. Really
I cannot but smile through my tears—it seems so queer a development, and after all I dare say he will like the life well enough. Can't
you picture him correcting Greek verses at his desk and looking up
suddenly and saying with forced calm to some tiny boy "Hawksbury,
bring that piece of paper from under your desk to me! Come Sir,
this instant!" I can picture him too at supper, with his bearded
colleagues, implying that he went the pace at Merton and not being
believed. And then at the end of term walking over to his home
with a handbag. The Usher's Return. I feel that he was intended
by Heaven for something better than all this—but still it will be a
career of a kind: he will do something at any rate and he will enjoy
the Christmas holidays very much, though he may not like Usher-
ing in the New Year. Really it is sad: I think a letter from you might
comfort him. . . .

I am very fairly happy for my part. London is quite delightful
and I am within the indispensable stone's-throw of the Tivoli. But
I am constantly being reminded of Oxford by receiving notes from
Merton men whom I scarcely know and who say that they are just
"passing through" and would I care to look them up at the Sports
Club? When will friends understand that when one has not seen
them for some time one does not wish to see them for some time—
especially at a place with such a telegraphic address as "Sportella,
London"?

I have done a sweet drawing of Mistress Mere standing in a white,
guileless frock against a narrow background. The darkness of her
hair is echoed in a dark row of footlights beneath her. This morning
I took her to the framers and had reluctantly to leave her there. I
wanted very much to draw a picture of her chaperone and leave
it there with her, but perhaps it would have seemed silly and

over-anxious. I am going to call the picture "Lines suggested by Miss Cissie Loftus."[1] Isn't that reverent of me and modest?

Tomorrow Henry Arthur comes before Demos in the guise of a poet: it is well for him and for the theatre that I am not Demos but only a very exquisite individual, for if it were otherwise his poetry would not be repeated many times by the mummers and even then to a running accompaniment of the "*pastoricia fistula.*" As it is I expect a great hit will be made.

Ah! I await in breathless eagerness the return of the White Girl's photographs: I hope she will sign them prettily.

Ever yours MAX

... Are you as charming as ever? I look forward to your presence: *adieu.*

I send you an arrangement in pen and ink, which does its best to remind me of the lady Cecilia as I saw her at the Tivoli: please keep it in reverence though it is very bad.[2]

[*21 September 1893*]   *19 Hyde Park Place*

The first night was brilliant beyond compare.[3] But first let me tell you that I think your poem full of a very great charm, and that I envy you such a valve of emotion as must be yours in the power of writing it. Certainly you must publish a little volume and I must design the title-page. By the way, John Lane wants me to write the letterpress of a fantastic book of which Aubrey Beardsley is doing the illustrations: but the whole thing so far is rather complicated and vague, so that I will tell you no more till we meet. I feel that I have the germs of success in me and shall leave the disease to run its course. The book, which would be rather long, would not be produced until next year. It would be called *The Masques.*

[1] This drawing (here reproduced opposite p. 49) appeared in the *Sketch* on 9 May 1894.   [2] See illustration opposite.
[3] *The Tempter,* by Henry Arthur Jones, was first produced at the Haymarket Theatre on 20 September 1893, with Tree as the Devil, supported by Mrs Tree, Fred Terry, Julia Neilson and Irene Vanbrugh. It ran for seventy-three nights.

Aubrey is doing some of the pictures already and I am to write as my fancy guides me.[1]

Well, as I say, the first night was brilliant beyond compare. Though September is upon the town, the stalls were positively infested with politicians; and peeresses in their own right were hustled into tiny boxes above the chandelier. Meredith was to have come but could not: also Zola was to have been there but, being travel-worn, was not,[2] and his place was filled by Sir William Harcourt[3] and other Romanticists. Just behind us were Mrs Lawson and your brother: I thought he looked rather ill and worn but he seemed in rather good spirits and as you may imagine did *not* like the play. I suppose you will have read what the papers say of it: so let my criticism be one of the exquisite, unwritten things. Oscar was in town but went to the Alhambra with Bosie Douglas.

In future I shall not mind being the bearer of ill-tidings, knowing that I shall not be believed. But really it is all true about the ushership. . . . Fancy a man of any culture or power of life following in the footsteps of Dr Arnold and Mr Squeers—going out into the desert to live amongst those poor little creatures, half-formed in body and half-formed in mind, that we call boys: getting up every morning at six-thirty to frighten them till night-fall: making himself the tyrant of their miseries and the sharer—if he be an athlete like our friend—of their wretched pastimes. . . .

I am designing you a yellow overcoat, am intensely in sympathy with your love of Miss Cumberlidge, am very angry with my darling

[1] This project came to nothing.
[2] Emile Zola (1840–1902) had already published all twenty volumes of his Rougon-Macquart series of naturalistic novels, and in 1888 and 1889 his English publisher, Henry Vizetelly, had been first fined and then imprisoned on their account. Now Zola was visiting London at the invitation of the Institute of Journalists. He arrived on 20 September and was welcomed by Sir Edward Lawson, who made a speech in French at Victoria Station. He was entertained at the Imperial Institute, the Crystal Palace, and by the Lord Mayor at the Guildhall. On 28 September the Authors' Club gave him a dinner, which was attended by eighty literary men including George Moore, Frank Harris, Oscar Browning, Jerome K. Jerome and H. D. Traill.
[3] The Rt. Hon. Sir William George Granville Venables Vernon Harcourt (1827–1904), lawyer and Liberal politician, was Chancellor of the Exchequer 1892–95.

for not sending her photographs when she must have received them
by the first post on Tuesday, have quite forgiven her and am

Your affectionate MAX

P.S. *Voilà un mot.* Young Henry Irving was speaking of Zola last
night. "He is stupendous, he is superb," he said; "he sweeps everything before him!" "So does a scavenger," I suggested inimitably.

Friday [Postmark 22 September 1893]   *19 Hyde Park Place*

My dear Reg,

Mistress Mere has sent me the portraits: they look ever so beautiful with her name across them and the simple, unaffected and very
gratifying avowal that she is mine—mine very sincerely. I asked
her to write a line out of "Susey Toosey" upon the two where she
is mimicking Eugene Stratton and she has done so with the obedience of an artist. On one she has written "My scrumptious Soosey
Toosey" and on the other she has made herself say "Oh you can't,
'cos the fire's out *too*." What a good hand she writes! I think she
must be very clever. Does Miss Cumberlidge write a good hand?

But (said he, scarcely pausing for a reply) I almost wish she had
not given me the exquisite things so soon. I love the passive ardour
with which one hangs upon every knock that falls from the postman's finger, when one is waiting for anything so sweet. However
. ..

I am very much *intrigué* about Aubrey and the book and the
long Lane that has no Elkin.[1] When I have seen some of the pictures
I shall know what kind of thing is expected of me. It is rather a
compliment for me. I am so glad the publisher came to me and not
I to the publisher.

Oscar is still in town, dancing attendance upon Zola's attendants.

My love to you. I wonder *how* many letters I have written to you
since we parted and how much of them you have read.

Yours affectionately MAX

It seems that John Lane is furious with Will Rothenstein, whose
guest he has been for a few days in Paris. After conducting his
publisher to the Louvre, taking him into every room and listening

[1] John Lane's partner in the Bodley Head was Elkin Mathews.

with great attention to his detailed opinions of all the pictures, he suddenly turned upon him with pent-up fury and insolence and told him never to mention Art again: inasmuch as he knew nothing whatever about it and probably cared less. John Lane is extremely bitter about him now in consequence and is probably going to get someone else to design a book-plate, instead of one for which he has already paid Will Rothenstein. Isn't it rather sad?

[23 September 1893]   19 Hyde Park Place

My dear Reg,

Is love an illusion as they say or is it a series of disillusionments, as my reverence of Cissie Loftus has been? Am I always to be at the mercy of such things as I saw last night when she came upon the stage—a large and carefully frizzled fringe; eyes standing out, surrounded by pigments, in bold relief from the face: a dress of salmon-pink with a dash of orange in it? Why cannot she still be as when I first saw her, "endeavouring," with features of wistful ivory and hair combed as they combed it in the convent, "to give us a few imitations of some of our leading music-hall artists"? It is nonsense what I used to say about all actions being justified by personality— that one's queen could do no wrong. Everything she does is wrong and hateful in the sight of her lover. When I saw Cissie first and loved her I said unconsciously "Here is Perfection." And so every step she has taken since then has been, in my eyes, a step towards the ground. I *wish* she were still the same: I wish Cupid had shot his arrow not to quicken my heart but to make rigid her limbs, lest life should change the form or pose of them. However the photographer did something of the kind when he clicked his camera before her: she went to Elliott & Fry and was taken by them at her best and most beautiful—just as she was at first. Forgive me, dear Reg, for meandering so far: I am sure there must have been times when you have wished Miss Cumberlidge to be petrified for an "eternal moment." The Lady Cecilia certainly *has* changed and her fringe and her frock are quite terrible: I suppose it is all due to the absence of Miss Mahrie Loftus who is in Edinburgh. She, I think, understood her child's charm, but the child itself wishes no doubt to be

even as her elders and betters in appearance—Miss Jenny Valmore[1]
and the rest of them. For the moment she has succeeded.

Even the audience had the good sense to resent the change in her
last night: the applause that followed her mimicry—did I tell you
that she calls herself "the mimetic marvel" in the advertisements?—
was ominously less. But in the end all was well. You would have
loved her when a man gave an irresistible peal of laughter as she was
imitating R. G. Knowles. She laughed too and could not catch up
the music: she blushed and broke down and had to finish the song
in silence abashed. As she went off in a storm of laughter and
applause, I could see her throw herself down on a little chair at the
wings and bury her face in her hands. She was roaring with laughter
herself. My heart mingled with hers.

Ever yours affectionately MAX

P.S. Give me some news of Miss Cumberlidge. It is absurd the way
I go on writing to you so continuously. You must forgive me. You
see you are more sympathetic than a diary. The fault is yours.

I have heard from Will Rothenstein who is painting out in the
provinces: with him he has a model whom he loves: he says she is
quite "a note in art" and "quite 1830."

Mistress Mere is only fifteen.

Some day these effusions by me must be published under the title
of "Misdirected Love-Letters."

Friday [Postmark 29 September 1893]   *19 Hyde Park Place*

My dear Reg,

How charming it was—your dinner after so long a parting the
other night—and how nice your rooms are and how enviable you.
After I left you I could not resist the Shrine, where was also Bobbie[2]
a-worshipping with his brother: we went on, when the young goddess had vanished in thunder, to "The Crown,"[3] a literary tavern

[1] Described in an advertisement of January 1893 as "The People's
Idol" of the Canterbury, Paragon, Tivoli, and Pavilion music halls.
[2] Robert Ross.
[3] A public house in the Charing Cross Road, where according to Will
Rothenstein, "we usually met in a little room, away from the bar, where
we could talk. Hot port was the favourite drink." (*Men and Memories*,
1931, vol I, p. 238)

full of young nameless poets and cocottes and old men who have been ministers of the Church of England and are no longer. Such a dull, suspect place it is. Bobbie loathes it and so do I, but we must go together some night to cure your mind of any Bohemian hankerings that still lurk within it. Let us both try to be quite ordinary and to make money and never do anything wrong. Above all let us purge our minds of literature: it leads to no good. Bobbie has offended Oscar most *fearfully* by telling him that whatever his shortcomings may be—and they are many—no one can deny that he is a gentleman of the old school. Isn't it exquisitely funny? There *is* something rather Georgian in Oscar's deportment.

By the way, it is all over. I hate Cissy Loftus, or rather I can see her now with no emotion but regret—cold regret. I saw her last night and she had gone a step *too* far. She had piled a Pelion of rouge upon an Ossa of powder: her eyes shone again and she had even abandoned the little prologue about "kind permission" and "a few of our leading music-hall artists." Anything less mere I have never seen, nor anything less like that sweet creature with the grace of a fawn and the *gaucherie* of a young elephant—the white girl that I worshipped. Do you remember "the fate that foolish Harriet befell" in the nursery book? How that she would play with the matches till one day she caught fire and nothing was spared by the flames except her two shoes?[1] Oddly enough Cissie Loftus still wears those yellow shoes with the little straps over the instep that she wore from the first—they are all that remains of poor Mistress Mere: why would she go so close to the footlights? She has been burnt partly by her own fault like "foolish Harriet" and partly in deference to public opinion, like Joan of Arc. Certainly the audience at the Pavilion received her more rapturously than ever she was received in the old days. At the end of her songs, someone threw her a bouquet and she seemed very pleased with it, though I don't think she deserved it. The flowers were very lovely and were intended I am sure for Mistress Mere, not for the tawdry creature made in her image. I say "someone" threw her them, but I do not mean that it was I—on the contrary it was a rather pretty demi-mondaine in a box full of

[1] "The Dreadful Story about Harriet and the Matches" in *Struwwelpeter* by Heinrich Hoffmann (1809–74), first published in German 1845, in English 1848.

men. Poor Lady Cecilia, poor Small Saint, how she has changed—her very photographs are fading: but don't imagine I have meant a word of all that I have been saying. If you did I should be obliged to call in all the copies of this letter and as I am sending them to friends in all parts of the kingdom it would be very inconvenient indeed.

In spite of her, I think I love Cissy Loftus more than ever: I love her for having been so beautiful and for all the good she has done me unknowingly and for the pain and happiness that I have had by reason of her. And I love her because she is still far more beautiful than anyone else in the world. Your affectionate MAX

There are 25 copies of this letter of which this is copy number 17. Forgive these blots.

[*Postmark 2 October 1893*]   *19 Hyde Park Place*

My dear Reg,

How did you like the 'Ogarth? I think it is rather a cosy little place—odd without being squalid or Bohemian in the bad sense of the word. And to us with our literary wishes it will be very very useful I suppose. How do you like Bobbie? He too is cosy I think and useful also. Oh I have written a delightful paragraph about *le jeune* Henry Irving—how that at Oxford amongst his intimates he had a reputation for ability and that since that time "he has not allowed the grass to grow under his feet—seeing that he has played a part twice under the auspices of his father's old friend Mr John Hare, has read for the Bar in Mr George Lewis's office and has written for the *Albemarle Review*." I longed to add "though his article, which dealt comprehensively with the question of crime, was not accepted by the editor," but did not dare and wished him all success instead.

My people tell me that Oscar's message about the caricatures was seriously intended! Fancy! I had taken it as the merest and most obvious of pleasantries. How I wish he had written to me on the subject and how I could have crushed him. Don't you think it fearful cheek on his part? So long as the man's head interests me, I shall continue to draw it. He is simply an unpaid model of mine and as such he should behave. Mr Swift MacNeill and his "technical assault" must have suggested the idea.[1] Are all Irishmen so sensitive, I wonder?

Tomorrow I am going to Drury Lane:[2] I grudge every evening spent away from the Tivoli, and I am quite reconciled to whatever change Mistress Mere may choose to make in her appearance. One coating more or less of paint upon the lily—what does it matter? Like poor Muffat in Zola's book,[3] I have given up wishing to keep my love perfect: I forgive her again and again. Unlike Muffat, however, I have no religion upon which to fall back: Cecilia is the only saint I know and a small one at that. How charming it is to be in love. Why do you say I am not sympathetic with you about your love? The very fact of my writing to you every day all about myself is proof enough of my sympathy.

On Tuesday—do you remember?—you asked us to come to tea. So I shall see you then and we can talk about everything that is delightful. Your affectionate MAX

[Postmark 13 October 1893]   19 Hyde Park Place

My dear Reg,

I found your nice, amusing letter when I came home the other day: also today I had a nice note from the Warden[4] who says that

[1] John Gordon Swift MacNeill (1849–1926), Anti-Parnellite M.P. for South Donegal 1887–1918. On 26 August 1893 The Times reported that he "feels aggrieved at a caricature which appears in the current issue of Punch, and meeting Mr Harry Furniss in the Lobby [of the House of Commons] last night, he demanded to know whether that gentleman was responsible for it. Mr Furniss admitted that the sketch complained of was his work, whereupon Mr MacNeill denounced him with some warmth, and, seizing him by the shoulders, committed what might be construed into a technical assault." Three days later Furniss wrote to say that the assault was "more loving than aggressive."
[2] Where A Life of Pleasure, a spectacular drama of modern life in five acts by Sir Augustus Harris and Henry Pettitt, had opened on 21 September, with Henry Neville, Lily Hanbury and Mrs Bernard Beere in leading parts.
[3] Count Muffat de Beuville in Nana (1880), who allowed his passion for Nana to destroy him.
[4] The Hon George Charles Brodrick (1831–1903), second son of the seventh Viscount Midleton, was Warden of Merton College, Oxford, from 1881 until his death.

the College gives me leave.[1] Isn't the weather too *dreadful?* But I forgot—you do not mind cold weather: to me it is instant death.

My sister-in-law saw the Lady Cecilia to talk to yesterday and liked her very much. She is going to the Haymarket next Tuesday and I am going too—isn't it nice? But I am not going to write to you about her any more: you were rather unkind to me about her when I last saw you, and I had thought all along, all the time I was writing about her to you, that you were sympathetic. I feel like a man who, on his knees, has been whispering his soul-secrets to a confessor and peers at length through the grill of the confessional only to behold the grinning or yawning face of a sceptic. I confess I was rather hurt and must find another confidant. After all, why should you not have been kind? If you did not really think I had more capacity for being in love than H, you need not have said so— nor need you have said that you have been *épris* of little artistes yourself, nor that I could not love anyone whom I knew so little. Surely love is not a question of letters of introduction or invitations to tea or any other of the symbols of acquaintance.

However, I am not going to write any more about the Lady Cecilia. *Parlons d'autre chose.* I am going to begin reading: don't knock yourself up by taking no exercise.   Yours MAX

The series of "Misdirected Love-Letters" concludes with this letter. I am afraid they were "misdirected" in more ways than one— *hélas.*

Saturday [14 October 1893. Postmark 15 October]
19 Hyde Park Place

No, my dear Reg, of course I do not think you are angry with me. Why should you be? I don't think I have done anything to make you angry. After all the whole "incident" or whatever one would call it comes to very little: simply that I had been writing long letters to you chiefly about one subject thinking you very sympathetic about it: then, when I spoke to you about this same subject, I thought you rather less sympathetic than might be, and felt—not

[1] To stay down from Oxford for the term, ostensibly to work for his degree, for which Max never sat.

unnaturally—rather foolish and, rather unwisely, said so. You say that you were not really at all unsympathetic except in manner and I quite believe you were not and there is an end of it! I hate being the aggrieved party and it was quite refreshing to me when I came to that part of your letter where you speak of your sympathy being quite equal at least to anything I ever showed or am likely to show for things or people which interest you. Now we resume our old footing once more. I the cruel monstrous egoist with not a word except in scorn or a glance except in derision for any of the thoughts and interests of poor, silent, shrinking you. I am quite myself again. Your picture of our intercourse always flatters my vanity, though I am afraid the shorthand reporter might not quite bear you out. I am sure Mr Bull knows shorthand—why not station him behind the screen whenever I am going to see you and in time perhaps I shall become less conceited than you tend to make me. Really, dear Reg, I think you are rather morbid, though I tremble for the consequences when I call you so. Let us be friends again for the present.

Will Rothenstein is on his way from Oxford at this moment to draw my brother in chalks upon brown paper during the *entr'actes* of *The Tempter*! I fear the thing may be a terrible failure. Mrs Tree thinks Rothenstein the ugliest man in the wide world: I think he is rather nice to look upon with his huge spectacles and his thick raven hair combed over the forehead. He looks like a creature of another world. I wonder if he will succeed? He ought to if anyone ought to, I think. Such utter self-confidence I have never seen. Did I tell you that he has no heart-line on his right hand?   Yours MAX

That is an admirable maxim of yours, that one should always try to say the thing that pleases one's friends most. I think really that I have always tried to act upon it in all my friendships—and thereby have thrown away much of sincerity. Most of my true words are spoken in jest and I don't think you quite discriminate between the offensiveness of chaff which is generally small and the unkindness of serious criticism which can be great.

P.S. Of course I saw the other day that you were "*distrait* and wanted to work" and I felt rather a beast for staying so long: but alas I had no umbrella and had spent my last eighteenpence in the world upon the cab that brought me to Clement's Inn—*voilà*.

My dear Reg,

Of course the story about Wallace was as complete a fiction as you imagine my love of the Lady Cecilia to be. Amusing things like that very seldom happen and I was rather charmed that you did not utterly disbelieve my little tale. Also I was rather touched by your cross-examinatory attempt to trip me up by asking whether I had yet heard from Geo. Do not leave off telling the tale however: such are the straws that go to form the bricks in the walls of the temple of my fame that is to be.

Our little controversy is becoming most funny, delightful and droll—and loses nothing of its charm by the restored good humour of each of us. What could be very much more piquant than your protest that "*when 'you' do happen to take an interest in 'me' and 'my' loves*" I am not duly thankful, though to your "own idea" you have quite "*sufficiently proved*" your sympathy? It is the first time I have heard of a man "proving" his sympathy to his own satisfaction and I think the idea very sweet. Evidently the law is beginning to tell upon you—but I shall not really drop my contention till you have made an affidavit, witnessed by Crackanthorpes Senior and Junior,[1] to the effect that you really were very sympathetic. In a case like this of course one cannot be too careful: I must not accept any sympathy that is not formally proven, nor of course must I reject it thus without forfeiting my position as sympathiser. And really when you suggest that "the manner in which for weeks you received the misdirected love letters" is sufficiently final evidence in your favour, I must remind you that I scarcely know what that manner was, though to judge from your phrase it must have been a very long-suffering sort of manner! Certainly you never forbad me to go on writing to you, but then neither did the pillar-box at the corner of the street refuse to harbour my envelopes. Of course you asked me from time to time how was the Lady Cecilia, did I still adore her and so forth, and very nice of you it was, but how in the name of courtesy could you have done otherwise? *Besides* I never complained

[1] Presumably Dayrell E. M. Crackanthorpe (b. 1871), who was a Merton undergraduate 1890–93, and his father Montague Hughes Crackanthorpe (formerly Cookson), Q.C.

of your conduct at a distance: only of what appeared to my lay mind to be rather unsympathetic in your speech and manner at Clement's Inn the other day. Indeed it was for the very reason that I had thought you sympathetic all along that I resented what I took to be a sudden change in you. However, you say that you were awfully nice to me. So be it. I have made a terrible mistake. As it is, I await your affidavit eagerly. I was a fool to walk in the garden with closed eyes, else I should have seen the little butterfly with its wings in a flutter of sympathy: at least it will be something that I have the butterfly with a pin through it and a label under it and over it a case of glass!

. . . I hope you are not over-reading, and am

Your affectionate* MAX

* (Charming)

My sister-in-law has given me a note which she has received from Cissie (or is it Cissy—or Cissey?) asking for seats at the Haymarket. It is written in bright red ink and is, in my fevered opinion, a misdirected love-letter. Wednesday is the day to be honoured by her visit, so I am living in the near future.

You need not be alarmed about love making me unhappy—at all events it is not doing so just now. Is that necessarily a sign that it is growing less, my dear Reg? Are all Cupid's arrows arrows of poison? If I said that I loved her the less for the greatness of her fringe, I did not mean it. One may carp and carp at every little action of one's mistress and, as I have said, to carp and carp is most natural, but forgiveness comes always at the same time. If I had first seen the Little Writer in Red Ink as now she is in all her frippery and finery, I might never have thought of her except as an incomparably poignant mimic—as an ape, as a parrot.

But it is quite otherwise with me, you surely understand: she was so sweet that I love every ringlet now in her fringe and all that is sophisticated or sweet in her voice and bearing.

But I must not detain you: I am beginning to presume upon "the way in which for weeks you received" the poor vagrants of my pen. Do I really love you so very much? I wish you would not say so at any rate. Look up the word "confidant" in that dreadful "Lover's Lexicon" in the *P.M.G.* Or haven't they got so far yet? They had just got to "bridegroom" when I last saw the paper.[1]

Another P.S. How exciting about your letter to the *Chronicle*.[2] Have you seen the comment upon it in this evening's *P.M.G.* in the Literary Notes? You have woken up and found yourself famous! How happy you should be. Poor Oscar went to bed and found himself infamous. More fireworks!

Saturday [*Postmark 21 October 1893*]   *19 Hyde Park Place*

My dearest Reg,

I think your note very sweet: the nightingale herself might envy you. But the picture! How fearful, how unconscious of the prettiness of the Little Writer in Red Ink! Besides I am quite, quite sure she has not got Gus Elen and *ces autres* upon the brain: don't let the foolish picture mislead you.

Here is the way in which the picture should have been drawn [*see p. 80*].

By the way, do you know what disappointment is? In my unregenerate days I was far too much of an egoist to seek pleasure in anything but introspection and, taking myself as the standard of

[1] "The Lover's Lexicon" by Frederick Greenwood was appearing at intervals in the *Pall Mall Gazette*. It consisted of a series of apophthegms with headings in alphabetical order. The issue of 5 October contained FRIEND, GALLANT and HABITUDE. The whole thing was reprinted as a book before the end of the year.

[2] On 14 October the *Daily Chronicle* had published a review of *Europe: 1789–1815*, by H. Morse Stephens, and on 16 October the following letter:

Sir, So far from "loading the memory of Robespierre with unnecessary invective," Mr Stephens has been wont to place him in too high a niche among the virtuous, a view which has been somewhat severely handled by eminent critics of Mr Stephens's book on the French Revolution. The best, the truest estimate of Robespierre's character is surely to be found in Mr John Morley's essay, where with marvellous intuition he lays bare the narrowness, the pedantry, the mediocrity of a man who must always be something of a mystery, but can never be a hero.

                                        I am, etc.
                                        Reginald Turner

2 Clement's Inn, Strand, Oct. 14.

perfection, thought myself perfect utterly—and was never, never disappointed. But now I have become a tuist and all is changed. Last Wednesday—that should have been the day of days—I looked in vain for the Small Saint at the Haymarket: the chaperone sat in her place with some hideous creature but no Small Saint had come! And again today: waking dimly in the morning I remembered that tonight was the first night of the burlesque[1] and I should see her in the white kirtle of Haidée: when I opened my paper I found Geo. Edwardes' dastardly notice of postponement "owing to an accident to one of the leading performers." Heigh-ho: I suppose there is such a thing as "Saturday next"—but how long hence!

I went to the Gaiety and asked to whom the accident had happened, what accident was it? It was not, as I half hoped, the Small Saint who had broken her heart—only Mr Robert Pateman who had sprained his ankle. I went drearily to lunch alone at Solferino's and tried to forget sorrow under a crown of vine-leaves which—alas—merely served to cast a deeper shadow over my brow. Pity me, dear Reg: my love is a very dolorous sequence. But I am very sympathetic with your liking for Miss Cumberlidge and like you for liking her. How charming to be near her with nothing to prevent you from seeing her all day long and no unladylike profession to be scoffed at by your friends and no silly outworn poses of your own to be called up against you! Nobody believes in *me*! Even R, a professional believer and on the eve of starting for Africa expressly to trade upon his own credulity, scoffs. I wish there were not anything so inherently vulgar in suicide, for it is the only logical conclusion to my career.

Do write to me again. My people saw Cissie in a box at *Sowing the Wind*[2] tonight: I was, of course, at the Trocadero. My luck is simply abominable.

The Trocadero is a fearful swindle. They advertise a gorgeous programme with "all the stars" and when you get inside you find

[1] *Don Juan* by James Tanner, with lyrics by Adrian Ross and music by Meyer Lutz, eventually opened at the Gaiety on 28 October. Cissy Loftus played the part of Haidée, her first appearance on the regular stage.
[2] A play by Sydney Grundy which opened at the Comedy Theatre on 30 September 1893, with Cyril Maude, Brandon Thomas, Winifred Emery and Rose Leclercq in leading rôles.

that it consists of Miss Maggie Mayhew and Mr Tom Robbins and that all the rest are extra-turns. No stars but any number of asterisks. However—   Your affectionate MAX

[*On back of envelope*] *Oscaris versus mirifica voluptate mea pectora implent. Librum assidua cura adhuc conservo.*[1]

Sunday [3 December 1893. Postmark 5 December]
19 Hyde Park Place

My dear Reg,

And so we parted with no formality! I had fully intended to come the next evening to say good-bye, but I had rather a headache, and it was, you may remember, ever so cold and I thought the streets would be rather un-cosy and so could not come. I wonder what sort of a voyage you are having and in my heart of hearts I rather hope— but psychology to the winds: I am sure you will enjoy Egypt and can imagine you raving about the pyramids in a way that would irritate me: also terrifying the Egyptians.[2]

I am sending you the *National Observer*, which has in it a superbly poignant article about Le G's book: you must read it.[3] I went yesterday to the first night of *Captain Swift*[4] which was damned well received. The Custs were there in the front row and never exchanged one word the whole time: such is matrimony, Reg. Apparently the lesson of the play was too much for their consciences,

[1] Oscar's poems fill my heart with wonderful pleasure. I am still keeping the book with assiduous care.
[2] Reggie was visiting Egypt with Frank Lawson.
[3] On 2 December 1893, reviewing Richard Le Gallienne's *The Religion of a Literary Man*, the *National Observer* wrote:
"Here at last is a book that should have a vogue. For it is a book that meets the spiritual needs of the age. The tea-tables of the suburbs have been crying out for a Moses to lead them into the Promised Land where prigs are. And here is Mr Le Gallienne to bring them over Jordan under the twin banners of Literature and Religion. His book is just the article to supply the want. As a conjunction of pretentiousness and cheapness, affectation and simplicity, shallowness and foppery, it is all that the Heart of Woman could desire."
[4] This play by C. Haddon Chambers, originally produced by Tree in 1888, was revived by him at the Haymarket on 2 December 1893.

for they left before the fourth act, like the King and Queen of Denmark. Afterwards, at the Garrick, I met for the first time Clement Scott.[1] Possibly I may have seen commoner and stupider men but I can't at this moment recall any such. His fat fingers were loaded with huge glassy-looking jewels and he wore two bracelets. Also his conversation—heavens! My brother told him with a white little wave of his hand that I also was going in for literature: to which Clement Scott replied that he only hoped I would, as he seemed to be fighting all alone for his dramatic creed. I smiled with genial deference. Do you see me as the henchman of the man?

Well, dear Reg, I must end as I have to go out into the cold with my people. Do write—write me a real letter and tell me all about Africa. Yours MAX

P.S. I suppose you will have written to Lady Brooke, asking her to turn over a new leaf now that she is a Countess.[2] Outram Tristram is taking over the *Whitehall Review* and wants me to do an illustrated article for it.[3] I suppose I shall be advertised with the other contributors! Hurrah!

Tuesday [*19 December 1893*] *19 Hyde Park Place*

Dearest Reg,

I had your nice letter yesterday: why was it written the Sunday before last and yet did not arrive before? Also have you had *my* letter which I sent to the care of Messrs Cook some time ago? How

[1] Clement William Scott (1841–1904) was dramatic critic of the *Daily Telegraph* from 1872 until 1898 (see note p. 127). He also edited a monthly magazine, the *Theatre*, 1877–97, wrote some plays and translated others, including Sardou's *Diplomacy* (1878). A violent opponent of Ibsen.
[2] Frances Maynard (1861–1938) married (1881) Francis Richard Charles Guy Greville, Lord Brooke (1853–1924), who succeeded his father as fifth Earl of Warwick on 2 December 1893. Lady Brooke had been the subject of a quarrel, and almost a duel, between the Prince of Wales and Lord Charles Beresford. As Lady Warwick she was later famous as a Socialist.
[3] William Outram Tristram (b. 1859), author and playwright, may well have become the new editor of the *Whitehall Review* at this time, but I can find nothing by Max in it.

glad I am that you are enjoying yourself in Cairo. I was quite sure you would and so am not disappointed. But all the same I hope to see you again at home before any unconscionable time elapse: do not settle down as that perpetual bore Robert Louis Stevenson has done in Samoa and flood the weekly papers with "Mr Turner in his Egyptian Home," "Mr Turner in Exile" and so on, to the exclusion of more fascinating matter.

Of me there is nothing great to tell. . . . Bobbie Ross has returned to this country for a few days and of him there have been very great and intimate scandals and almost, if not quite, warrants: slowly he is recovering but has to remain at Davos during his convalescence for fear of a social relapse. I must not disclose anything (nor must you) but I may tell you that a schoolboy with wonderful eyes, Bosie, Bobbie, a furious father, George Lewis,[1] a headmaster (who is now blackmailing Bobbie), St John Wontner,[2] Calais, Dover, Oscar Browning,[3] Oscar, Dover, Calais, intercepted letters, private detectives, Calais, Dover and returned cigarette-cases were some of the ingredients of the dreadful episode. Bobbie, it may amuse you to hear, was watched to our house that night you were here and then on to the Hogarth, so you may yet be something to posterity. The *garçon entretenu*, the schoolboy Helen "for whom those horned ships were launched, those beautiful mailed men laid low,"[4] was the same as him of whom I told you that he had been stolen from Bobbie by Bosie and kept at the Albemarle Hotel: how well I remember passing this place one night with Bobbie and his looking up sadly at the lighted windows and wondering to me behind which of the red curtains lay the desire of his soul. From the data which I have supplied, you will doubtless form a fair notion of the trend of the catastrophe, of which more when we meet.

[1] George Henry Lewis (1833–1911) was head of the firm of Lewis & Lewis and one of the most successful and fashionable solicitors of the time. He was knighted 1893 and made a baronet 1902.
[2] 1842–95. Partner in Wontner & Sons, Solicitors, the firm founded by his father, Thomas Wontner, which for more than sixty years acted for the Home Office, the Treasury and the Commissioner of Metropolitan Police.
[3] 1837–1923. Eton master 1860–75, Cambridge don and "character" 1876–1909. Author of many books, mainly historical.
[4] Oscar Wilde, "The Critic as Artist," Part I (published in *Intentions*, 1891).

Oxford won the football match[1] and the scene at the Empire that evening was extraordinary. I went afterwards with some men to the "Mandoline," a little dancing-club which teemed with Merton men. . . .

Dear Lady Cecilia, how I do wish I were still in love of her: for I never was so happy before nor have been since the time: "one should always be in love" said Lord Illingworth[2] and I think he was right. I am sorry to say, too, that *Masques* has begun to depress me and I think after all of having a try for the service: of course I am a bit too old for Sandhurst: but they say the Militia is a much easier and freer way and, *I* think, *much better training*: what does trigonometry and algebra and the rest of it do for a soldier: a soldier has to be ready to fight and defend himself, not to waste his time among a lot of musty school-books. Don't *you* think so? Poor Rothenstein, his series *"va très lentement:"* at present he has rented for a month the loveliest little house and studio in Tite Street: it is like a glorified 19 Merton Street and on the staircase hangs a huge oil-painting by Whistler, a scurrilous caricature of his old enemy Leyland,[3] seated on the White House with a horrible pattern of gold covering his face and hands, which are claws. Yesterday I went to see H. and found it rather ghastly, as I sat there, to feel that underneath was your room, dark and cold and tenantless. As I went down, I touched the electric bell at your door and waited, half expecting the door to open upon your broad smile cosily bisected by an amber-held cigarette. But the bell had vibrated in darkness and I had to go away at last, feeling rather what Jerome K. Jerome calls mournful.

Well, au revoir and mind, another charming letter very soon for me.

——————

Xmas Day. Your letter and charming card have just come. My mother thanks you immensely for the card you sent her. Also I am

[1] In the University rugger match on 13 December 1893 Oxford beat Cambridge 3–0.
[2] In Act III of Oscar Wilde's *A Woman of No Importance* (1893).
[3] Frederick Richards Leyland (1831–92) was a wealthy self-made Liverpool ship-owner, for whose house in Princes Gate, London, Whistler (largely unasked) painted his famous Peacock Room. The decorations included a caricature of Leyland as a grasping bird with its claws on a pile of money.

not going to give you your present till you come back—so make haste and let no modern Pharaoh detain you in Egypt. . . . Sorry I have no card for *you*. All shops are shut up and I did not get you one before, remembering what an antinomian you were and how you once said that you "disliked conventional greetings." So I have no card. Antinomianism never pays, you see. All love.

All this was written before your Christmas letter arrived.

Monday [*1 January 1894*]*   *19 Hyde Park Place*

My dear Reg,

What an amusing letter and a charming! Many thanks for it, but why did it take such a fearful time to reach me—eight days! Surely Egypt is nearer than all that. I am very sorry indeed that the *National Observer* never reached you, but surely you did not expect *me* with my beautiful helpless ways to *send* it to you as I promised—sending it would have meant string and stamps and postal wrappers and corners left open to shew that it really was a newspaper, and many such things quite out of my line. Really, dear Reg, I think you are a little unreasonable: however, I am very sorry you did not receive it (I had hoped some chance might throw it into your hands without my intervention) for really the critique of the *Religio Scriptoris* was ever so funny and unjust to a fault:[1] it said amongst other things that it was the work of a prig and a charlatan, that the style was "a curious blend of the *Daily Telegraph* and the New Testament; 'the world and the kingdoms thereof' jostles 'the Corvine Valkyrior' (which means 'rook')" and so on. Of the whole preface it makes cruel work, speaking of "the rooks, or 'the poor dead cawers' as Mr Le Gallienne calls them in his literary way" and of "Mr Le Gallienne (why does the man's very name sound ungrammatical?)" Again and again it is lovely, but there are a few of its flowers.

I suppose that Bosey[2] has told you all about Bobbie's troubles, which I sketched in silhouette in my last letter. (I suppose it has in no wise reached as I write this one.) All of it is rather sad, don't you think?

[1] See note, p. 82.   [2] Douglas was in Egypt with Reggie.

By the way Rothenstein has given me a charming pastel of myself and is going to paint me in oils. Tomorrow is the first sitting. The thing will be shewn at the Grafton[1]. . . . Dear Bosey, all love to him. I am afraid his father's marriage must have been rather a shock and a grief to him.[2]

Last night being New Year's Eve, I drank in the New Year with the Trees at Sloane Street (do you remember those happy days shut out from the world with our little jokes and our laziness and our Austin Dobsons in Merton just two years ago?). . . . Well, I drank in the New Year and that awful Nisbet was there. When I left— about two o'clock—two pretty harlots accosted me a few yards from the house and we talked together for some time. Ever since, I have been racked with fear that the Trees may have been looking out of the window—which would have been awkward, especially as it would seem an odd beginning to the New Year.

I must tell you a sweet tale of Oscar told me by Will. Will and Oscar were conducted by Sherard[3] to a kind of thieves' cellar in Paris, where they mixed freely with the company—mostly cut-throats. Sherard, as is his wont, got drunk and frightful and rising from his chair assumed an attitude of defence, saying in a loud voice that anyone who attacked Mr Oscar Wilde would have to reckon with *him* first. "Hush, Robert, hush!" said Oscar, laying a white hand of plump restraint upon Sherard's shoulder, "hush, you are defending me at the risk of my life!" Isn't it lovely?

As a result of an interview I had with 'Arry Cust—who, it may amuse you to hear, drinks like any fish—I am writing an article about cosmetics for the *PMG*. The article will be amusing and perfect I think—probably I call it "The Philosophy of Rouge."[4] But oh the *PMG* itself has very terribly got on my nerves—such

[1] Unidentified. Rothenstein drew and painted many more portraits of Max than have yet been traced and listed.
[2] The eighth Marquess of Queensberry, having been divorced by his first wife in 1887, married in 1893 Miss Ethel Weedon, who obtained a decree of nullity against him in October 1894.
[3] Robert Harborough Sherard (1861–1943), author and journalist. Early friend and first biographer of Oscar Wilde.
[4] This essay appeared in the first volume of the *Yellow Book* (April 1894), entitled "A Defence of Cosmetics." Much revised, it was reprinted in *Works* (1896) as "The Pervasion of Rouge."

priggishness and pedantry as have never been. . . . However, I'll change all that.

Fool, you *must* do Talma (or is it Cavour?).[1] An admirable subject. I know you won't go on with a novel. Really it is silly of you. And now with all nice wishes to you and to your brother.

Ever yours in affection   MAX BEERBOHM

Dandy[2] is very well and happy and is now known as "Hilda" or sometimes as "Unruly Puppy." My people send their love. Dear Cissie, how sweet those days were. I suppose the name of Miss Cumberlidge arouses nothing but comparative indifference in you by this time. Do you remember your quarrel with the Marshalls and that terrible unburdening of your mind to me, you looking out of the corner of your eyes the whole time to see if I was laughing and the terrible scene of bitterness when you caught me at last?

This week the *National Observer* has an article on the pantomimes beginning "The boast that Sir Augustus Harris[3] has really surpassed himself is this year justified indeed. Positively his pantomime is more tedious than ever." The Beardsleys are becoming suspects, but they are very charming and think a lot of me.

PS. John Lane is just going to start a quarterly magazine called *The Yellow Book* with Harland[4] as Editor and Aubrey as Art Editor. It is to make all our fortunes. I am both to caricature and write for it. . . .

[*Postmark 21 February 1894*]   *Merton College*

My dear Reg,

You cannot think how pleased I was to see your familiar handwriting (much improved by the way) upon my breakfast table today.

[1] Presumably a suggested biography, or play, based on the life of the French actor François Talma (1763–1826) or the Italian statesman Count Camillo Benso di Cavour (1810–61).
[2] A Manchester terrier belonging to Max's sister Constance.
[3] Augustus Harris (1851–96), manager of Covent Garden and for many years of Drury Lane, where he specialised in melodrama and pantomime, into which he introduced Dames and Principal Boys. Knighted 1891 as a Sheriff of the City of London when the German Emperor visited it.
[4] Henry Harland, American author and journalist (1861–1905). He edited all thirteen volumes of the *Yellow Book* (1894–97).

All the more so because I had no idea you would be already back. In your last letter you hinted so gravely about your health that I imagined you had left Cairo and sought some skilled medicine-man in the desert and goodness only knew when you would return. Just before that I had written you a letter to Clement's Inn, which perhaps was forwarded as you do not mention it, full of compliments and reminiscences and invitations. For though alas there is not a room at the Macfies[1] I can get you one in Merton Street, if you would like that, and we could be very happy. Do come but not merely for a wretched 48 hours. That terrible old fallacy about your being the heart and soul of our friendship and my being a cold, unresponsive but calculating acquaintance prevents me from saying much—but really I do want to see you and shew you and ask you and tell you very many things. Rothenstein comes to Y. Powell[2] on Saturday and you know how exacting he is, and how divided my company—though not my heart—would be, so do not come before next Wednesday, but *do stay* then. Possibly you have important things to do in London and it would be foolish, but we are at the age when foolish things should be done. I ought to read every moment of my time now, but I would far rather see you.

The White Girl figures largely upon my mantelpiece. How goes *your* love? You have not mentioned it lately. Do you remember asking me blunt-point-blank "Are you still in love or not?" and my exquisite reply "I still *reverence* the Lady Cecilia." Do you still reverence the Lady Cecilia perhaps? I know how love does tremble at time and space and how that even the photographer's art may not prevail against leagues and aeons—but still I hope you are not *défrisé* as yet, dear Reg.   Yours MAX

[*8 March 1894*][3]   *Merton College*

My dear Reg,

Many thanks for your sweet letter: also for the nice things you say about me in your letter to Bosie, who, as I suppose you know, is

[1] Presumably lodging-house keepers.
[2] Rothenstein stayed with York Powell at Christ Church.
[3] This date appears to have been added by another hand, but the contents of the letter fit in very well with those of the two succeeding letters. Hitherto Douglas was believed to have returned from abroad at the

up just now—very charming, always beautiful and seldom sober. He has taken his name off the Magdalen books, resenting their resentment at his presence in the University. Also Will Rothenstein is up and has done a lithograph of me for the Oxford Series: it will appear in the next number with Walter Pater—the two stylists.[1] It is rather touching: you know how angry old Henry Acland was at the libellous portrait of him and how that Walter Pater refused to sit at all?[2] Well, poor Rothenstein has turned idealist, in consequence—has done a second thing of old Henry who, no longer an old village-dotard, appears exactly like Gladstone, only far firmer, and Walter Pater, who as you know is a kind of hump-back *manqué*, figures as a young guardsman with curly mustachios—just what Kendal[3] must have looked like twenty years ago. Isn't it rather touching? I too who write am a child of fifteen and quite god-like. A terrible *rencontre* took place today in my rooms. Enter upon Bosie, Will and me, John Lane, gentleman. Will, who has heard that John Lane, gentleman, has said various things against him, bowed very very stiffly and relapsed Byronically into an arm chair, what time Bosie attacked the Publisher about the awful quarrels and so forth that have been. Imagine me! walking swiftly and suavely up and down the room talking about anything that came into my head while John Lane sat very red and uncomfortable on a high chair. Figure him moreover in very new dog-skin gloves, a citron-coloured bowler and a very small covert-coat beneath which fell the tails of a braided black coat. Poor me. What a position.

I was so glad you enjoyed yourself last week and I hope you will come often and often next term. I owe you £3, dear Reg: but, at this moment, fear I cannot repay it, having lost all I have at roulette. I wonder could you possibly lend me a further sum of £7, making it

---

beginning of April, but I know of no concrete evidence to that effect, and he may well have returned at the beginning of March.
[1] Rothenstein's lithographed portraits, *Oxford Characters*, were issued serially in batches before being published in a limited edition by John Lane in 1896. Max and W. H. Pater were two of the subjects.
[2] Both Pater and Sir Henry Acland, Bart, the Regius Professor of Medicine, objected to their portraits. Acland's was redrawn, but Pater died (30 July 1894) before he could insist on similar treatment.
[3] William Hunter Kendal, stage name of W. H. Grimston (1843–1917), English actor and manager.

£10? Why do I ask you? You may imagine I would not do so unless hard pressed: at the present moment I cannot ask my people for more: and must pay certain debts before the term's end. I shall repay all within *three* weeks: the date is not merely a hazard one, for at the end of that time I shall have plenty to go on with. If it is in the *least* inconvenient to you just now, please say and I can manage otherwise. It seems horrible to have a man up to stay with one and to treat him as a moneylender at the same time. However— if you can and will, please let me hear as soon as possible. "To-morrow I start for America."[1]

My people give me no knowledge as to what they intend. I wish they would go into the country and I could come, as you sweetly ask me, to Clement's Inn, which I should dearly enjoy: are you making your mark at the Bar? I hope so.   Yours MAX

*12 March 1894**   [*Oxford*]

My dear Reg,

I have many things to thank you for—a charming letter, a delight-ful cheque, a kind invitation and the loveliest ring in the world. Many thanks for all. In the morning when my hand is white the ring is a heavenly blue—it looks like a glimpse of sky through the little window of a white tent: in the evening my hand is a delicate kind of pink and the ring upon its third finger grass-green. All my friends are very envious and most of them leave Oxford today for that reason. "A few remain" among whom I till tomorrow—how can I leave a place that I love so much at any fixed academic date? There is absolutely no reason why I should stay but I must do so. Dear Bosie is with us. It needed but that we should wait.[2] Is it you who have made him so amusing? Never in the summer did he make me laugh much, but now he is nearly brilliant. Also is it you who have made him so abnormally, damnably, touchingly conceited about his poetry? Never was he so in the summer. The dons objected to his coming up, so he took his name off the books and

[1] Possibly the exit-line of some earlier borrowers of money.
[2] Cf. "Artifice is with us. It needed but that we should wait." ("A Defence of Cosmetics," *Yellow Book*, vol I, p. 70)

91

wrote to Warren[1] at the time saying that one day it would be Magdalen's proudest boast that she had for a time harboured him within her walls, her greatest shame that she had driven him forth —or something to that effect. I like his sonnet about the Sphinx.[2]

I have been doing my Collections cosily in my own room, surrounded by my books—and with an imaginary chill which I think I said was on the liver. I am a real strategist. No man has ever avoided Collections so often nor so cleverly as I. My people, dear Reg, are still in town. . . . They have taken rooms at 14 Old Quebec Street, Marble Arch, preparatory, I suppose, to seeking that Fool's Paradise, the country. I am brilliant. When they go I should love to come to you if you will have me.   Yours MAX

[*Postmark 16 March 1894*]   *14 Old Quebec Street, London*

My dear Reg,

Many thanks for your letter. My people go away I think at Easter from Thursday till Monday: so that if you repent not of your nice invitation I should love to come then: let me know however if there be any other plan you would rather make for yourself and I could go quite well into the country: my people are so enamoured of these rooms and so hate the idea of *la campagne* that they think of staying here for some time after Easter: I am very happy as always.

Aubrey has done a *marvellous* picture for the *Yellow B*: "*l'Education sentimentale*" he calls it. A fat elderly whore in a dressing-gown and huge hat of many feathers is reading from a book to the sweetest imaginable little young girl, who looks before her, with hands clasped behind her back, roguishly winking. Such a strange curved attitude, and she wears a long pinafore of black silk, quite-tight, with the frills of a petticoat showing at the ankles and shoulders: awfully like Ada Reeve, that clever malapert, is her face —you must see it. It haunts me.[3]

[1] Thomas Herbert Warren (1853–1930) was President of Magdalen 1885–1928. He was knighted in 1914.
[2] This sonnet, written at Cairo in January 1894 and dedicated to Reggie, was published in Douglas's first book, *Poems* (1896).
[3] This drawing appeared in the first volume of the *Yellow Book* (April 1894) and was reproduced in *The Early Work of Aubrey Beardsley* (1899).

This time tomorrow, I take it, you will be in love, cynic that you are. I am so sorry if you do not like the interest I take in your character, career, conduct, past, future etc. etc. Next time you must talk a lot about me—I shall not be angry. Will R. is going tomorrow to do a heavenly and elaborate pastel of me, sitting straddle-legged over a chair, my hat tilted back, a white carnation and trousers of a very pale gray. It will be in his exhibition.[1] Cannot you imagine the public pausing before it and exclaiming "Is *that* Max Beerbohm?" and thinking of the paper on Cosmetics?

Do come and see me and my people whenever you have time.

Yours MAX

12 April 1894[*]   *19 Hyde Park Place*

My dear Reg,

I am feeling very home-sick—sick of being at home—after my sweet staying with you in the quiet inn, and envy you keenly your rooms and repose and general content.

The *Yellow Book* dinner is on Monday next at half-past seven and at the Hotel d'Italie, 52 Compton Street, and I hope you will come. But we shall meet before then. Did you see the interview with Harland and Beardsley in this week's *Sketch*?[2]

Everybody is very much excited by the news of *Sala's Journal*.[3]

Your affectionate MAX

[24 April 1894. Postmark 25 April]   *19 Hyde Park Place*

My dear Reg,

Certainly, certainly. I will search among my shirts and return you your own when we meet (if you like) at the 'Aymarket.[4] For I

---

[1] I have been unable to locate or identify this portrait.
[2] An anonymous interview in the *Sketch* of 11 April, entitled "What the *Yellow Book* is to be," and reproducing the cover of the first number.
[3] On 30 April 1894 there appeared the first number of *Sala's Journal, A Weekly Magazine for All*, edited by the prolific journalist and author George Augustus Sala (1828–95). It survived only until April 1895.
[4] Where *A Bunch of Violets* by Sydney Grundy, founded on *Montjoye* by Octave Feuillet, was produced on 25 April, with the Trees and Lily Hanbury in the chief parts. It ran for more than three months.

am staying up for tomorrow's fiasco and if you by chance do not succeed in getting a stall, you will delight my people by coming to Box 10—over the Royal Box or over the one opposite. What a poor play and *what* a poor part for my brother and *what* well-deserved hisses in store for that blancmange Miss 'Anbury.

A tantôt MAX

The *World* is rude about me this morning, have you noticed?[1] Like Meredith or Keats or any great striker of new notes, I am rejected at first. But so long as I attract notice I am happy—and so long as I can do beautiful work, and have a little following that calls me "Master."

[*Postmark 7 August 1894*]   *19 Hyde Park Place*

My dearest Reg,

Thanx very much for your letter, from which I am glad to hear that you are having such a good time—by the sea.[2] Here I am in my room upstairs, writing to you from my sofa. The day is extremely and even tropically hot but I am covered by a large railway-rug, which makes me very cosy though over-heated. Also it makes me feel as though I were upon my way to the Engadine or somewhere, where I could forget life and be happy. As it is, I do not suppose I shall get further this week than the Tivoli, where the programme is quite splendid. Do you remember the bank-holiday in August last year and how we spent the day together and how in the evening we visited the Tivoli and heard the Loftus sing? The

[1] Reviewing the first number of the *Yellow Book* on 25 April, the *World* commented:

"Who wants these fantastic pictures, like Japanese sketches gone mad, of a woman with a black tuft for a head, and snake-like fingers starting off the keyboard of a piano; of Mrs Patrick Campbell with a black sticking-plaister hat, hunchy shoulders, a happily impossible waist, and a yard and a half of indefinite skirt. . . . Then, for the letterpress how little is there to be said. Mr Henry James in his most mincing mood; a Mr Beerbohm, whose 'Defence of Cosmetics' contains such humorous phrases as 'the resupinate sex,' 'the veriest sillypop,' 'Rome in the keenest time of her degringolade,' and is otherwise pure nonsense."

[2] Reggie was staying at the Hotel Metropole, Cromer, Norfolk.

heat of the auditorium, if I remember correctly, was too much for you and we parted rather abruptly, much to my terror. You see, I live very much in the past already. I was miserable throughout my schooldays, and then Fate let me run away by myself for two or three years, and now she has caught me with her velvet-paw and sharp-claws again: no longer am I light-hearted. But I have an equable and careless temper, which prevents me from being so very unhappy. I think I shall go to the Tivoli tonight in memory of last year.

Oscar and Bosie lunched with me today in the Royal Coffee House[1] and were very charming. Oscar was just in the mood that I like him—very 1880 and withal brimful of intellectual theories and anecdotes of dear Lady Dorothy Nevill[2] and other whores. Bosie came in a Homburg hat—dove-coloured—and wearing a *very* sweet present from you in his shirt-cuffs. I thought the club especially fascinating and insisted upon his changing it to the outside of his right sleeve. Oscar also was all admiration and said that he supposed that "dear Reg's present to him was in some way delayed." I am meanwhile hard-at-work upon *Georges Quatre*. Henry Harland wants to lead off the third volume with it.[3] I am becoming very fond of *eau-de-Cologne*.

Bobbie has returned to London but I have not seen him. Do write me a *longer* letter very soon. One learns nothing of your soul from so short a letter as I had this morning. Many thanks for Cosmo Posnor's caricature of Alexander which I thought very clever indeed.[4]

I am going to call upon Mrs Lawson early tomorrow afternoon. How is your brother? Have the Alexanders come over yet? Do talk about nothing except the splendour and charm and sweetness of Mrs Patrick, and say that the man who would omit a leading lady's name, except in the way of kindness, etc. etc.

[1] i.e. the Café Royal.
[2] Authoress (1826–1913), daughter of the third Earl of Orford (of the second creation) and widow of Reginald Harry Nevill.
[3] This essay, "A Note on George the Fourth," duly appeared in the third volume of the *Yellow Book* (October 1894) and was included in *Works* (1896).
[4] Untraced.

I have been drawing Gus Elen, Herbert Campbell[1] and Dutch Daly[2] for *Pick-Me-Up*.

Excuse an egoistical letter, I am not usually an egoist.

Your affectionate   MAX

P.S. Your links have arrived, looking much improved, from the jewellers. Shall I send them on to you or keep them till you return?

A heavy downfall of rain has just commenced. I hope it may teach these shop-people not to take a mean advantage of their ill-gotten privileges.[3]

Oscar liked the "Fry."[4] The *Westminster Gazette* was very charming about it. So is the *Illustrated London News*.[5]

*12 August 1894**   *19 Hyde Park Place*

My dear Reg,

Thank you, thank you for your wholly delightful letter. Do you really like my letters? I rather doubt it, seeing how very little *real* interest you ever show in hearing of my literary works, and seeing also that I discovered from something you said the other day that you could not have read the whole of a letter I wrote when you were at Richmond. However, I leave dear London for dear Broadstairs tomorrow, very loth. I have been doing many drawings for

[1] Music-hall performer. Appeared regularly in Drury Lane pantomimes from 1882, often as massive foil to the diminutive Dan Leno. I have failed to find a caricature of him by Max in *Pick-Me-Up*, but Max spoke admiringly of him in his 1942 broadcast, "Music Halls of my Youth" (printed in *Mainly on the Air*, 1946). Max's caricature of Gus Elen appeared in *Pick-Me-Up* on 15 September 1894.
[2] Stage name of William James Daly, English music-hall performer (b. 1848). Max's caricature of him appeared in *Pick-Me-Up* on 29 December 1894.
[3] Gained by a new interpretation (1894) of the Shop Hours Act of 1892.
[4] C. B. Fry (1872–1956), the great athlete and cricketer, was still an Oxford undergraduate when Max interviewed him. The interview, entitled "Fry of Wadham," appeared in the *English Illustrated Magazine* for August 1894. Max himself had gone down from Oxford in June.
[5] The *Westminster Gazette* printed a few favourable words on 2 August, and on 4 August the *Illustrated London News* wrote: "Mr Beerbohm's portraiture of young Oxford is excellent in every way."

Pick-Me-Up.[1] They are going to appear in a long (I hope) series.
One and a half guineas each. Isn't it nice? Raven Hill[2] seems to
admire me intensely. I went to the first night of *Little Jack Shep-
herd*.[3] Also I have been several times to *Little Christopher Columbus*,[4]
where the Ulmar[5] is *quite*—to me *quite*—delightful. John Lane wants
me to do a book of caricatures for him in the Autumn. Oscar has at
length been arrested for certain kinds of crime. He was taken in the
Café Royal (lower room). Bosie escaped, being an excellent runner,
but Oscar was less nimble.[6] The other night at *Little Christoph*: I
saw in a distant box, whom do you think? the Loftus—in pink with
short sleeves and two-button dog-skin gloves. Extremely sweet and
with one of her strangely-gloved hands supporting her chin. She
had a younger sister with her as chaperone, and looked wonderfully
1893 . . .

    Do write to me again.   Yours sincerely MAX

[*Circa 25 January 1895*]*   *The Waldorf, New York*[7]

Darling Reg,
    N'York is too terrible. Very many thanks for your wires. The

[1] Between September 1894 and April 1895 Max contributed thirty-one
caricatures to *Pick-Me-Up*.
[2] Leonard Raven Hill (1867–1942), artist, *Punch* cartoonist, and art-
editor of *Pick-Me-Up*. He wrote an introduction to Max's first book of
drawings, *Caricatures of Twenty-Five Gentlemen* (1896). A caricature of
him by Max appeared in *Pick-Me-Up* on 3 November 1894.
[3] A burlesque by H. P. Stephens and W. Yardley, with music by Meyer
Lutz, originally produced in 1886, was revived at the Gaiety on 11
August 1894, with Seymour Hicks and Ellaline Terriss in the chief parts.
[4] A burlesque by G. R. Sims and C. Raleigh, with music by Ivan Caryll,
first produced at the Lyric Theatre on 10 October 1893.
[5] Geraldine Ulmar, American actress and singer (1862–1932). She had
sung in many of the Gilbert and Sullivan operas, and was now playing
the principal part in *Little Christopher Columbus*.
[6] This all-too-prophetic joke almost certainly refers to the police raid on
a club at 46 Fitzroy Street, London, on this very day, when eighteen men
were arrested, including two in female dress.
[7] Beerbohm Tree's first American tour opened in New York on 28
January at Abbey's Theatre with performances of *The Red Lamp* by
W. Outram Tristram, and *The Ballad Monger*, adapted by Walter
Pollock from Théodore de Banville's *Gringoire*. After a month in New

voyage was too terrible. Lionel Brough[1] had a cabin opposite to, not with, me and, strangely enough, could not go to sleep without smoking a pipe, the fumes of which added a terror to life. I was ill off and on all the time. It is quite surprising how one feels the motion on those great vessels. Also there was a terrible thin brother of Marston[2] on board—very like Marston but thinner and with an eyeglass. He terrified Mrs Tree on the first day by settling down beside her and saying "I am a great gossip." He is going to be married to a girl in New York next week and has asked me to his wedding. He told me the girl had a cold in the head but hoped she would be all right.

Oh the voyage! Oh the arrival and the drive through the hideous and ill-paved and noisy streets—and the coming to this hideous hotel, where everything is worth a king's ransom. I sleep in an enormous double drawing-room which is furnished like a Pullman Car. There are lots of common, coloured prints in very massive frames on the wall—no electric light or bell near the bed—nothing set to rights when one goes from one's room in the morning or when one has dressed at night. One returns and finds shirts and débris scattered all over the floor. From this Zolaesque piling-up of details do you understand that on the whole I think N'York loathsome, and am wretched—and long for you and cosiness and refinement and peace and laziness? I live in a whirl of dreary sordid intrigues about theatres and companies. I am going to write a slashing article upon "N'York" for the *Y Book*. Meanwhile I am doing an ardent series of sonnets *à la* Oscar in Italy—"Sonnet upon hearing the whistle of an elevated railway for the first time. Jan '95."—"Nay Lord, not thus," and sonnet about Chicago—"We stepped down from the car; my heart did burn, Chicago, my Chicago at thy name."[3] I am sick of pretending to the inhabitants (the country is inhabited) that I like their things and ways.

York, during which four more plays were presented, the company moved to Chicago, Philadelphia, Boston, Washington, Baltimore and back to New York. Max was ostensibly employed as Tree's secretary.
[1] English actor (1836–1909), who specialised in Shakespearean and low comedy parts.
[2] See note, p. 56.
[3] Parodies of the title and opening lines of Wilde's sonnets "On Hearing the Dies Irae sung in the Sistine Chapel" and "On Approaching Italy."

At any rate, it is a blessing that I am ashore—home is the bad sailor, home from the sea—or rather I soon shall be home. I put my veto this morning upon an idea of prolonging the tour till June. Cissie Loftus, poor little dear, is much liked here. . . .

The hotels are stifling hot but the streets are as cold as death. I hate (in the words of a poet for whom I care not at all) the iron ground and the day that closes with never a sound nor a song.[1] I have such lots of letters to write before catching the mail that I must desist. I hope you have written to me and will write often. I will write again directly and tell you more.

Yours with much love   MAX

[*Postmark 22 February 1895*]   *The Waldorf, New York*

My dearest Reg,

Forgive me for not having written. I have written so much to everybody else that I have no news.

However I send you a copy of this week's *Vanity* (have you read my two first articles?). I think this one will amuse you, if only on account of the way I have dipped certain Oxford flies in my American amber.[2] . . .

I have had a charming time here—New York has given itself to me like a flower. Tomorrow I must throw away the petals, for we start to Chicago, which everyone says is quite a beastly place. I *long* for news of old Oscar's new farce—the papers here announce it a huge success.[3] Also I see that Oscar has *really* been to Paris at last. I wonder how he liked it. Do ask him about a dear playwright

> [1] I hate the iron ground,
> And the Christmas roses,
> And the sickly day that dies when it closes,
> With never a song or a sound.

is the third stanza of "A Winter Sunset" by Lord Alfred Douglas, first published in the *Spirit Lamp*, vol. 3, no. II, 17 February 1893.
[2] *Vanity* (New York) published Max's essay, "Dandies and Dandies," in four parts on 7, 14, 21 and 28 February 1895. They formed the basis for the essay of the same name in *Works* (1896).
[3] *The Importance of Being Earnest*, which had opened in London at the Haymarket Theatre on 14 February.

named Clyde Fitch,[1] of whom I have seen much and who is one of my greatest admirers and not unlike Denis Browne.

Herbert has been in great form here. Really his success has been wonderful. I have no time to write more lest I should lapse into brilliancy—I must keep my brilliancy for this beautiful town. I am certainly going to settle here for some years when we have finished the tour. You can come out and see me, if you really miss me.

I really miss you.

Your loving MAX

[Postmark 3 March 1895]   *The Chicago Club, Chicago*

My dear Reg,

Poor, poor Oscar! How very sad it is.[2] I cannot bear to think of all that must have happened—the whisperings and the hastenings hither and thither—before he could have been seduced into Marlborough Street. I suppose he was exasperated too much not to take action. I am sorry he has not got George Lewis, wonder if Bosie has returned, what evidence will be brought in for the defence—and so forth. It is awful not to be upon the spot. Do let me hear *real long* details—*full accounts*. Do please not mind writing many pages—I am parched for news—the head-lines are so short here and so relentless: "Gives Oscar what's-for," "The Pretty Poet and the Mocking Marquis," "Mrs Wilde sticks to him," etc. etc.—quite dreadful. Do not, I beg you, get mixed up in the scandal. I was *so* deeply interested in your account of the first night, but do not curtail anything about this matter.

Dear Chicago! I quite like it and am being rather lionised. I am (not a word to dear Mrs Leverson[3]) in love with a certain Miss Conover[4] in my brother's company—a dark Irish girl of twenty,

[1] American dramatist (1865–1909).
[2] On 1 March 1895 Oscar Wilde obtained a warrant for the arrest of Lord Queensberry on a charge of criminal libel.
[3] Ada Esther Beddington (1862–1933) married Ernest Leverson, the son of a diamond merchant. She contributed witty pieces to *Punch* and other periodicals, and later published successful novels.
[4] Grace (Kilseen) Conover, believed to have been the daughter of an Irish immigrant to the U.S.A. and a Danish mother.

very blunt and rude, who hates affectation and rather likes me. We only knew each other during this tour and have seen a good deal of each other. On the car from N. York to Chicago we sat together all the time. I made her cry on the first afternoon by telling her circumstantially that she was known at the Garrick as "Kill-Scene-Conover"—and immediately fell in love with her. There were two sleeping cars, one entirely for the actors and the other for the actors and actresses, who slept in berths partitioned off by ineffectual curtains that were perpetually withdrawn to let people pass. Miss Conover looked extremely pretty in her night-gown and gave me an apple from her hamper. Miss Cockerell,[1] who slept by her in the same berth, looked very pretty too, I am bound to confess. Miss Cockerell threw me a banana. It was like being in a girls' school. Do you remember the big girls' school on the road to Rouen and our speculations about it? Here in Chicago I see Miss Conover perpetually and have asked her to be my wife, but as we have always been upon terms of chaff, she is only just beginning to realise that I am in earnest—which perhaps I am not—who knows? I took her to a theatre here last night and in the cab home we held each other's hands all the way. I have her photograph in my little green case now. I really am very much in love with her and she will be very much in love with me, I think, soon. Do be sympathetic.

The climate, you will be sorry to hear, does not agree with Charles Allan.[2] He cannot get bread-and-milk well made here and has to substitute negus at night. (He says that negus comes extremely expensive.) I heard him use the expression *"Fiddle-de-dee"* to a black waiter the other day.

Last night Herbert gave a large supper to the critics: afterwards Herbert and I and Brough were taken to see a town-ball—a scene of vast and hideous debauchery. Also we visited certain houses where black-women danced naked to the sound of the piano—and one where French women gambolled with one another in a room cushioned with blue silk, just as the bells began ringing for early

[1] Una Cockerell (1875–1944), younger sister of Sydney Cockerell (Director of the Fitzwilliam Museum, Cambridge, 1903–37). She acted with Tree off and on until 1900, when she married Captain Charles Low and left the stage.
[2] An actor in Tree's company.

mass. I did not get to bed till six, just as the sun began his daily task of painting and gilding.

This is Sunday evening at six and I feel rather feverish as I used to feel on the Sunday after a wine. I wish that this huge club in which I am writing were the little room at Adamson's and that the younger X would soon come in stamping in his great-coat and Y with the debauch of last night in his small blue eyes and Z looking forward to his champagne, and you smiling at me. Dear Oxford! Dear Chicago! My great love to you.   Ever your MAX

[*Postmark 3 May 1895*]   *19 Hyde Park Place*

My dearest Reg,

I am very sorry I have not written before. Ever since I arrived I have been all day at the Old Bailey and dining out in the evening—and coming home very tired.[1] Please forgive me. Oscar has been quite superb. His speech about the Love that dares not tell his name[2] was simply wonderful, and carried the whole court right away, quite a tremendous burst of applause. Here was this man, who had been for a month in prison and loaded with insults and crushed and buffeted, perfectly self-possessed, dominating the Old Bailey with his fine presence and musical voice. He has never had so great a triumph, I am sure, as when the gallery burst into applause—I am sure it affected the gallery. Public opinion too has undergone a very great revulsion, so everyone seems to think—nine out of the twelve jurors were for him. Today they renew application for bail, but I don't think they can get it. Somebody has written to Ned Clarke[3] offering Oscar the sole use of his house and grounds at Camberwell or somewhere. Ned Clarke has done splendidly and is very much implected with Hoscar—and talks of shaving his whiskers. Hoscar

[1] The jury in Oscar Wilde's first trial disagreed on 1 May and a new trial was ordered. On 7 May Wilde was released on bail. His second trial opened on 20 May, and on 25 May he was found guilty and sentenced to two years' imprisonment with hard labour.

[2] "I am the Love that dare not speak its name" (from "Two Loves" by Lord Alfred Douglas, first published in the *Chameleon*, an Oxford undergraduate magazine, in December 1894).

[3] Sir Edward Clarke, Q.C. (1841–1931), was Wilde's Counsel in all three trials.

stood very upright when he was brought up to hear the verdict and looked most leonine and sphinx-like. I pitied poor little Alfred Taylor[1]—nobody remembered his existence, and Grain[2] made a very poor speech and he himself a poor witness. Hoscar is thinner and consequently finer to look at. Willie[3] has been extracting fivers from Humphreys.[4] It was horrible leaving the court day after day and having to pass through a knot of renters[5] (the younger Parker[6] wearing Her Majesty's uniform—another form of female attire) who were allowed to hang around after giving their evidence and to wink at likely persons: Trelawny[7] is raising money for the conduct of the case. Leverson[8] has done a great deal. Clarke and Humphreys are going to take no fees. The Leversons have got the full-length portrait of Hoscar and Rothenstein's pastel of Bosie and also of him and a larger nude picture by Ricketts.[9] Rothenstein is

[1] Alfred Waterhouse Somerset Taylor (b. *circa* 1862). His house in Westminster had been used as a meeting-place for male homosexuals. He refused to turn Queen's Evidence against Wilde, was tried at the same time, and received the same sentence.

[2] John Peter Grain (1839–1916) appeared as Counsel for Alfred Taylor in both trials.

[3] Willie Wilde.

[4] Charles Octavius Humphreys (1828–1902) was Wilde's solicitor throughout his trials.

[5] Slang term for men who participate in male homosexual affairs for a reward (originally perhaps for their rent).

[6] A young man who gave evidence at Wilde's trials.

[7] Edmund Trelawny Backhouse (1873–1944) had been at Merton with Max. Rothenstein describes him as an eccentric undergraduate who collected jewels and was such an admirer of Ellen Terry that he once took a whole row of stalls and filled it with undergraduate friends. He went out to China, was present at the Siege of the Legations at Peking during the Boxer Rebellion of 1900, became Professor at Peking University 1903, and head of the school for Chinese Studies at King's College, London, 1913. He presented 27,000 Chinese books and manuscripts to the Bodleian Library, and wrote (in collaboration with J. O. P. Bland) *China Under the Empress Dowager* (1910). Succeeded his father as second Baronet 1918.

[8] Ernest Leverson. He and his wife took Wilde into their London home when he was out on bail and no other house would take him in.

[9] These pictures were bought by Leverson at the forced sale of Wilde's belongings on 24 April 1895 and later restored to him. The portrait of Wilde was by Harper Pennington, and the nude was not by Ricketts but by his friend C. H. Shannon.

most sympathetic and goes about the minor clubs insulting everyone who does not happen to be clamouring for Hoscar's instant release.

I saw Bosie the night before his departure.[1] He seemed to have lost his nerve. The scene that evening at the Leversons' was quite absurd. An awful New Woman in a divided skirt (introduced by Bosie) writing a pamphlet at Mrs Leverson's writing-table with the aid of several whiskey-and-sodas: her brother, a gaunt man with prominent cheek-bones from Toynbee Hall[2] who kept reiterating that "these things must be approached through first principles and through first principles alone:" two other New Women who subsequently explained to Mr Leverson that they were there to keep a strict watch upon New Woman number one, who is not responsible for her actions: Mrs Leverson making flippant remarks about messenger-boys in a faint undertone to Bosie, who was ashen-pale and thought the pamphlet (which was the most awful drivel) admirable: and Mr Leverson explaining to me that he allowed his house to be used for these purposes not because he approved of "anything unnatural" but by reason of his admiration for Oscar's plays and personality. I myself exquisitely dressed and sympathising with no one.

Dear Miss Conover! I see a great deal of her and love her very much. I think you would like her. *Do*, for God's sake, come back again. I long to have a cosy day or two at *l'Auberge Clement*. Also I am sure it would be much better for you, as I suppose you must have been more or less talked about as you were in the garden of Gethsemane at the supreme moment.[3] Why not shew yourself on English territory.[4] I must say I think it is rather bad luck that you— a comparatively new friend of Oscar—should have been with him at that unpleasant crisis. Do come back. How is Charley Hickey?[5] Do come back. Your loving MAX

[1] Douglas crossed to France on 25 April, the eve of Wilde's first trial. He went unwillingly but at the urgent request of Wilde's lawyers.
[2] A social settlement in Whitechapel, erected in memory of the economist and social reformer Arnold Toynbee (1852–83).
[3] Reggie and Robbie Ross were with Wilde when he was arrested at the Cadogan Hotel on 5 April.
[4] Like other friends of Wilde, Reggie had deemed it prudent to go abroad, and was now staying at Bois Guillaume.
[5] A young friend of Reggie, Wilde and Alfred Douglas.

Thursday [?2 April 1896][1]   *Berkeley Hotel, Bognor*

My dear Reg,

I take the following from next Sunday's papers: "Yesterday Mr Max Beerbohm passed through London. In the morning he was engaged in transacting business at his residence and after luncheon was driven to Paddington, proceeding by the ordinary afternoon express to Maesllwch Castle,[2] the residence of Mr Frank Lawson. A small house-party had already assembled to meet him, including Miss Helen Forsyth[3] and Mr 'Regie' Turner."

I wish I could get away tomorrow and come down on Sat. morning, but for various reasons I must be here till Sat. I hope you will be charming and amusing and I look forward to Maesllwch very much indeed. I bring a *shoal* of MSS to be alternated with your play. I foresee very long evenings together after the retirement of the guilty couple.

Please remember me to Frank—and also to Miss Forsyth, if she has arrived yet.   Yours   MAX

Thursday night [?April–May 1896][4]   [*London*]

My dear Reg,

I am sending you this by messenger early tomorrow. Could you ask somebody else to go in my place tomorrow? I told Kilseen on the way home and asked her if she minded my going with H.F. Of course she told me to go and not mind what she felt, and so on. But evidently she thought it in bad taste that I should be seen in a

[1] It is impossible to date this letter with confidence, but the visit to Maesllwch may conceivably have been the Easter one referred to in the letter of 18 April 1897. In 1896 Easter Sunday was on 5 April.

[2] Near Glasbury in Radnorshire.

[3] English actress (d. 1901). She had been on the London stage for some ten years when in January 1895 she created the part of Mrs Marchmont in Wilde's *An Ideal Husband*. Now she was clearly having a love affair with Frank Lawson, but on 14 October 1898 Reggie wrote to Max from Rome: "Helen Forsyth is living in Calais, I hear, and calls herself the Comtesse Quelque Chose."

[4] This letter is difficult to date within six years. Assuming that H.F. refers to the Helen Forsyth of the previous letter, I have chosen this as a possible date.

public place with H.F. and so I told her that I would not go. Probably you will think her view very absurd—and so do I—but I suppose it is a fact that if one is engaged to be married one ought to observe certain absurd conventions. And Kilseen has such lots of worries and disappointments that I should like to please her in this instance. You know how I should have looked forward to going and how I should have enjoyed myself with you there, and what a horrid thing it is to give up. But you'll understand my slight act of heroism. You can easily get somebody else to go instead of me. I suppose it is natural of Kilseen not to wish me to be seen with a lady of frayed hem, but I expect she will send me a letter tomorrow saying that she does not really mind. In any case, please forgive me for accepting with effusion and then changing my mind—it seems stupid.   Yours MAX

[*Early August 1896*]   *Berkeley Hotel, Bognor*

Dearest Reg,

   I am so sorry I did not keep my promise of writing to you directly, but there has been absolutely *no* news to tell you. Bognor is a very nice and well-behaved little place, but unstimulating to the mind. I have been drawing a good deal, some caricatures for the Xmas Supplement of the *Saturday Review*—Carson, William Watson, Barnato and Devonshire.[1] *Also* (this is more interesting) I really did write "The Story of the Small Boy and the Barley Sugar" all in one day—a gem of about 2500 words. Really charming.[2] Of course I shall tell everyone 'twas your plot *à vous*—and you must consent to share the profits. I hope you are not angry. You know

[1] The first Illustrated Supplement of the *Saturday Review*, which appeared on 15 December 1896, contained only one Max caricature—of Wilson Barrett as Marcus Superbus in *The Sign of the Cross*—and six parodies; of Marie Corelli, Richard Le Gallienne, H. G. Wells, Ian Maclaren, Alice Meynell and George Meredith. Will Rothenstein, who edited the Supplement, says that he rejected some of Max's caricatures.
[2] First published in *The Parade*, an Illustrated Gift Book for Boys and Girls, edited by Gleeson White (1897). Reprinted in *A Variety of Things* (1928 and 1953). The original idea of the story had clearly been Reggie's, since in his copy of *The Parade* Max wrote: "Given by Max Beerbohm to Mr R. T. the Onlie Begetter of the only good story it contains."

you would never have written it, and it will amuse you now to see the press-notices of it. Why not subscribe to Romeike?[1] Also I have finished "Yai and the Moon," which I have re-christened "Moons and Lilac."[2] Also Henry's want me to do a monthly article, a kind of causerie, for *Tomorrow*.[3] I tell you all these things in the dearth of other news. Connie and Dandy and I have been all alone as yet, but today the others are coming. Dandy likes Bognor fairly well, and is in good spirits, barking furiously at everything. Yesterday Connie had gone out and I found him on the sofa growling at a fly that was crawling over a cushion. Kilseen writes to me and I to her every day. She is still in France and is feeling stronger and seems to enjoy herself. She comes back very soon. And how did you enjoy Dieppe? Do write and tell me. Did Ada[4] mash[5] the band much? And was Justice tempered with mercy about the railway-tickets? I suppose you at Maesllwch already. If so give my kind regards to Frank. Is he all right again? I shudder at the approach of autumn, and I don't think I shall live through another winter—and I am writing in great discomfort, an eyelash having got into my eyelid. I wish you could come down here from S. to M.[6] if you are in London, but I suppose you are not.

My letter to the *D.C.* has had quite a little success—mentioned in many places.[7]

[1] See note, p. 114.
[2] As "Yai and the Moon" this story appeared in *The Pageant* (1897) and was reprinted in *A Variety of Things* (1928 and 1953).
[3] Max contributed eight essays and reviews to *Tomorrow* during the last quarter of 1896. Five of them were revised and reprinted in *More* (1899).
[4] Ada Leverson.
[5] Slang for fascinate.
[6] Saturday to Monday. The word "week-end" did not come into general use till well into the twentieth century.
[7] This letter, which appeared in the *Daily Chronicle* on 29 July 1896, ran:

A PLEA FOR DEAD WALLS

Sir,—Are they really, as you suggest, going to raze the wall that hides Devonshire House from Piccadilly? I hope not. The unseen courtyards that still remain before a few of the greater residences in London—Devonshire, Lansdowne, Marlborough, and other Houses—always strike me as peculiarly charming and impressive. I wonder that you, sir, who have so often and so well protested against the destruction of interesting pieces of architecture, should say no good word for these walls, also. Are

Isn't the *D.T.* Commemoration thing *sickening*?¹ I have composed a rather charming letter to be sent under an assumed identity, but I suppose it wouldn't do. It is as follows:

Sir, For more than two years the only man who ever loved me has lain a prisoner in Her Majesty's Gaol, Dartmoor. I count the hours to his release, but meanwhile I am growing old and it may be that, when he is free, I shall no longer find favour in his sight; he will have forgotten, perhaps, the happy times we had together. Would it not be a gracious act to celebrate the long reign of our dear Sovereign (herself but a child when she married the good Prince Consort) by granting a free pardon to all persons convicted under Cap. 4, Section 3, of the Criminal Law Amendment Act?² I am, sir, your obedient servant

Flossie (aged seven).

---

they, like the toll-gates, an insult to democracy? To me, it seems that they are only an odd relic of days when the people were so democratic that they actually broke ducal windows, of days when Disraeli could put into the mouth of an Eton boy that fine speech, "My father says that every nobleman's house should have a courtyard." I have known many persons of taste, notably the late E. W. Godwin, distinguished among architects, who held the arrogant mystery of these walls to be one of the most fascinating things in London, and I am told that Mr William Morris (surely no champion of the *noblesse*) has often praised them. I hope they will stand. As for the "improvement" of Piccadilly, to that the razure of the Duke's wall could hardly contribute. Devonshire House itself is one of the ugliest sights in London.

Yours obediently Max Beerbohm
19 Hyde Park Place, W.   July 28

Max referred to this letter and enlarged on its theme in his "Ex Cathedra II" (*Tomorrow*, October 1896), which later formed the basis of "If I Were Aedile" in *More* (1899).
¹ On 23 September 1896 Queen Victoria's reign became the longest of any English monarch, and from 22 July to 8 August the *Daily Telegraph* ran a lengthy correspondence headed THE QUEEN'S REIGN/LONGEST IN HISTORY/HOW TO CELEBRATE IT.
² This Act of 1885 was "to make further provision for the Protection of Women and Girls, the suppression of brothels, and other purposes." Henry Labouchere was responsible for including in it Clause 11, dealing with male persons, under which Oscar Wilde was tried and sentenced.

I am not quite sure yet how long I shall be here, but do write to me at this address within a few days, and tell me various amusing things.   Yours MAX

I did three illustrations to the "Small Boy" story—an initial design, a tailpiece and a full-page—the two children in each.[1]

*15 August 1896** *Berkeley Hotel, Bognor*

My dear Reggie,

I should like to come to Maesllwch immensely—please thank Frank for the kind invitation. *But* I am afraid I could not come before tomorrow week, when we leave this place, as Kilseen is coming probably to stay here next week. If, by any chance, she should stay on in France, I would let you know at once and ask if I could not come after all. Otherwise I should like to come tomorrow week and return when you return. Maesllwch must be looking delightful just now. How is Frank?

I am going to do the soliloquy every month for *Tomorrow*, under the heading of "Ex Cathedra." Mrs Meynell will be my first topic, and September the first occasion of my appearance.[2]

Maud Tree is going to have another child in December,[3] and cannot therefore go to America with her old man—nor, of course, can Viola. It is a great surprise to everyone. Please write me another nice letter.   Yours MAX

Monday [7] September 1896 *19 Hyde Park Place*

My dear Reg,

I shall be charmed to dine with you tomorrow—7.30 I suppose? And I hope you have enjoyed Hassocks. I saw Travers Humphreys[4]

[1] All three appeared in *The Parade*.
[2] "Ex Cathedra I" (*Tomorrow*, September 1896) was a review of Alice Meynell's book of essays, *The Colour of Life*, headed, MRS MEYNELL'S COWSLIP-WINE.
[3] The Trees' third daughter Iris was born on 27 January 1897.
[4] Barrister and judge (1867–1956), son of C. O. Humphreys the solicitor. He and Reggie had read for the Bar together, and he had been junior defence counsel for Oscar Wilde in all three trials.

this morning in the Strand—pale but determined. I was in a cab so could not speak.

I lunched alone with Mrs Lawson, and we talked a good deal of you. My Meredith appears on the 24 of this month.[1] My article on Clem next Saturday.[2]   Yours MAX

[21] *September 1896.* [*Postmark 22 September*]
                                                    19 Hyde Park Place
My dear Reg,

Have you seen the *Sun* today? I suppose you have. It quotes a lot of your letter.[3] Also Blanchamp[4] has written to me for further things and says "Turner's letter was excellent." Are you not pleased? The ball is at your feet. Go on brave boy, your trembling foot is pure.

But Kilseen comes back tomorrow, so I cannot come and dine, as I should have otherwise been charmed to do. Let us all three dine somewhere before the end of the week. Are you disengaged?

                                                    Yours MAX

[*On back of above*]
My dear Reg,

Kilseen and I came, on the chance that you might be in, and we have waited in case you should come in, and are sorry not to see you. Can't you come and dine at H.P.P. on Saturday?

                                                    Yours MAX

Glad to see *Vanity Fair*. Is Meredith being framed?

[1] This caricature, entitled "Our First Novelist," appeared in colour in *Vanity Fair* on 24 September 1896, and was reprinted in *Max's Nineties* (1958).
[2] "An Unhappy Poet," an ironical account of Clement Scott's book of poems, *Lays and Lyrics*, appeared anonymously in the *Saturday Review* on 12 September. It was Max's first contribution to the paper.
[3] To keep up the fun, and in hopes of provoking an answer, Reggie had contributed to the *Saturday Review* of 19 September a letter signed A LOVER OF FAIR PLAY, in which he ironically pretended to defend Clement Scott from his anonymous assailant of the previous week. On 21 September the *Sun*, after quoting two paragraphs of Reggie's letter, commented: "Most people will think that the '*Saturday's*' young men might find something better to do than the piling up of this cheap and laborious irony."
[4] The manager of the *Saturday Review*.

My dear Reg,

It was very nice of Frank to wish me to come, and I hoped very much I might be able to do so. But, this afternoon, I found that I could not get the pictures for the Exhibition[1] done and framed and so forth (two I have to do anew) unless I stayed on the spot, and as they have all to be ready-framed by next Friday and as I could not afford to let slip the chance of exhibiting them, I had to send my unwilling wire of this afternoon. I should so much have liked to come. Please explain to Frank, to whom messages.

I saw Frank Harris[2] this afternoon. He is delighted with the Wilson B., which is well reproduced. The *Saturday* Supplement will be the most *beautiful* and *distinguished* thing ever published— and only a shilling! It ought to be ten shillings. They have a lovely Gainsborough, reproduced from a mezzotint. Fry, of *Vanity Fair*,[3] wants me to shew him other drawings. I have written suggesting Barney Shaw.[4] No news of Miss Maarie Corelli—I am afraid she must be ill.[5] Nor shall I probably have anything in the next *Saturday*,

[1] "A Century and a half of English humorous art, from Hogarth to the Present Day," which was presented by the Fine Art Society at 148 New Bond Street during October 1896. The sixty-six artists included Hogarth, Gillray, Rowlandson, Cruikshank, Thackeray, Leech, Keene, du Maurier, Caldecott and Phil May. Max contributed six caricatures (of Richard Le Gallienne, George Meredith, Henry Chaplin, Frank Harris, Beerbohm Tree and George Moore). So far as is known, these were the first drawings he exhibited.

[2] James Thomas (Frank) Harris (?1856–1931), author, editor and adventurer, had bought the *Saturday Review* in 1894.

[3] Oliver Armstrong Fry (1855–1931). Originally a barrister, he recorded in *Who's Who* that, having had as a pupil the first Siamese ever called to the English Bar, he was offered a judgeship in Bangkok, but preferred journalism. He was editor of *Vanity Fair* 1889–1904.

[4] G.B.S.

[5] Marie Corelli was the pen-name of Mary Mackay, best-selling English novelist (1864–1924). In his review of Mrs Meynell's essays (see note, p. 109) Max had written: "There are they who write, like Mrs Meynell, over the level of the ordinary critic. They who write, like Madame Sarah Grand, on that level. They who write, like Miss Corelli, beneath it. The third grade conquers the public most swiftly, needing no loud puff from the critics above." This brought forth an angry letter from Miss Corelli in the *Westminster Gazette* of 17 September, saying that she had *not* rented Killiecrankie Cottage, Pitlochry, for the shooting, did *not* ride a

as Augustine[1] is a personal friend of Frank, and Rosebery's former speech on Burns elicited an article entitled "Lord Rosebery's True Vocation."[2] Possibly I may do my article on *Punch*.[3] I *am* an Egoist—I *know* I am.

What news of Mr Watson? My friendliest greetings to Caftangioglu, the unscrupulous Greek.[4] And to yourself, always charming.

Yours   "MAX BEERBOHM"[5]

[*Postmark 9 October 1896*]   *19 Hyde Park Place*

My dear Reggie,

I shall be most happy to dine on Wednesday—and will bring Kilseen. Such excitement! Clem's article in the *Era* beyond all bounds of himself.[6] I shall probably have a long reply next week,

---

bicycle, and had *not* invented a bicycling costume for women; "and though my dear critics, according to comical Mr Max Beerbohm, have decided that I am 'beneath the level of their criticism,' as they can get no more 'gratuitous' copies of my books 'for review,' I am still misguided enough to prefer 'poet's ideals' to blatant feminine vulgarities." Max answered with a polite little letter in the *Westminster Gazette* of 18 September, and followed it up with an anonymous article called "Our Lady of 'Pars' " in the *Saturday Review* of 26 September, in which he pointed out that Miss Corelli obtained more paragraphs in the press by not doing things than her rivals—Hall Caine, Crockett and others—achieved by a hard programme of lecturing and other effort.

[1] Probably Augustine Birrell (1850–1933), writer and Liberal politician.
[2] Actually "Lord Rosebery in his True Role," in the *Saturday Review* of 25 July 1896. The anonymous writer insisted that Rosebery's home was in literature rather than politics.
[3] Max's essay on *Punch* first appeared in *Tomorrow* in July 1897, and was reprinted in *More* (1899).
[4] John (Ioannis) Caftangioglu or Caftanzoglu (d. 1929), lived in England from some time in the 1890s till 1910. In 1911 he married and settled down in Athens. A caricature of him by Max is in the possession of his son, Mr Lysandros Kaftanzoglu, the Greek Ambassador to Libya.
[5] These quotation marks, like the ones round Madge Kendal in the next letter but one, are clearly part of the same (now inexplicable) joke.
[6] In the *Era* of 3 October Clement Scott had risen to the bait and attacked the anonymous ironist of the *Saturday Review* in a long article headed COME OUT OF YOUR HOLE, RAT!

but it depends on Herbert. I am sending you an *Era*. Read *every* word. How are Frank and Caftangioglu? Yours MAX

P.S. Clem takes your defence seriously![1]

[*On back of envelope.*] Dear Reg, Sorry not to find you. Look out for *tomorrow's Saturday*.[2] Mrs Humby[3] tells me you have written to me. MAX

Wednesday [*Postmark 14*] *October* [*1896*]   *19 Hyde Park Place*

My dear Reg,

Thanks for your charming letter. When I said Friday or Thursday, I forgot I had promised to dine with Sickert[4] on *Thursday*. Are you free Friday—or Saturday? I hope so. Have your Pellegrinis come?[5]

I have had an amusing letter of warm encouragement from "Madge Kendal."[6] Yours MAX

---

[1] In his *Era* article Clement Scott had quoted from Reggie's letter in the *Saturday Review* and referred to its author as "one of my loyal defenders."
[2] In the *Saturday Review* of 10 October Max replied to Scott's *Era* attack in a signed letter headed HOLD, FURIOUS SCOT! He ended: "Both in the *Era* and elsewhere, he has been hinting darkly that there was some one, some desperate relative, who had urged me on to assail him. But herein, to adopt his own mode of speech, Mr Scott has planted his cloven hoof upon a mare's nest." This explains the reference to Herbert [Tree] above.
[3] Presumably Reggie's housekeeper.
[4] Walter Richard Sickert, English painter (1860–1942).
[5] Carlo Pellegrini (1839–89) began his caricatures signed "Ape" in *Vanity Fair* in 1862. Max greatly admired his work, examples of which hung in all Max's workrooms from Merton to Rapallo.
[6] English actress (1849–1935). On 12 October 1896 from the North Western Hotel, Liverpool, in a letter marked "Private," she had written:
Dear Mr Beerbohm,
I have just been told of your quarrel with *Mr* Scott! I have just finished reading your reply,—you will find many *friends* in the wainscot happy to scratch with you—and let us hope one day to bite! When rats do, their teeth meet, I'm told, if they please. I like your sentiments.
Wishing you all health and success, to fight this [?] Loren of the Sewers, where we rats reside, I remain, yours faithfully
Madge Kendal
A Female Rat.

Yellow Book probably appears on Friday.[1]
How absurd Bobbie is![2]

5 November 1896   *Berkeley Hotel, Bognor*

My dear Reg,

Did you know that I had come here, with Connie? I had no time
to come and say good-bye to you, though that does not matter
much, seeing how soon—Monday—I shall be back. My people have
let their desirable house in H.P.P. and are moving into rooms. Do
write to me. No news to tell you.

Romeike has only sent me snippets from *Yellow Book* notices, so
I don't know what the critics think of you. I wish you had subscribed to Romeike. He is not really ridiculous.[3]   Yours MAX

[1] Volume XI of the *Yellow Book* (October 1896) contained Max's story
"The Happy Hypocrite," and his caricature of Henry Harland in the
guise of "The Yellow Dwarf," besides a short story by Reggie called "A
Chef-d'œuvre."
[2] In his letter of Tuesday [13 October 1896] Reggie had described a
visit to Robert Ross:
"He is delighted at the great name you are making, but enquired
anxiously how you were taking it, and if you were spoiled. I reassured
him. He is in very good spirits and excellent humour. I told him you were
the author of 'Our Lady of Pars,' which had struck him much. He warned
me against imitating you; he said he had noticed a certain striving after
epigram in my letters to him, and he told me I was not properly equipped
for imitating you with any success. I certainly should not try to do so. I
know your style imitated would be terrible, and so if I did do so it was
unconscious. He was rather sinister about it, but very kind, saying he only
told me as I had a distinct humour of my own etc. which made it worse.
He had not seen the Meredith. He is looking much better. I think he half
expected that you would have almost dropped me and your undistinguished friends, but I said you would always be the same. I hope I was
right, but he has given me an uncomfortable feeling that you may be
growing too large for me."
[3] Messrs Romeike & Curtice, the well known press-cutting agents. On
19 April 1890 Whistler wrote in a letter to the *Scots Observer*: "I only
regret that the ridiculous 'Romeike' has not hitherto sent me your agreeable literature." On 25 May the firm wrote to Whistler demanding an
apology and pointing out that they had in fact supplied him with 807
cuttings. The same day Whistler wrote back to Mr Romeike, over his
butterfly signature: "Who, in Heaven's name, ever dreamed of you as an
actual person?—or one whom one would mean to insult?" He published
all three letters in *The Gentle Art of Making Enemies* (1890).

8 November 1896   *Berkeley Hotel, Bognor*

My dear Reg,

You are becoming quite a letter-writer, in the best sense of the word. My congratulations. But why all this absurd and morbid nonsense about waning friendship? I am sure I am always coming to see you—if only at dinner because dinner is the only time I am sure to find you in. And you know how I delight in your company. Your sense of humour alone—but I suppose that is not what you want. Anyway, I am sure I am always seeking your company, and as to our respective lives, I think you are in very many ways to be envied enormously.

All this is to pave the way to asking whether I might come and stay in Shorter's room on Wednesday? Say no, if you think you know me well enough.   Yours MAX

[*Postmark 24 December 1896*]   *46 Connaught Square, W*

My dear Reg,

I am childishly delighted with your beautiful present—the thing is such a lovely shape, so very modish and swiftly impressive. Thanks so much for it. It certainly must not establish a precedent, and I am determined to give you something vastly inferior. But what? What would you like? Books? If so, what books? Do let me know. Kilseen was delighted with the book you gave her. I hope you are having a nice Christmas. Tell me when you are coming back.   Yours affectionately MAX

[*Postmark 12 January 1897*]   *46 Connaught Square*

My dear Reg,

I shall be charmed to come and dine tomorrow—dress, I presume.

Horrid fog, isn't it? London is like some monstrous daffodil, as Oscar would say.   Yours MAX

My dear Reg,

I send you the *D.M.* and the *S.R.* The latter has nothing by
me, but the former has me and Clem—rather exquisite, seeing that I
have made the first half of my article a parody on Clem.[2] Won't he
be *furious?* How are you enjoying Rouen? Do write to me. I shall
be here till Wednesday at any rate. Tell me all about your visit and
whether you have seen Madame and so on. This is rather a nice
place. Very large and comfy. Several other people staying here besides John Lane. William Watson has most of his meals here—he is
very nice.[3] I foresee what Kilseen calls "a gushing friendship." John
Lane got rather drunk last night and said that "Milton was a finer
artist than Shelley"—whose name sounded at the moment as if it
ought to be pronounced Selley. You will be glad to hear that he had
an awful *contretemps* the night before last. As the ladies rose from
dinner Lane rushed gallantly to open the door for them, coming
down with a *tremendous* crash on the parquet floor. I wish you
could have seen him—it was exquisite. I have been bicycling this
afternoon: it reminded me so of Maesllwch last Easter. Have you

---

[1] J. Lewis May in his *John Lane and the Nineties* (1936) says that "some
friends of Lane's, who had a house in the most delightful part of Windermere facing the Langdales, invited him to spend Christmas there in 1896,
and to bring with him any three men he chose. He took Aubrey Beardsley,
Max Beerbohm and William Watson." Clearly his date is wrong (see
letter, p. 115), and Beardsley was certainly not there in April 1897, but
this was the house.

[2] Since 5 December 1896 Max had contributed twenty articles to the
Daily Mail, each headed "A Commentary made by Max Beerbohm,"
and followed by an editorial disclaimer: "Our readers will understand
that we do not accept the very wide responsibility of identifying ourselves
with Mr Beerbohm's opinions." The last of them ("Envoi") appeared on
17 April 1897 and began: "There come in the course of every career
certain moments when retrospection is pardonable, when a man may (to
borrow, once more, the best manner of Mr Clement Scott) cry 'halt!'
and, resting on his oar, brush away a tear with his last breath, as he looks
back longingly at the distant spires of the old homestead." The same issue
of the *Daily Mail* contained three columns of reminiscence and anecdote
by Clement Scott about the destruction by builders of the public and
private gardens of North London.

[3] English poet (1858–1935). Knighted 1917.

heard about a seat for the first night?[1] If we have a box, of course you must come. I wish you were up here. The men here are nice but not what *I* call clever—not what I call clev— As we sit over the wine, I keep thinking of Oscar's conversation. Do write.

Yours MAX

[*Postmark 16 May*] *1897*   *Folkestone*

My dear Reg,

Many thanks for your amusing letter. You are becoming quite the letter-writer. I have sent Bobbie the books.[2] Mind you keep your eye on Mr Pigeon—keep the net round him till I come back and pluck his plumage at leisure. I think he will be the best thing we have been on since Trelawny Backhouse. The "Conservative" is famed for its clarets—we'll empty the cellar.

Folkestone is very full, but I have had a great personal success. The *Folkestone Journal* was brought in yesterday by our landlady who had marked a paragraph in which my presence in the town was chronicled—"the clever, original and pleasantly cynical young author"—with a hope expressed that I should "write one of my famous articles about Folkestone, unless I were too deeply engrossed with my eloquent pen."[3] Quite a *succès*! You may imagine that my head is by way of being turned—Max Beerbohm!

Today is Mr Holland's[4] last Sunday in prison—aren't you glad?

[1] Of *The Seats of the Mighty*, by Gilbert Parker, with which Tree opened his new theatre, Her Majesty's, in the Haymarket, on 28 April 1897.
[2] Oscar Wilde had asked Robert Ross to collect some books for him on his release from prison. Max sent four, including his own *Works* (1896) and *The Happy Hypocrite* (1897).
[3] This paragraph appeared in the *Folkestone Herald* of 15 May.
[4] Wilde's wife and children had changed their name to Holland, but he never used it himself. He was released from prison on the morning of 19 May 1897, and crossed that night with his friend More Adey to Dieppe, where Reggie and Ross were waiting for him. As they waited, Reggie wrote to Max:
"Robbie and I are cosily sitting here discussing a citronade and writing letters. Oscar missed the train this morning and went down to Newhaven with More during the day, so though your picture of seeing the steamer arrive will hardly be realised, we shall be on the quay at 4 a.m. tomorrow. Robbie and I have laughed a good deal today and have been talking of

Dora has enjoyed herself here, and has played a great many paper-games and games of Halma with me. Tomorrow we return. Shall I come and see you on Tuesday afternoon? ...

Yours affectionately MAX

I enjoyed Clem's Inn immensely.

31 May 1897   *48 Upper Berkeley Street*

My dear Reg,

I shall be charmed to come on Wednesday, bringing with me some tiny gift. Pray build no hopes. Also I will bring to show you a very nice letter from Mr Melmoth.[1] It came this morning. Last night I dined with the Jones's.[2] Mrs Cyril Maude[3] was given the place of honour, on my right hand. On my left, Lady Dorothy Nevill, who is a dear. After the "vile participations"[4] of the evening before, I felt quite like George Robey with "the lady Flo" at the Garden Party:

"They wanted *me*!
They wanted *me*!"

When I see you I shall have to strike my boot with the male-bamboo, which is still at Clement's Inn, by the way. Cissie M'Carthy—*née* Loftus—sat near me.[5] Also the Bram Stokers[6] and the dear Morrises—Irish Law Lord.[7]

---

your *mots* and dilating on your great sanity. Oscar, we are informed by telegram, is charming. In his room we have put a lot of flowers. All the books we have collected are on the mantelpiece, and your own two works are in the centre to catch his eye. In another room we have ordered sandwiches and a bottle of red and a bottle of white wine to be placed."

[1] Sebastian Melmoth was the name Wilde used in the early days of his release. His letter to Max, thanking him for the books and criticising *The Happy Hypocrite*, is printed in *The Letters of Oscar Wilde* (1962), p. 575.

[2] Presumably Henry Arthur Jones, the playwright, and his wife.

[3] Winifred Emery, English actress (1862–1924), married the actor Cyril Maude in 1888.

[4] *1 Henry IV*, Act III, scene ii.

[5] In 1894 Cissy Loftus had married Justin Huntly M'Carthy, dramatist, novelist and historian (1861–1936). They were divorced in 1899.

[6] Bram Stoker (1847–1912), business manager of Irving's Lyceum and author of *Dracula* (1897), had married Florence Balcombe in 1878.

[7] Michael Morris, first Lord Morris (1827–1901) had been Lord Chief Justice of Ireland 1887–89 and was Lord of Appeal in Ordinary 1889–1900.

Goodbye till Wednesday. I have done a beautiful little caricature of Whistler.   Yours   MAX

Berkeley Hotel, Bognor

My dear Regie,

I need not say how sorry I am to have delayed so long in writing to you. I have meant to write every day, but what with one thing and another have not written till today. I will make amends by writing more regularly. Much as I dislike letter-writing, I shall be buoyed up by my love of receiving letters. I hope you will write to me. Many thanks for your last amusing letter. I hope you are going on all right, and that you can dispense with the doctor's advice for a while, and that you are taking care of yourself and will soon be in a position to drop one of the initials after your name. It is simply a question of time.

Are you writing at all? That play of which you told me seemed very promising, I thought. (Do not imagine that I am simply playing the sterling old friend.) I really do think that you ought to have a great future in play-writing.

My Hall Caine had rather a *succès*, hadn't it?[1] I am writing another thing about Clement Scott for the *D.M.*[2] at Harmsworth's[3] own suggestion. Harmsworth is wholly delightful. I stayed with him in Kent last Saturday to Monday. Mrs Harmsworth also very nice. They have a charming house, and many, many servants. Furse the painter[4] was there, and a man called Pollen, of the *Westminster Gazette*, very amusing,[5] and some other people. Stephen Crane[6]

[1] Max had witheringly reviewed Hall Caine's new novel, *The Christian*, in the *Daily Mail* of 11 August.
[2] This appeared not in the *Daily Mail* but in the *Saturday Review* (see note p. 123).
[3] Alfred Charles Harmsworth (1865–1922) was at this time proprietor and editor of the *Daily Mail*. Created Lord Northcliffe 1905, Viscount 1917. His country house was Elmwood, St Peter's, Kent.
[4] Charles Wellington Furse (1868–1904), member of the New English Art Club.
[5] Almost certainly Arthur Joseph Hungerford Pollen (1866–1937), business man and writer on naval affairs.
[6] American author and war correspondent (1871–1900).

was asked but couldn't go. My toilets knocked 'em all silly. On Sunday, flannel coat, white waistcoat, purple tie with turquoise pin, duck trousers and straw hat. My scarab was a great centre of attraction. Altogether a very pleasant visit, and I got away without tipping more than one person. I hope to see much of the Harmsworths —cigarettes and a telephone by one's bedside, and an enormous peach with one's morning-tea, and a glass of sherry-and-bitters on one's dressing-table at nightfall, and bound volumes of *Vanity Fair* in the library, and two small alligators in one of the innumerable hot-houses, and generally all the things which are indispensable to a scholar and a gentleman. Talking of *Vanity Fair*, Sickert has done a new caricature of me, which has been accepted. Don't know when it appears.[1] You *must* have it opposite my Meredith.

Kilseen may have an engagement from Hawtrey;[2] otherwise she will go on tour with Bertie Tree. The weather here is rather awful, but the place is as sweet as ever. The parade is always crowded with "flowers." . . .

I hear that that ass Oscar is under *surveillance*—I suppose he is playing the giddy goat. Can't someone warn him to be careful?

Do write to me as soon as possible. . . . When do you return?

Yours affectionately MAX

[Late] August 1897*   *Berkeley Hotel, Bognor*

My dear Reggie,

It is all very well for you to talk about silver match-boxes which have been much admired by the Princess of Wales, but *where is mine?* My birthday is behind me and I am still carrying my matches loose in a breast-pocket. I hope you'll "advise" your jeweller. Also I hope you are not giving me the jubilee match-box which Mrs Frank gave you. Do have my present sent to me very soon. . . .

I had seen in some paper that Mrs Atherton was going to Rouen, but I am intensely interested to hear that she is under your roof.[3]

[1] Signed "Sic," it appeared in colour in *Vanity Fair* on 9 December 1897.
[2] Charles Hawtrey, actor and manager (1858–1923). Knighted 1922.
[3] Gertrude Atherton (1857–1948) was an American novelist of unblemished reputation. At this time she had published three novels and

With love
Grace Conan.

KILSEEN

No. 239.—Vol. XIX.   WEDNESDAY, AUGUST 25, 1897.   SIXPENCE.
By Post, 6½d.

MR. RICHARD LE GALLIENNE IN HIS CYCLING COSTUME.

FROM A PHOTOGRAPH BY RUSSELL AND SONS, BAKER STREET, W.

Who recommended her to you? Do tell me all about her, and tell her all about me. I had heard that she had a daughter over the sea. She herself started life behind a bar in St Louis—then went to San Francisco, where she used to dance naked in one of the dime-shows. Also she was kept for some years by President Garfield.[1] When he was assassinated, she became an authoress. This letter is written with a special view to its being read aloud across the table at *déjeuner*.

If I possibly can, I will come to Rouen for a few days, but my plans still depend greatly on Murray Carson,[2] who is acting at Folkestone this week. I send you a page from the *Sketch*, which I think you would not like to miss.[3] . . .

Yours affectionately   M A X

I have written about Clement Scott's new book—probably in the *Daily Mail* Thursday.[4]

---

was to write forty more. On 24 August Reggie had written from Bois Guillaume:

"There is an American novelist staying here, Mrs Gertrude Atherton by name, and she is the person who reviewed your *Happy Hypocrite* for *Vanity Fair*, a criticism which gave you so much pleasure. Fortunately for me she keeps her room all day except at meals. She seems nice and 35 but I shall find out both later. She is a widow (like Lottie Collins) and has a daughter (in California). It is rather an Ibsen ménage. Do write to me, as having boasted of our intense intimacy it would be awful if I got no letters from you. . . . I have never read anything of Gertrude Atherton's except her criticism of you, and I told her so with engaging frankness, scorning worldly compliments. She has already (I arrived last night) confided to Madame her hope that she will not like me *too* much. It is a hope I quite reciprocate. She is a friend of Lane's fiancée, and does not like Henry Harland or George Moore."

[1] James Abram Garfield (1831–81), twentieth President of the U.S.A. After only a few months in office he was assassinated in a Washington railway station.
[2] English actor and playwright (1865–1917).
[3] Almost certainly the full-page photograph of "Mr Richard Le Gallienne in his Cycling Costume" on the first page of the issue of 25 August, here reproduced opposite.
[4] See p. 123.

My dear Regie,

Please forgive my not having written sooner to thank you for the delightful book of Forain's.[1] I have not been ungrateful, all the same, and have been revelling in the drawings. How funny your meeting must have been with Sebastian and the "Infant Samuel."[2] Did Oscar order any of those liqueurs about which he was so very bitter in the historic letter, and did he refer at all to "Bobbie's beautiful action" at the Bankruptcy Court?[3]

I am here till Tuesday, when I go to London. On Sunday I start with Murray Carson who is going to act *Gudgeons*[4] with his Company at Harrogate. Thence we go to (probably) Paris. What a pity you could not still be at Rouen—we might have seen much of each other. Please let me know when you come exactly to London. How is your play progressing? The match-box has never arrived, but I am living in hopes. Kilseen has acted a small part in *The Taming of the Shrew* at Birmingham, and seems to have done well.[5] Herbert's tour is a great success. Murray Carson came down here for a night on Thursday—very full of the play and very elastic and "vital." I wish immensely I could have come to Rouen as you suggested,

---

[1] Probably *La Vie*, a book of coloured drawings by Jean-Louis Forain (1852–1931), with captions, published in 1897.

[2] i.e. Wilde and Lord Alfred Douglas. This sentence and the next one show that Robert Ross must have shown to Max and Reggie the long letter from Wilde to Douglas known as *De Profundis*, which Wilde had handed to Ross on 19 May.

[3] "When I was brought down from my prison to the Court of Bankruptcy between two policemen, Robbie waited in the long dreary corridor, that before the whole crowd, whom an action so sweet and simple hushed into silence, he might gravely raise his hat to me, as handcuffed and with bowed head I passed him by. Men have gone to heaven for smaller things than that." (Wilde to Douglas, from Reading Gaol.)

[4] A modern comedy by Thornton Clark and Louis N. Parker, originally produced at Terry's Theatre on 10 November 1893, with Murray Carson in the cast.

[5] *Katherine and Petruchio*, Garrick's one-act adaptation, was part of the large repertory with which Tree opened his two-months tour at Birmingham on 30 August. Tree and his wife played the name-parts, with Lionel Brough as Gremio, Charles Allan as Baptista, Gerald du Maurier as Biondello and Kilseen as Bianca. When the play opened at Her Majesty's on 1 November Kilseen had been replaced by Margaret Halstan.

but it was impossible for one reason and another. I look forward to seeing you very much. How is Gertrude Atherton? I always confuse her with the person who sang the laughing song.[1] . . .

Yours affectionately MAX

I send you the article on Clement Scott from the *Saturday*.[2] I also had an article on scenery last week, which I have mislaid.[3] Will give you a copy for your collection.

[*Late September 1897*]   *Hotel du Port, 34 Quai Gambetta*
                                        Boulogne-sur-mer

My dear Reg,

Excuse this absurd envelope on which I am writing. I am writing in a little and absurd *café chantant*, which is the only thing in Boulogne. Carson and I and his valet and his secretary came out, full of hope, to Bruges, of which Carson sickened, and so we came here. The collaborator and his staff have returned to England, so I have now to do the play by myself[4] and to fold my own clothes and to write my own letters, which is a great hardship. The Marquis de Leuville[5] is in Boulogne, quite superb, representing the old French

[1] Alice Atherton, English actress (1847–99). In a burlesque called *The Babes, or Whines from the Wood*, by Harry Paulton with music by W. C. Levey, produced at Toole's Theatre in September 1884, Miss Atherton and her husband William Edouin performed a laughing song together.

[2] "An Appreciation" (*Saturday Review*, 4 September 1897), in which Max made fun of Clement Scott's new book of essays, *Sisters by the Sea*.

[3] No. XIII in a series of articles called "The Best Scenery I Know," which appeared in the *Saturday Review* on 28 August 1897. It was reprinted, revised and entitled "Prangley Valley" in *More* (1899). Other contributors to the series included Arthur Symons, W. H. Hudson, Selwyn Image, Herbert P. Horne and May Morris.

[4] The only collaboration between Max and Murray Carson which came to anything was a three-act comedy called *The Fly on the Wheel*. It was produced at the Coronet Theatre, Notting Hill Gate, on 4 December 1902.

[5] 1843–1908. C. B. Cochran described him as a "Fleet Street and Strand notoriety . . . It was creditably reported that his real name was Oliver and that his father was a barber. After his assumption of the marquisate— a wealthy widow was supposed to have bought it for him abroad—he thought it necessary at times to lapse into broken English . . . He scented himself copiously, wore a huge cameo in his black satin scarf, high heels

aristocracy, of which we hear so much and see so little. Also the Dowager Lady Cadogan,[1] who is a great comfort to me and sits near me at *table d'hôte* in the Hôtel des Bains, which is my address. I return on Sat. morning, and am going to the first night of a musical play in an illicit production for which Claud Nugent has written the lyrics or the libretto, and in which Mackay of my brother's Co. is also involved.[2] Two stalls have been reserved for me. Would you, if you are in London, like to come with me? You might write me a line to *UBS*.[3] It would be nice if you could come with me. What have you been doing? Anything in the way of plays? I wish you would. I am sure you have the dramatist's [*two words illegible*]. Boulogne is a horrid place, I think. As I write, a man with a false nose and a blouse is just beginning the usual peasant's recitation.

Hope you can come on Saturday.   Yours MAX

[*Circa 8 November 1897*]

My dear Reg,

I have waited for you. Will you come and dine *chez* Carson on Wednesday—or Friday? And come to the *V.K.*[4] afterwards. He is very anxious to know you—and liked your face. (I have promised that you will do your imitation of Irving.) Write please *tout de suite*, and I will let you know the hour. Do come. I think you'd like them. May I take with me your collection of my works, for a day

---

to his boots, and was reported to have the biggest appetite in London." (*Showman Looks On*, 1945, p. 17.) He published several volumes of "passionate verse" and gave many public recitations.

[1] There was no Dowager Lady Cadogan at this time. Max must have meant the wife of the fifth Earl (1840–1915). She was born Beatrix Helen, daughter of the second Earl of Craven. She married in 1865 and died in 1907.

[2] *The Mermaids*, a submarine musical fantasy by Gayer Mackay, with music by Claud Nugent and additional lyrics by Charles Brookfield, opened at the Avenue Theatre on 2 October 1897.

[3] Upper Berkeley Street.

[4] *The Vagabond King*, a play in four acts by Louis N. Parker, which had opened at the Court Theatre on 4 November with Murray Carson in the principal part.

or two? I will guard them most jealously, for my sake as well as your own. This is an autograph letter from Max Beerbohm—lucky rogue!

Yours MAX

I had an article in the last *Sat. Rev.* which you ought to have.[1]

30 November 1897   *210 Cromwell Road, S.W.*

My dear Reg,

Thanks for your nice letter. I think I score off Whistler next Saturday.[2] Shall we dine at Monico 7.15 that day and go to Her M's?[3]

[1] "How to Behave," largely an ironical review of *The Art of Conversing; or Dialogues of the Day*, by A Member of the Aristocracy (*Saturday Review*, 6 November 1897).

[2] In a signed essay called "Papillon Rangé" in the *Saturday Review* of 20 November 1897 Max had written ironically about the news that William Heinemann had "induced Mr. Whistler to consent to the issue of another edition" of his *Gentle Art of Making Enemies*, originally published in 1890. This provoked a letter from Paris from Whistler the following week, called "An Acknowledgement," in which he referred to Max as "your new gentleman—a simple youth, of German extraction" and proceeded to make fun of a slip in Max's French and his use of an unusual English word. In the "Notes" on the first page of the *Saturday Review* of 4th December appeared the following paragraph which must have been written by Max:

> In our last week's issue there appeared a letter from Monsieur J. McNeill Whistler criticising our contributor Mr Max Beerbohm. The letter was in M. Whistler's best butterfly style; it fluttered gaily, poised itself delicately for a moment for a slip in French or a somewhat unusual English word, and then flitted away. We will not imitate M. Whistler's manner; the airiness of the youthful irresponsible beau is antiquated now; the white plume that used to stand out so bravely against the dark locks is now almost indistinguishable, the boyish impertinences even have lost their charm as do the girlish gigglings of a maiden aunt; but "it intrigues us vastly," if we may imitate without understanding M. Whistler's English; we are, in other words, curious to know why M. Whistler should parry thrusts that do not, he avers, go near his skin.

[3] Her Majesty's, where on 1 November Tree had presented a double bill, consisting of *The Silver Key*, adapted from Dumas *père's Mademoiselle de Belle Isle*, by Sydney Grundy, and *Katherine and Petruchio*.

The *More Works* are perfectly safe and shall be religiously returned. Is it true that you are going to Egypt? I hope not.

Excuse hurried note; I am immersed in the play: reading of
second act to Wyndham[1] on Thursday. He liked the first act very
much.   Yours affectionately MAX

Do come and call here. The Carsons were bowled over by you, and
I am afraid they may be feeling offended.

Have you seen Bryan's picture of me in the Xmas *World*?[2]

[*?December 1897*]   210 *Cromwell Road*

My dear Reg,

Can't send a wire, for I am literally penniless, but the seats will
be all right. Enquire at box-office. Reserved in my name. Wish I
could come too, but I am engaged.

I was much gratified by the idea of booming my costume—and
should have liked it immensely—but I feel I don't deserve it: my
wardrobe is so very slender and the honour ought to go to a worthier
man. There is Lord Chesterfield[3]—also Colonel Brabazon:[4] you
might suggest them to Murphy.[5] I should be delighted to be
"honourably mentioned" from time to time in connection with the
subject in the *Journal*. My hat ought to make rather good copy—
also my frock-coat. But I don't think I ought to be insisted upon.

[1] Charles Wyndham, actor-manager (1837–1919). Knighted 1902.
[2] This number, which was dated 25 November, contained a long article
in prose and verse by Mostyn T. Pigott, called "Une Cause Célèbre,
1897 versus 1837," in which various topical celebrities, including Max,
Edison, John Burns, Lord Esher and Johnston Forbes-Robertson are
produced as witnesses before Mr Justice Time. The drawing of Max by
Alfred Bryan shows him in a box at the theatre, smoking a cigarette with
gloved hands, his top hat resting on the ledge beside him. For Max's
opinion of Bryan's work, see the essay "A.B." in *More* (1899).
[3] Edwyn Francis Scudamore Stanhope, tenth Earl of Chesterfield (1854–
1933), had been Treasurer of the Queen's Household 1892–94.
[4] Col. John Palmer Brabazon (1843–1922) had served in many overseas
campaigns. A.D.C. to Queen Victoria 1889–1901, when he retired with
the rank of Major-General. K.C.B. 1911.
[5] Unidentified, except that he seems to have been the London represent-
ative of the *New York Journal*.

The Americans might see through me! Tell Murphy I shall be delighted to place any knowledge I have at his disposal.

Yours MAX

Wednesday [Postmark 12] January 1898   Windlestone, Ferry Hill
[Co. Durham]

My dear Reg,

Forgive my silence since your welcome and very amusing letter. I am glad Bobbie would not like Pau and I gather that you are having a nice time there.

Not much has happened since you went away. I did not go to Terriss's funeral, though the papers accused me of doing so.[1] Ned Lawson[2] was really there, however. By the way, Irving is going to head a deputation to Lawson about Clement Scott—perhaps you have heard.[3] Murray Carson has been very active in the matter, bursting with indignation. He wants a Royal Charter to be granted to the Actors' Association. I am afraid he is not an artist, in Ranger Gull's sense of the word.[4]

Observe this note-paper. I write from the Stately Home of a Baronet of Jacobite creation, Sir William Eden,[5] in the County of Durham. Walter Sickert is here as my sponsor, and I have a smoking-suit of purple silk, with dark red facings—and am rather

[1] William Terriss was murdered by a disappointed actor outside the stage-door of the Adelphi Theatre on 16 December 1897. His funeral at Brompton Cemetery on 21 December was attended, according to *The Times*, by 50,000 people.
[2] Reggie's putative cousin (1833-1916). See p. 7 *et. seq.*
[3] In an interview in *Great Thoughts* Clement Scott had been quoted as saying "There is no school on earth so bad for the formation of character, or that so readily, so quickly draws out all that is bad in man and woman as the stage" and more to the same effect. Somewhat reluctantly Irving saw the manager of the *Daily Telegraph* on behalf of the Actors' Association, and Scott resigned his position as dramatic critic and retired to the Continent.
[4] Cyril Arthur Edward Ranger Gull (1876–1923) was on the staff of the *Saturday Review* 1897–98. He later became a prolific and successful novelist under his own name and as Guy Thorne.
[5] Seventh Baronet (1849–1915), landowner, painter, eccentric, one-time friend of Whistler, father of the Earl of Avon.

light-headed, I am afraid. W.S. has acted in *Dream Faces*[1] with Lady Eden for a charity. He was not at all word-perfect—she was quite so. Sir W is a delightful and surprising man. We get on very well together. I sat beside him on the bench at Petty Sessions on Monday, wearing my check-suit and a fancy waistcoat—very bluff but at the same time very intellectual, and with my chin resting on a beautiful white hand.

The house is very comfortable and distinguished. In the Hall is a Visitors' Book over which I spend most of my leisure-moments—a Debrett in MS. The dear Ormondes, the dear Londonderrys, the dear Zetlands, and many others too numerous and too distinguished for me to mention in a private letter to an old friend. I am going to ask Sir W to let me have the book for my little nephew who has begun a collection of autographs.

Do write to me, dear Reg, at Upper Berkeley Street. London was very dull without your genial and talented presence. I look forward to seeing you, untitled though you are. Kilseen tells me you have written to her. Goodbye.   Yours affectionately MAX

[*Postmark 31 January 1898*]   *4 Trinity Crescent, Folkestone*

My dear Reg,

I am here with the Carsons, in my usual capacity of led captain— nor do we leave before the end of the week at earliest. So I can't dine with you on Wednesday, as I should much like to do. But couldn't you come *via* B and F,[2] staying a night or two at the West Cliff Hotel which is quite adjacent? Had I a penny or two you should be my guest. But I have not and so you cannot. I am sure the Carsons would rejoice to see you, as they are so fond of you. And now my heartfelt congratulations (not untempered with envy and alarm) on your new career. I think it will be great fun for you, and you certainly ought to galvanise the remains of the *D.T.*[3] We are all very much excited. I only wish that you were about to pour the

[1] A one-act play by Wynn Miller, originally produced in 1888.
[2] Boulogne and Folkestone. Reggie was staying at 25 Boulevard de Capucines, Paris.
[3] Reggie had taken a job on the staff of the *Daily Telegraph*.

purple wine of your wit into a worthier gourd, as "our friend"[1] would say. Ernest[2] will be awfully impressed when he hears about the affair. I have already got a red-backed case for the Works of Reginald Turner. It will be fun "spotting" what is yours every day.

I hope you are not being very Capucin in Paris after your Pau campaign. Did you see my caricature of Pinero in the *Daily Mail*?[3] A very good one.   Yours affectionately   MAX

24 May 1898   *48 Upper Berkeley Street*
My dear Reg,
I am very sorry I can't lunch with you on Thursday—pray ask me some other day. I have done a series of eleven *Gladstone in Heaven* drawings, which I will send down to you.[4] Müller[5] can have the series for ten guineas (very cheap *if he wants them*) but I can't sell 'em separately. Many thanks for your note.
                                       Yours   MAX
Ten guineas *down*, as I am so hard up—otherwise they would be £105.

Thursday [*26 May 1898. Postmark 27 May*]
                                    48 Upper Berkeley Street
My dear Reg,
As you may imagine, I was immensely delighted to have your letter and Müller's cheque. I have written to thank Müller. To you many thanks for being go-between. I think £12.12. a very good price considering how quickly I had done the series. You must have a meal with me! When can you come?   Yours affectionately   MAX

[1] Oscar Wilde.
[2] Ernest Leverson.
[3] Published on 21 January 1898.
[4] These eleven drawings, "Mr Gladstone goes to Heaven," were first exhibited in the Guedalla exhibition at the Leicester Galleries in 1945, and first reproduced in *Max's Nineties* (1958). The originals are in the Junior Carlton Club. Gladstone had died on 19 May.
[5] Unidentified.

My dear Reg,

I wonder whether you could possibly "accommodate" me to-morrow night? I have to dine with Alf Harmsworth and don't want to return so late up this interminable hill. If you can't I can easily go to the Charing X Hotel[2] or elsewhere. Anyhow I will call in the afternoon—you might leave me a note to say whether I shall come or not. *"Clyde"*[3] is in England, and has asked me to lunch on Monday.

How are you? Hampstead is very nice. Dandy is very happy on the Heath, and wishes to be remembered to you, though he cannot say so.   Yours MAX

[Postmark 27 June 1898]   *4 Holly Mount, Hampstead*

My dear Reg,

Thanks for your charming letter. I *was* so pleased with it. Shall you be in at tea-time tomorrow? I am going with Kilseen to *Pelléas*[4] and I might bring her to tea—or why don't you go to *Pelléas* tomorrow? You must positively go, sooner or later, and it stops on (I think) Friday.

I am going to write *Zuleika Dobson*[5] and cut Maeterlinck out.

Yours affectionately MAX

P.S. Here is my Leiter from the *D.M.* of Saturday.[6]

---

[1] The Beerbohm family was temporarily living here while their own house in Upper Berkeley Street was let.

[2] All his life Max particularly enjoyed staying in the big London railway hotels, and always did so on the least excuse.

[3] Clyde Fitch.

[4] Maurice Maeterlinck's play, *Pelléas et Mélisande* (1892), was first produced in London in an English translation by J. W. Mackail, with special music by Gabriel Fauré, at the Prince of Wales Theatre on 21 June 1898. Nine matinée performances were given, with Johnston Forbes-Robertson, Mrs Patrick Campbell and Martin Harvey in the leading parts.

[5] Not finished until 1911 (see p. 204).

[6] Joseph Leiter (1868–1932). Wealthy American, brother of the first Lady Curzon. Max's caricature of him appeared in the *Daily Mail* on 25 June 1898.

23 August 1898   *Townshend House, Cowes,*
                                           Isle of Wight[1]

My dear Reg,

I am so sorry not to have answered before. I have been awfully busy here re-arranging my essays,[2] and have felt obliged to devote all my spare moments to getting bronzed. It is terrible to think how soon I shall be once more pallid in the garish light of *foyers*, talking to Morton[3] and nodding to Joe Knight.[4] . . .

I must plead guilty to having abstracted your *Playhouse Impressions*[5] and forgotten to notify same. Please let anger be swallowed up in relief that it is all safe in my keeping. "Vengeance is mine, saith the Lord," as the absurd Colonel Hamborough says.[6]

When do you "take" your holiday? How is Bobbie? Please give him some mulierastic[7] equivalent for my love.

Ranger Gull has written to me. He sends a dummy number of the new paper[8] and seems to think me a big artist—as I suppose I am.

It is very cosy here and charming. My white ducks are received with great attention and respect. Sickert is still in Dieppe and has seen Whistler, but not to speak to. My essays appear in October or are supposed to, and you shall have a copy. The binding will be bright green.

Do communicate with me again.

                                    Yours affectionately   MAX

[1] On 20 August Max had published an article called "At Cowes" in the *Saturday Review*.
[2] For publication in *More* (20 April 1899).
[3] Edward Arthur Morton (d. 1922), dramatic critic of the *Referee*.
[4] Joseph Knight (1829–1907), dramatic critic of the *Globe* and the *Athenaeum*. Editor of *Notes and Queries* from 1883. Max had been appointed dramatic critic of the *Saturday Review* in May 1898 and was to hold the post for twelve years.
[5] A book of collected dramatic criticism by A. B. Walkley (1892).
[6] Reference untraced.
[7] i.e. heterosexual. Wilde called it "Robbie's immortal phrase."
[8] *London Life*. To the first issue, which appeared on 17 September 1898, Max contributed a self-caricature and an essay called "Many Happy Returns," in which he linked his own twenty-sixth birthday with the paper's birth.

48 *Upper Berkeley Street*

My dear Reg,

Thanks very much for your letter. I was so glad to hear from you, but sorry that you had not been well at first. I hope you have quite recovered and are having a good time—by which I do not mean an *immoral* time. I fear that some fair *contadina* may have seduced you into living a light life, but I hope that you will keep to that straight and narrow way which you usually patronise, and which is always open to visitors at Naples. I send you last week's *Saturday* (I had nothing in the previous number). Also an article of Archer's which may amuse you. My article is partly a reply to it.[1] The stupid title of the article is not mine, but was impudently inserted by Runciman[2] or one of the other drunkards of *la Rue* Southampton.[3]

You must enjoy being with Bobbie. Which of you has said the better things? And have you had any of those awful coolnesses which sometimes marred our enjoyment in the Rouen days? You were invariably in the wrong. Do you remember that occasion when I asked you not to "wait dinner" for me—and the very sinister scenes that ensued?

I am reading *Aylwin*, Theodore Watts's belated novel.[4] It is of

[1] Max's article, which appeared in the *Saturday Review* of 15 October 1898 under the title "Max, Mr Archer and Others," was partly a review of *The Adventure of Lady Ursula* by Anthony Hope (first produced at the Duke of York's Theatre on 11 October) and partly a rejoinder to Archer's article in the *World* of 12 October, in which he had taken Max to task for suggesting a "close season" for those overworked classics, *Hamlet, Romeo* and *Macbeth*, and for "fabricating" authorities and opinions.
[2] John F. Runciman (1866–1916), outspoken music critic of the *Saturday Review*, and author of books on music. In 1896 he caused a storm by describing the Royal Academy of Music as "a cesspool of academic musical life." Bernard Shaw described him as "young, clever, and quite genuine, but, like many middle-class Bohemians, without a notion of public or private manners. He drank, died, and is forgotten; but he held his own among us for a time."
[3] The offices of the *Saturday Review* were in Southampton Street, off the Strand.
[4] Published in 1897, by Walter Theodore Watts (1832–1914), who in that year changed his name to Watts-Dunton. He had spent many years on it, and its success was immense, twenty-two editions being called for in

entrancing and surpassing beauty. Do read it as soon as you come back. It is rather P.B.¹-ite, but very amusing. The sort of thing Pater would have written if he had been a *man* and not an old woman, as he was. Rothenstein is in his new house, which is very pretty—and the hot meals are a great comfort after the corned-beef and the meagre salads of Glebe Place.² Everyone sends love to you and to Bobbie. Do write to me again. Ask Bobbie to write to me too, if he will—but I stipulate that he write legibly. I hear that Wyndham has been in Paris, and given Oscar a definite commission for a play, and that Oscar has already begun to write it.³ I wonder if that is so.   Yours affectionately MAX

21 November 1900   *48 Upper Berkeley Street*

My dear Reg,

   Please forgive me. All I can say is that I will write again to-morrow. I hope you are having a happy time in Paris, and especially a *chaste* time, and keeping out of mischief. Are you writing at all? I have looked at the *World* and have seen some Paris notes once or twice, but I don't think they are by you. Do write a *play*: I know you are a dramaturgist at heart, and that you would write successful plays—plays not for the "closet."

   Turning for a moment to myself, I enclose a cutting from the *Daily Mail* of today, which tells its own story.⁴ The story is not a

---

seven years. Oscar Wilde pronounced it "on the whole a capital book to give to one's parents at Christmas time."
¹ Preraphaelite Brotherhood.
² Rothenstein had just moved from Chelsea to Pembroke Cottages, Edwardes Square, Kensington.
³ Charles Wyndham (see note, p. 126) had visited Wilde at Berneval, near Dieppe, in July 1897 to discuss an adaptation of Eugène Scribe's play *Le Verre d'Eau*, but in September Wilde turned down the idea. There is no record of Wyndham's visiting Wilde in Paris, but early in 1900 they were still in correspondence about possible plays.
⁴ "It is announced that, at the request of Mrs Patrick Campbell, Mr Max Beerbohm has dramatised his pretty little fairy story, *The Happy Hypocrite*, into a one-act play, and that it will shortly be produced by Mrs Campbell in front of *Mr and Mrs Daventry* at the Royalty Theatre."

very thrilling one to me; however, I *may* make £225—at any rate, not less than £125, even if the play is a fiasco. Meanwhile, I shall have to attend rehearsals, which will be painful affairs, I expect. Tomorrow I am sending you the Xmas *World*—the day of its publication. Let me know if you like my part in it.[1]

I dined with Hardwicke[2] last night. I met at dinner (and impressed favourably) George Wyndham[3] soon after you left England. I am going to be a "Celebrity At Home" in the *World* in a few weeks,[4] *unberufen*.[5] Will R. has a painting of me at the New Gallery.[6] I am going to have a new dress-suit. I am looking fairly well.

And now let us turn to higher things. I suppose the Rosses have left Paris. I have not seen Alec[7] since his return. How is Oscar? Do you see him often? Do write and let me know all about your doings. By the way, it may amuse you to hear that Rendle of the *D.T.*[8] has been making everyone very furious by attacking *everything* that has been produced. I am told that "Edward"[9] himself is vexed, and that there is an influential cabal working for Rendle's downfall.

---

[1] The Christmas 1900 issue of the *World* was solely illustrated by Max, in some twenty-seven caricatures and drawings. In addition eight full-page caricatures, reproduced in colour, were issued in a folder as a supplement. They were of the Bishop of London, Lord Kitchener, Sir Edward Carson, J. S. Sargent, Lord Charles Beresford, M. de Soveral, Sir Henry Irving and Stephen Phillips.

[2] Albert Edward Phillip Henry Yorke, sixth Earl of Hardwicke (1867–1904). Secretary of State for India 1900–2.

[3] Politician and author (1863–1913). He had been Conservative M.P. for Dover since 1889, and private secretary to Mr Balfour 1887–92. Under-Secretary of State for War 1898–1900. Published literary essays and an edition of Shakespeare's poems.

[4] This interview, which appeared in the *World* of 5 December is here reprinted as Appendix C on p. 297.

[5] This German equivalent to "Touch wood" was commonly used in polite English society at this time.

[6] Unidentified.

[7] Robbie's brother, Alec Ross.

[8] Thomas McDonald Rendle (1856–1926), who had been on the parliamentary staff of the *Daily Telegraph* since the early eighties, succeeded Clement Scott as dramatic critic and held the job until 1901.

[9] Edward Lawson.

Sidney Colvin[1] "is very angry"[2]—also Courtney,[3] and Mrs Hulse.[4] London is horrible—wet and dark. I do envy you your deliciously irresponsible and elegant life in dear beautiful Paris. I should like to come over as soon as my bloody playlet has seen the light—I am only really happy in France. Where do you eat your meals? I think you said you only had coffee and roll in your rooms. Do write to me quickly, and I really will reply quickly, dully but quickly.

With best love. Yours MAX

Kilseen is not here, but I know she would also send her best love. She is at present very much excited, having ordered an astrakhan coat.

Saturday [Postmark 1 December 1900]

48 Upper Berkeley Street

My dear Reg,

I got your letter this morning, and read it before I read my newspaper—before I knew that poor Oscar really was dead.[5] I am, as

[1] 1845–1927. Slade Professor of Fine Arts at Cambridge 1873–85, Director of Fitzwilliam Museum 1876–84, Keeper of Prints and Drawings in the British Museum 1884–1912, knighted 1911, friend and editor of Robert Louis Stevenson, biographer of Keats.
[2] On 18 November 1901 Reggie wrote to Max: "I am greatly relieved to know that you are not, like Barry Pain on a famous occasion, very angry," and the phrase had clearly been a joke for many years. It may have originated in 1894, when Pain (prolific humorous author, 1867–1928), reviewing the first volume of the *Yellow Book* in his weekly column "In the Smoking Room" in *Black and White* on 28 April, described Max's essay on cosmetics as "the very rankest and most nauseous thing in literature that I have ever read."
[3] William Leonard Courtney (1850–1928) was a Fellow of two Oxford colleges before turning to journalism and authorship. For many years on editorial staff of *Daily Telegraph*. Editor of the *Fortnightly Review* from 1894.
[4] Edith Maude Webster Lawson, daughter of Sir Edward Lawson, the first Lord Burnham, married (1888) Edward Henry Hulse (1859–1903), Conservative M.P. for Salisbury 1886–97. He succeeded to his father's baronetcy 1899.
[5] Oscar Wilde died in Paris on 30 November 1900, aged forty-six. Robbie Ross and Reggie were with him. Reggie's letter to Max of 8 December, describing the event, is printed in *The Letters of Oscar Wilde* (1962), p. 858.

you may imagine, very sorry indeed; and am thinking very much about Oscar, who was such an influence and an interest in my life. Will you please lay out a little money for me in flowers for his grave? I will repay you, having (for me) quite a large sum of money in the bank.[1] I hope to be able to write something nice about Oscar in my next article for the *Saturday*.[2] Of course I shall have

[1] Reggie answered on 8 December: "I got your wreath. It was only ten francs, as we none of us had any money, but for ten francs you get very pretty flowers, and Oscar's coffin was covered with really beautiful flowers. We got one wreath of laurels which we placed at the head and tied all the cards to it."

[2] In the *Saturday Review* of 8 December, after reviewing a play called *The Swashbuckler* by Louis N. Parker, Max devoted the second half of his space to this necessarily guarded tribute:

"The death of Mr Oscar Wilde extinguishes a hope that the broken series of his plays might be resumed. The hope was never, indeed, very strong. Despite the number of his books and plays, Mr Wilde was not, I think, what one calls a born writer. His writing seemed always to be rather an overflow of intellectual and temperamental energy than an inevitable, absorbing function. That he never concentrated himself on any one form of literature is a proof that the art of writing never really took hold of him. He experimented in all forms, his natural genius winning for him, lightly, in every one of them, the success which for most men is won only by a reverent concentration. His native energy having been sapped by a long term of imprisonment, the chance that he would write again was very small. His main motive for writing was lost. He would not, as would the born writer, be likely to find consolation in his art. *The Ballad of Reading Gaol*, though it showed that he had not lost his power of writing, was no presage of industry. Obviously, it was written by him with a definite external purpose, not from mere love and necessity of writing. Still, while he lived, there was always the off-chance that he might again essay that art-form which had been the latest to attract him. Somehow, the theatre seems to be fraught with a unique fascination. Modern dramaturgy is the most difficult of the arts, and its rewards (I do not mean its really commercial rewards) seem to be proportionate to its difficulties. To it, but for his downfall, even Mr Wilde might have devoted himself. But for his death, he might possibly have returned to it. And thus his death is, in a lesser degree than his downfall, a great loss to the drama of our day. His work was distinct from that of most other playwrights in that he was a man who had achieved success outside the theatre. He was not a mere maker of plays. Taking up dramaturgy when he was no longer a young man, taking it up as a kind of afterthought, he brought to it a knowledge of the world which the life-long playwright seldom possesses. But this was only one point in his advantage. He came as a thinker, a weaver of ideas, and as a wit, and as the master of a literary

to ask Hodge, first, whether he has any objection.[1] I think he is the kind of man who will not place any obstacles. In this morning's *Chronicle* there is a rather nice obituary and editorial note.

I suppose really it was better that Oscar should die. If he had

---

style. It was, I think, in respect of literary style that his plays were most remarkable. In his books this style was perhaps rather too facile, too rhetorical in its grace. Walter Pater, in one of his few book-reviews, said that in Mr Wilde's work there was always 'the quality of a good talker.' This seems to me a very acute criticism. Mr Wilde's writing suffered by too close a likeness to the flow of speech. But it was this very likeness that gave him in dramatic dialogue as great an advantage over more careful and finer literary stylists as he had over ordinary playwrights with no pretence to style. The dialogue in his plays struck the right mean between literary style and ordinary talk. It was at once beautiful and natural, as dialogue should always be. With this and other advantages, he brought to dramaturgy as keen a sense for the theatre as was possessed by any of his rivals, except Mr Pinero. Theatrical construction, sense of theatrical effects, were his by instinct. I notice that one of the newspapers says that his plays were 'devoid of consideration as drama,' and suggests that he had little or no talent for construction. Such criticism as this merely shows that what Ben Jonson called 'the dull ass's hoof' must have its backward fling. In point of fact, Mr Wilde's instinct for construction was so strong as to be a disadvantage. The very ease of his manipulation tempted him to trickiness, tempted him to accept current conventions which, if he had had to puzzle things out laboriously and haltingly, he would surely have discarded, finding for himself a simpler and more honest technique. His three serious comedies were marred by staginess. In *An Ideal Husband* the staginess was most apparent, least so in *A Woman of No Importance*. In the latter play, Mr Wilde allowed the psychological idea to work itself out almost unmolested, and the play was, in my opinion, by far the most truly dramatic of his plays. It was along these lines that we, in the early nineties, hoped Mr Wilde would ultimately work. But, even if he had confined his genius to the glorification of conventional drama, we should have had much reason to be grateful to him. His conventional comedies were as superior to the conventional comedies of other men as was *The Importance of Being Earnest* to the every-day farces whose scheme was so frankly accepted in it. At the moment of Mr Wilde's downfall, it was natural that the public sentiment should be one of repulsion. But later, when he was released from prison, they remembered that he had at least suffered the full penalty. And now that he is dead, they will realise also, fully, what was for them involved in his downfall, how lamentable the loss to dramatic literature."

[1] Herbert Hodge (1862–1937) was editor of the *Saturday Review* 1898–1913.

lived to be an old man he would have become unhappy. Those whom the gods, etc. And the gods *did* love Oscar, with all his faults.

Please give my sympathy to Bobbie, and tell him how much less happily Oscar might have died.

In great haste.

Yours affectionately MAX

Will has just come in and sends his love to you both.

Tuesday [*11 December 1900. Postmark 12 December*]
Metropole Hotel, Brighton

My dearest Reg,

I have just been telephoned to and wired to that the *H.H.* is really a success.[1] Here am I, all alone, "remote, unfriended"[2] etc., in order to avoid the temptation of going before the curtain—a practice for which I have so often condemned those whom I may now call my fellow-dramatists. If I had been in London, I should have been horribly frightened, and could not have kept away from the theatre, and I should have been dragged on, pallid and deprecating, by Mrs P.C. This lady, by the way, really is a rather wonderful creature. As stage-manageress she has been absolutely intelligent and sweet and charming all through. I do wish you had been here (or there, rather) to see the production. I wonder what the papers will say. Rendle, I am sure, will say it was "very thin," and will ask why we should go back to the drama of bib-and-tucker. But I fancy the *Daily Mail* will praise it as being "pure." Archer, too, may possibly call it a humanity-poem, and will urge me to greater solidity. Meanwhile, I find myself very happy, and slightly tipsy, having finished a bottle of "the boy"[3] on my own.

I don't care a damn if the papers slate the affair. There were five "curtains" after the show. The public, after all, is the *final court of appeal*. The public is on my side. Come the four corners of the *D.T.* etc. etc.[4]

[1] *The Happy Hypocrite* was first produced at the Royalty Theatre on 11 December 1900, with Winifred Fraser and Frank Mills in the principal parts. Max noted that it played for forty minutes only.
[2] "Remote, unfriended, melancholy, slow" is the first line of Goldsmith's poem "The Traveller."
[3] Slang term for champagne.   [4] Cf. *King John*, Act V, scene vii.

Thanks awfully for your very nice letters—and your good wishes. It is the one thing lacking: your absence. *Porro unum est necessarium.*[1] You must come and see the play with me before it ends. Perhaps it never *will* end. Personally I imagine it is a dreary classic. We shall see it together, when we have grey beards topped with toothless gums. The fuss I am making really is absurd. After all, the thing is a "curtain-raiser." I wonder whether all writers of "curtain-raisers" make such a pother in the ears of their bosom-friends?

Malcolm Watson has a "curtain-raiser" at the Garrick next Thursday. It is "founded on an incident in one of Wilkie Collins's novels."[2] But I daresay he will be writing to someone some such letter as this after the production. Life really is rather absurd.

Dear Reg, I wish you were here.

You must have had an awful time in Paris. Poor Oscar! I wish he were here, alive and superb—the Oscar before the fall. I remember so well that dinner at the Monico, when you met him for the first time.

Do write to me. I am now going to bed, in order to curtail the distance between myself and the morning-papers. Fuss again! There will only be little perfunctory notices.

Yours affectionately MAX

Monday [Postmark 24 December 1900]   *Savile Club*
107 Piccadilly

My dearest Reg,

The little boxful of pearls is really delightful—the most *chic* thing ever designed. A thousand thanks. It was very sweet of you to send it to me. I am going to wear it always at the end of my gold chain, and whenever men see my face reflected in the mirror inside it they will think of that gracious undergraduate who gave it to me.

[1] "But one thing is needful" (Luke, x, 42). In 1908 Max wrote a little essay on Switzerland which he titled "Porro Unum." It was reprinted in *Yet Again* (1909).
[2] Malcolm Watson (1853–1929) combined dramatic criticism with playwriting. This curtain-raiser, *Church and Stage*, in fact opened at the Criterion on 13 December, preceding *The Noble Lord* by Robert Marshall.

My present to you—a comparatively sordid little affair—shall reach you in due course. Do write to me. How long are you going to be in Paris? I wish I were there with you.

I am going to send you all the Romeikes about my play: you will not have seen most of them. The play really has succeeded, I think. Archer has turned traitor, however. I wonder if you saw his notice?[1] A terribly flat-footed, stodgy, stupid, thoughtful, able, idiotic two-columns-ful. I sent him a caricature of himself in a kilt, his eyes bandaged with a tartan handkerchief, holding in one large raw hand a large cart-wheel, in the other a butterfly-net with which he was making wild lunges at the air. Far above him was flying a very graceful and exquisitely-coloured butterfly. On the drawing I wrote "My dear W.A., Breaking a butterfly on a wheel is all very well, but—you must 'first catch your' butterfly."[2] He wrote back very nicely, but I think he was rather frightened. Walkley has come out very well, in *The Times* and *Literature*—charming notices.[3]

Today is Kilseen's birthday. She lunched with me at Prince's. She had written to you, but not to the address you sent me on your card—to the Cambon address. I wonder whether you will have received the letter.

I wish you would write a play with me—you supplying the plot, and the characters and all the *du théâtre* business, and I doing the dialogue, or at any rate *punctuating* it. Let this happen when you come back to London.

Wishing you a very happy Christmas, dear Reg.

Yours affectionately MAX

[1] In the *World* of 19 December.
[2] This caricature, which is dated 18 December 1900, was reproduced in *William Archer* by C. Archer (1931).
[3] In *The Times* of 17 December A. B. Walkley began his review: "In his first dramatic essay, *The Happy Hypocrite*, Mr Max Beerbohm has done what beginners rarely do; he has contributed an idea to the scanty theatrical stock, a diminutive idea perhaps, *vagula, blandula*, but still—an idea." And in *Literature* on 22 December he wrote: "Here is something new and strange and audacious, something which must give every playgoer with the slightest tincture of letters a distinct 'thrill.'"

My dearest Reg,

Again I write with many apologies for not having written before
—also for not having yet sent you the little (mark the word *little*)
present. It *is* ordered, but has not yet arrived; as soon as it does, it
shall be sent on to you. This all sounds as if it was something expensive, but it isn't, you will be sorry to hear. I will send with it the
Romeikes. At present *The Happy Hypocrite* has been withdrawn;
owing to the Queen's death all the theatres are shut.[1] I shall insist
that when I die *More Leaves from the Highlands* shall be withdrawn
from circulation temporarily.[2] I am sorry the poor Queen is dead. . . .

I met Hardwicke at dinner the other night, and am going to meet
the dear Wests (Lady Randolph).[3] This is to be at a dinner at Frank
Schuster's.[4] I think you know him, don't you? Usen't he to go to
Mrs Frank Lawson's? He is very musical, and a finished coquette in
his manner; also very wealthy.

Talking of wealth reminds me that John and Ida Nettleship were
clandestinely married the other day.[5] The parents, and the Rothensteins, accept the *fait accompli*; but everyone is prophesying unhappiness for Ida. John still dresses like a tramp, but has bought a
pair of patent-leather-boots.

Kilseen has just come, and sends her love, and is going to write.
Stuart Conover[6] has gone to Paris (happy creature!) and is going
to call on you. How is your play getting on? I loved your idea for
a burlesque of *The Happy Hypocrite*. Also I do hope you really will

[1] Queen Victoria died on 22 January 1901, and all the theatres shut for a
fortnight. The Royalty Theatre reopened on 5 February, with *The Happy
Hypocrite* still in the bill as curtain-raiser, but the run ended on 23
February.
[2] *More Leaves from the Journal of a Life in the Highlands, from 1862 to
1882*, by Queen Victoria (1884). Max's copy was copiously "improved"
and annotated in a close imitation of the Queen's hand.
[3] Winston's widowed mother, Lady Randolph Churchill (1854–1921),
had married George Cornwallis-West in 1900. They were divorced in
1913.
[4] Wealthy music-lover and social figure (1840–1928).
[5] The wedding of the painter Augustus John and Ida Nettleship took
place on 12 January 1901.
[6] Presumably Kilseen's brother.

seriously do a Regency scenario. I can't think of any other news. Do write to me and give me *your* news.

Ever yours affectionately MAX

[*Postmark 1*] *February 1901*   *Savile Club*

My dear Reg,

I have delayed my answer to your letter, because I have been hoping I might be able to say I could come and stay with you in Paris. But one thing and another prevents me. I should have loved to come—Paris is among cities what you are to me among friends. The possibility of coming was very delightful; but it turns out to be an impossibility. When are you leaving Paris? And coming to London? You are an enviable person, staying there, instead of writing about it in the *D.T.* as the *ville lumière*. Don't you yourself feel this? London today is in a state of frantic excitement—full of trippers.[1] The block in Piccadilly quite impenetrable: stands being erected all along the line of route, beaming shop-keepers refusing £10.10. (ten guineas) for a seat in the back-row. I have never seen such an air of universal jollity. It is a city of ghouls.

Street[2] is the only person who seems genuinely moved by the Queen's death. His leaders in the *St James's* are quite heart-breaking.

Your little present came from the jeweller's the other day—all done absolutely wrong, hideous and tawdry. I sent it back furiously, with a scathing note. I am sending you something else instead of it. I wish I could come and give it to you. Do write to me again.

Ever affectionately MAX

[1] For Queen Victoria's funeral procession, which took place on 2 February.

[2] George Slythe Street (1867–1936), journalist and author of *The Autobiography of a Boy* (1894) and other books. He had just overlapped with Max at Charterhouse, but they never met there. Rothenstein recounts how "they met one night at Solferino's. Street, like Max, was something of a dandy. Each aspired to be more coldly aloof than the other; but finally warmth crept into the party, and there and then a close friendship began." (*Men and Memories*, vol. I, p. 287.)

My dear Reg,

I do wish I could have come; but I was too frightfully busy. Are you having a nice time? The "prooves" must be exciting.[1] And remember, the more you "sweat" the more likely is the book to be a public success. Every bead of perspiration means a copy sold. However, I expect the book is delightful in itself.

I go to Dieppe as soon as I can—probably *about* the 26th of this month. So do come as soon as you possibly can. Come straight from Foremark Hall.[2] At any rate, a day or two will be enough for you in London. I am writing to Lefèvre[3] to keep my room. Do write too, in case the place is going to be full. Sickert will be in Dieppe, I believe, at the end of the month: so we ought to have good fun. No, not Lane for *Zuleika*, I think; but the thing is not yet settled. The American people wrote me a long letter, asking me to take royalties. I climbed down to £75, my minimum, and await their answer. I have not yet seen the Rothenstein baby.[4] It is said to be very like the mother, but of course it may at any moment become very like Will. It is not to be reared in the tenets of any Church: Will has conscientious scruples. Bobbie, as you may imagine, is very much upset by this, and spends his whole time urging Will to have the child circumcised—"duly" as Pater would say. Will seems very pleased and interested in the child. . . .

Clyde Fitch is here, very very successful—eleven companies performing his plays in America. Also, partly owing to me, Herbert is going to produce a new play that he has written round Count D'Orsay—really a delightful play.[5] I wish you were here to hear it. You would like it—it is very *du théâtre*—though of a smaller

---

[1] The proofs of Reggie's first novel, *Cynthia's Damages* (1901), a story of the stage, which was dedicated "to Frank and Mary [Lawson]."
[2] A house near Burton-on-Trent in Staffordshire, which Frank Lawson had rented.
[3] A *pension* kept by the Lefèvre family at 1 Rue de l'Hôtel de Ville, Dieppe, and much patronised by Max, Reggie and their friends. For an undated and unpublished note on it by Max, see Appendix D, p. 302.
[4] The Rothensteins' first child, John, was born on 11 July 1901.
[5] *The Last of the Dandies*, first produced by Tree at His Majesty's on 24 October 1901.

theatre, H.M.'s perhaps. A splendid part for Herbert—D'Orsay, of course. . . .

Please give my love to Mrs Lawson, also to Frank, if he is on the spot. And write to Lefèvre. Also to me again.

Yours affectionately MAX

Monday [*22 July 1901. Postmark 23 July*]

48 Upper Berkeley Street

My dear Reg,

I am such a bad correspondent that it is quite refreshing to be able to write and reproach you for not answering my letter. How about Dieppe? Do come as soon as you can. I am going D.V. on Saturday morning. I look forward to it very much. Sickert will be there, I hope. Oswald[1] is going, I believe, and, I suppose also, the girl to whom he used to curtsey on the Terrace. The Martineaus also.[2]

I have been having a quiet Season, though with a slight flare-up at the end. I lunched last week *chez* Lady Elcho[3]—sat between her and Arthur Balfour,[4] George Wyndham on her other side. Altogether I felt quite the gentleman. It is funny that with really distinguished people I do not feel at all shy, though I feel shy with everyone else. My one difficulty is to keep myself in check. As it was, I distinctly patronised Balfour, drawing him out about the

[1] Oswald Valentine Sickert (1871–1923) was a younger brother of the painter. He published one novel, but later became an overseas traveller for the *Encyclopaedia Britannica* and wrote little more.
[2] Cyril (son of the painter Robert Martineau) and his wife Kitty (daughter of H. Savile Clarke, playwright), whom Max noted as "the prettiest girl I ever saw."
[3] Mary Constance, daughter of the Hon. Percy Wyndham and granddaughter of the first Lord Leconfield, married (1883) Hugo Richard Wemyss Charteris, Lord Elcho. In 1914 he succeeded his father as eleventh Earl of Wemyss. Lady Elcho was a close friend of Arthur Balfour.
[4] Arthur James Balfour (1848–1930), Conservative Prime Minister, 1902–5.

ventilating-arrangements in the House, and so forth. On Friday I lunch with Lady Féo Sturt[1] to meet Melba.[2] I have never called since the first meal. Evidently I am "in request."

Are you still correcting proofs? But I suppose they are finished by this time. Do write a play—you and Clyde Fitch really are the only two men I have ever seen of whom I could postulate that they were born to write for the theatre. But I am tired of repeating this to you always.   Yours affectionately MAX

Tuesday [30 July 1901. Postmark 31 July]   *Lefèvre [Dieppe]*

My dear Reg,

I have told the Lefèvres that you will be here on the seventh of August—or thereabouts. They are much pleased, and it will be quite all right about the room—a room *in* the hotel. Let me know exactly when you will arrive, and I will tell them. And do come as soon as you can. Why be in London when here it is so delightful? The two Evelyn Beerbohms[3] are in Dieppe—Julius has been. Mrs Nathan[4] has not been sighted. The Stormy Petrel[4] has. The Hannays[5] are here—a trifle *gênés*. The Martineaus are coming later on, I believe. Tommy Chaine,[6] who was at Lady Féo's the other day,

[1] Lady Feodorowna Yorke (d. 1934), daughter of the fifth Earl of Hardwicke, married (1883) the Hon Humphrey Napier Sturt (1859–1919), who succeeded his father as second Lord Alington 1904.
[2] Stage name (from her birthplace Melbourne) of the great Australian prima donna Nellie Mitchell (1859–1931). D.B.E. 1927.
[3] The wife and son of Max's half-brother Julius Beerbohm (1854–1906).
[4] Unidentified.
[5] Arnold Hannay (1854–1927) was a London solicitor, and his wife Alice was a painter. Each summer they spent some months in their Villa Séjour on the hill by the Castle overlooking Dieppe. Many of their friends were writers and artists, including Whistler and Sickert.
[6] Son of Lt.-Col. William Chaine and Maria Henrietta Sophia (née Phipps), both of whom held court appointments at Kensington Palace. In *Conversation with Max* (1960) S. N. Behrman gives Max's account of Tommy Chaine's life.

said he was coming for three days. (Soveral,[1] by the way, was also at the lunch—really a fascinating person.)

Is Alec[2] coming? He seemed to think he would.

Give my love to Bobbie. Get him to come too, if only for a few days.   Yours affectionately   MAX

Thursday [*Postmark 5 September 1901*]   *Dieppe*

My dearest Reg,

Many thanks for your nice and amusing letter. I am glad you have been having a nice time in Paris.

I am still here, as you see, and I shall return probably on Monday. . . .

Miss Beardsley[3] has also arrived, fresh from a provincial tour. She trails about, all day, in evening dress—low neck, no sleeves, and a train as long as the Rue de l'Hôtel de Ville, which she carries swathed over her arm. She creates a great sensation. This afternoon I was walking with her on the terrace of the Casino; Mrs Horace Nevill[4] passed, and I took off my hat, and Mrs Horace Nevill cut me dead! Sickert has had a chill, but is all right again. He had old Pissarro[5] to dinner last night—a great dear, very amusing and sweet and patriarchal. Makower[6] and all of us very respectful to

[1] Marquis Luis de Soveral, G.C.M.G., G.C.V.O. (1862–1922), Portuguese Ambassador in London 1897–1910, friend of King Edward VII and nicknamed the Blue Monkey, was a favourite subject of Max's caricatures.
[2] Ross.
[3] Aubrey Beardsley's sister Mabel (1871–1916). She was at this time on the stage and had toured in the United States with Arthur Bourchier. In 1903 she married the actor George Bealby Wright. She died after a long illness, during which she produced a good deal of journalism. W. B. Yeats's sequence of poems "Upon a Dying Lady" in *The Wild Swans at Coole* (1919) was addressed to her.
[4] Horace John Nevill (1855–1924), second son of Reginald Henry and Lady Dorothy Nevill, married (1880) Annie Harriet Martha Rowe (d. 1931).
[5] Camille Pissarro, French Impressionist painter (1831–1903).
[6] Stanley Victor Makower (1872–1911), English writer and music critic. He was a member of the *Yellow Book* group, contributing stories and one of the earliest studies of Yvette Guilbert.

him. When the dessert was on the table, and I had reached the stage of saying "*Je voudrais bien être peintre pour vous adresser comme cher maître,*" enter the awful young Evelyn, with a straw hat on the back of his head, saying "Less talking there, please!" He proceeded to sit down with us (much to Sickert's disgust), did not remove his hat, struck me a blow on the shoulder, and was generally a very false note. I dread going back to London and the theatres.

Do write me a letter to Upper Berkeley Street—to break my fall. Don't overdo the cure.[1] Tell the brothers of the Grande Chartreuse that your greatest friend—if I may so call myself?—owes his education to them. Yours affectionately MAX

The *Chronicle* had some extraordinarily inept but well-meant quotations about me on my birthday. I have just had them from Rom-eike.[2]

[1] At Uriage, near Grenoble.
[2] On 24 August 1901 the *Daily Chronicle* published this comment and list of quotations:
"To-day, when it is over, still leaves Mr Max Beerbohm in his twenties—though in the last of them. Years, however, it is consoling to think, will never deprive him of youth. Yet he has once been taken seriously. That was when his book *More* was bought by a Mother Abbess, who gave it to a novice to read aloud in the refectory, believing it to be an edifying biography of Blessed Sir Thomas More, the Chancellor. No caricaturist has been oftener caricatured by himself and others than has Mr Max Beerbohm. Yet once also he has been quite seriously presented to us. That was by Mr W. Rothenstein in his *Oxford Characters*. But the writer of the accompanying text made haste to get back to chaff. For "Max" was set down as "a dandy" seeing that he wears "boot-buttons in his cuffs.""
This is my birthday (Shakespeare).
MAX BEERBOHM, Aug 24, 1872.
I can do with my pencil what I know,
What I see (Browning).
All those *atomi* ridiculous (Ben Jonson).
Harlequin, splendid in youth, leaps down the throat of bewildered giants (Thackeray).
  Made it his care
To draw men—not as they are (Goldsmith).
Undeniably bright, witty and daring (Thackeray).
As much beloved in the side-box as on the stage (Thackeray).
Conscious of a well-fitting coat, relieved by a dandiacal hint of shirt-frill (Quiller-Couch).
My soul, Max! (Lytton).

Wednesday [*4 December 1901. Postmark 5 December*]
48 *Upper Berkeley Street*

My dear Reg,

I don't know *what* you can think of me for not having written sooner. My not writing is of course the result of my usual procrastination. I have put it off from day to day. Now at last I am writing to say how very much delighted I was with *Cynthia's Damages*—and with its success. From all the gloomy accounts of it you had given me, I expected that perhaps I should not like it. Therefore my delight in it was the more intense. The book really is most awfully funny. I think I like the trial-scene most of all. "And we shall shock them." That passage almost killed me. I am so glad you have been able all through the book to work *yourself* in—your own peculiar brand. "Go on, brave boy." Your trembling pen is not absolutely pure, perhaps. But that does not matter. In the *Saturday* this week I have twice referred to the book. I am sending you the article.[1]

By the way, what a leg-up you have given Sidney Ellison.[2] You ought to send him a copy.

London is too awful—fogs—depression—inanimation. Everybody is very poor, owing to the war,[3] also very nervous about the small-pox. Carfax[4] opens with my exhibition next Saturday.[5] Harmsworth is reproducing six of the John Bull series in the *D.M.*[6] I wonder what Edward Lawson will think of them? I am afraid he won't insist on Le Sage[7] noticing them favourably. *The Happy*

[1] "A Most Hard-Working Profession" (*Saturday Review*, 30 November 1901. Reprinted in *Around Theatres*, 1924).
[2] Ballet-master for George Edwardes at the Gaiety Theatre. Married the actress Kate Cutler.
[3] The Boer War, which had now lasted for more than two years.
[4] A picture gallery in Ryder Street, St James's, which had been started by John Fothergill and Arthur Clifton in 1898. Two years later Robert Ross became its leading spirit.
[5] The catalogue of Max's first one-man exhibition, at the gallery of Carfax & Co, is dated November 1901. Among the 110 drawings were the series of fifteen later published as *The Second Childhood of John Bull*.
[6] In the event only three of the drawings appeared in the *Daily Mail*, on 7 December 1901.
[7] John Merry Le Sage (1837–1926) was managing editor of the *Daily Telegraph* for many years. Knighted 1918.

Hypocrite is in rehearsal for America—Waring as Hell.[1] I dined with Lady Maud Warrender[2] the other night, and am dining with Lady Féo Sturt on Monday. I pretend to myself that such people are useful to me in my career. As a matter of fact they don't seem to be; and my pleasure in them is mere disinterested flunkeyism, I am afraid.

What a beautiful life yours is! Dieppe, Uriage, Geneva, Nice, Paris. For me Dieppe, London, London, London, with recurring dot. When do you come back? Do come soon. Write me another amusing letter, meanwhile.   Yours affectionately MAX

Mama sends her love. Also Kilseen, who is here. And Con and Aggie.

Thursday [*16 April 1903. Postmark 17 April*]
                                        48 Upper Berkeley Street

My dear Reg,

I am just half-way up *The Steeple*,[3] and I cannot wait till I reach the apex to congratulate you. I have been *shaking* with laughter and delight all the way—calling silence among my people whilst I read out this or that particularly delicious passage, and wishing that Matthew Arnold were one of my people, because he, of all men that ever lived, would have most delighted in the book.

The gentle affectionate banter of it, with flashes of irresponsible caricature, is so like his own manner—absolutely delightful! And in my opinion distinctly your masterpiece, so far as I have read. I hope it doesn't fall off in the second part. Certainly the middle is as

---

[1] *The Happy Hypocrite* (its leading character is Lord George Hell) was announced as part of the repertory with which Mrs Patrick Campbell opened a season at the Republic Theatre, New York, on 13 January 1902 (with Herbert Waring in the company), but I can find no record of its production there.
[2] Lady Maud Ashley-Cooper, younger daughter of the eighth Earl of Shaftesbury, married (1894) George John Scott Warrender (1860–1917). He succeeded his father as seventh Baronet 1901, and ended a distinguished naval career as Vice-Admiral and Commander-in-Chief at Devonport 1916.
[3] Reggie's third novel (1903). His second, *The Comedy of Progress*, had appeared in 1902.

good as the beginning. Tell Greening[1] to send *Street* a copy—83 Marine Parade, Brighton. He would love the book. Also, hadn't you better send Parker[2] a copy? The *Spectator* is important. I will write again.　　　　　　　　　　　　　　Your affectionate　MAX

Friday [24 April 1903. Postmark 25 April]
　　　　　　　　　　　　　　　　　　　　48 Upper Berkeley Street

My dear Reg,

I hear you are in Paris. Do please forgive me for not having written before. I did write to you to tell you how immensely I appreciated *The Steeple*. I ought to have written afterwards to tell you how much all my people and friends admired it. Far and away the best of your books, so far: "that seems to be the verdict," as Clement Shorter[3] would say. I do look forward to seeing you, dear Reg, again. I have had a harassing and unhappy time of it, on the whole,[4] and it has been no great comfort to imagine you at large in sunshine and holiday-mood.

　　　　Love from my people and from your affectionate　MAX

4 June 1903　　　　　　　　　　　　　　　　　　　　*Savile Club*

My dearest Reg,

What a ghastly thing it is.[5] I am so very truly grieved. I have written to Mrs Lawson; also to Frank, whose address I cannot remember, and it is too new to be in the Red Book; so will you address this letter to him?

I hope your next birthday will be a very much happier one, and that you will have a very great number of very happy birthdays after it, dear Reg.　　　　　　　　　Your affectionate　MAX

[1] Reggie's publisher.
[2] Eric Parker.
[3] Clement King Shorter (1857–1926), author and journalist. Founded the *Sketch* (1893), the *Sphere* (1900) and the *Tatler* (1903). Edited the *Sphere* 1900–26.
[4] Breaking off his six-year engagement to Kilseen Conover.
[5] On 2 June 1903 (Reggie's birthday) Frank Lawson's eldest son Lionel died in a fire at Eton, where he was at school.

Wednesday [*8 July 1903. Postmark 9 July*]

48 *Upper Berkeley Street*

My dearest Reg,

I do so hope your neuralgia is better: in any case, the change is sure to take it away. I wonder if you will be angry at my bothering you about the matter to which the enclosed letter refers. You will be on the spot and speaking French with fluent grace; I shall be here, with an unintelligible pen.

The question is this: shall Constance[1] and Mrs Roscoe[2] and Mrs Roscoe's child (with nurse) occupy the rooms to which Titine[3] refers?

What they want is three rooms to sleep in, and one to sit in. So far, so good; and the price seems very reasonable: it "works out" at about ten shillings per day for the whole suite. But then, (and that only you can decide, being on the spot) are the rooms decently light and clean?—habitable? They need not be more than that. Also, could the whole party have its meals *chez* Lefèvre, at a reasonable tariff? All this I am asking on my own responsibility. Titine's letter has only just arrived, and I haven't yet seen Constance; I am just going to write and tell her the situation. And would you, as soon as you can, after your arrival, write to me and tell me what you think had better be done: whether the rooms are nice, and how much the food would come to. I am so sorry to throw this burden on you; only I know you would like Constance to have a nice time and not a too expensive time, and that she is one of the things you are looking forward to in August. And, as I say, I can't judge, at this distance, what is best.

By the way, Constance and party will arrive on the *27th*, not on the *17th* as they had hoped and as I had told Titine.

And now *bon voyage*, dear Reg and *bon* (*?bonne*) *santé*.

Your affectionate MAX

[1] Constance Collier, English actress (1878–1955), had been engaged by Tree in 1902 to play Pallas Athene in Stephen Phillips's *Ulysses*, and acted with him for six years.
[2] Flora, wife of Henry Lincoln Roscoe, partner in Messrs Field, Roscoe & Co, solicitors.
[3] Either Madame Lefèvre of the Dieppe *pension* or her daughter.

Saturday [Postmark 11 July 1903]   *48 Upper Berkeley Street*

My dearest Reg,

You will have had my wire. I went to Constance this morning to tell about the raised price; but meanwhile Mrs Roscoe had decided that with the nurse and child she had better be in a regular hotel. So the whole party are going to the Familles. I believe they have already written to engage rooms there. I am so very sorry you have had all this bother for nothing. But, after all, in Dieppe and in this weather, nothing can be a serious bother. I do trust the weather isn't wearing itself out. I watch it so jealously, like an heir to a patrimony that is being squandered. To you, who can flutter in sunlight all the year round in lovely places, my anxiety for August must seem strangely pathetic.   Yours affectionately MAX

Monday [13 July 1903. Postmark 14 July]

48 Upper Berkeley Street

My dearest Reg,

Evidently I must reconsider Cosmo Gordon Lennox (Cosmo Stuart).[1] I wish to Heaven I could get away and reconsider him on the spot. But I shall have to be here till about the 25th, at any rate.

Give my love to Walter,[2] when you see him again. And do write again to me and let me know what is going on.

Your affectionate MAX

Constance *et Cie* have, I think, secured their rooms at the Hôtel des Familles. If you see that little secretary of the Casino (I forget his name) I wish you would tell him to post me a card of admission to await me at Lefèvre's. Last year I applied by letter from here, and was notified that a card would be given me when I came to Dieppe.

[1] Cosmo Charles Gordon-Lennox (1869–1921), wealthy grandson of the fifth Duke of Richmond. Actor (as Charles Stuart), playwright and successful adaptor of French plays. His greatest success was *The Marriage of Kitty* in 1902. He married the actress Marie Tempest (1866–1942) in 1898. Reggie had written to Max from Dieppe on Sunday [12 July 1903]:

"Cosmo is very charming. He delivered a great eulogy of you yesterday, saying how delightful you were, how simple and kind-hearted, and how perfect a gentleman. I did not let on that you had hard thoughts of him."

[2] Sickert.

MAX AND CONSTANCE COLLIER AT DIEPPE,
1903

Helen McCaul
Elizabeth Dickson

H. Victoria Street,
Westminster, S.W.

Max from Reg
Oct. 1902.

But the first few days after my arrival the secretary was never in his office, and I had to pay for several *abonnements* for the day. Remind him of me (if you see him, and if it is no trouble). Remind him that I am *romancier, dramatiste, journaliste, causeur, conférencier, caricaturiste, beau garçon, clubman, cher ami de Boulestin,*[1] etc.

Thursday [Postmark 23 July 1903]   *48 Upper Berkeley Street*

My dearest Reg,

Thank you, thank you, for your wholly delightful letter. This one is a frantic scrawl, written while I am writing about *Prince Pierrot* for the *Saturday.*[2]

Enclosed is the note to Bloch.[3] I start on Saturday morning. I have a grey Homburg hat with a black band, but no new suits. Delighted to dine with Mrs F. on Saturday if she wants me. I am, of course, praising *P.P.* which is indeed most delicious; only running down the performers.   Your affectionate   M A X

Tuesday [Postmark 1 September 1903]   *[Café des] Tribunaux*
                                                        [Dieppe]

My dearest Reg,

Titine showed me your postcard, and I suppose you will be staying in Paris for a little while. Has Herbert Horne[4] arrived? I

---

[1] Xavier Marcel Boulestin (d. 1943) was music-critic, novelist, actor, caricaturist, and designer before he found fame in England as restaurateur and cookery expert. In 1905 he published a French translation of *The Happy Hypocrite* as *L'Hypocrite Sanctifié.*
[2] *Prince Pierrot,* a mime play composed by Reggie, with music by Dalhousie Young, was produced in the West Theatre of the Albert Hall on 21 July 1903, with an amateur cast, headed by Mrs Arthur Clifton. Max praised the play and damned the performers in the *Saturday Review* of 25 July.
[3] Isidore Bloch, the secretary of the Dieppe Casino (see previous letter).
[4] Architect, writer and connoisseur (1865–1916). Before 1900 he went to live in Florence, where he wrote a biography of Botticelli (1908) and set up the Museo Horne in the Via dei Benci. Will Rothenstein records Reggie's saying: "Dear Herbert Horne! poring over Botticelli's washing bills—and always a shirt missing!"

look to him to keep you out of mischief. I am on the verge of departure. It is just 11 o'clock, and I go by the day-boat. My things are packed, but I dread the bill and the tips and the *à l'année prochaine* and the registering of luggage and all the other horrors. But they are as nothing to the horror of staying another moment in Dieppe, cursing the sunshine that would have made my August so lovely, mooning around talking to myself because there is no one else to talk to (though the place is still as full as it was in race-week). It is odd, but the departure of Constance and you and the others has quite pricked the bubble of my self-importance. I really did feel as if the place belonged to me, so long as my "set" was here: *now* I am a pariah—uniform with the man who was turned out of the diplomatic service. Lindemann[1] engaged me in conversation just now, but only in a side-street: I wished we were on the terrace. I shall see Constance tomorrow afternoon, and will give her your love. Do write to me at Upper Berkeley Street. How soon do you return? I hope sooner than I expect.   Your affectionate MAX

Monday [*9 November 1903. Postmark 10 November*]
48 Upper Berkeley Street

My dearest Reg,

All last week I had been expecting you to appear and have some meal. Only today, from Alec,[2] at the Savile, did I hear that you had been seedy. I am so very sorry. But why didn't you let me know? Whom do you expect to come and see you if not your Old Friend? He proposes to come tomorrow afternoon—about four o'clock— and is   Your affectionate MAX

Wednesday [*Postmark 30 December 1903*] *48 Upper Berkeley Street*

My dearest Reg,

By the way: please don't breathe to Bobbie or anyone about my engagement to Constance. I want it to be a *dead secret*. The

[1] A Franco-Bavarian Count who was much enamoured of Lady Cardigan, the widow of the leader of the Charge of the Light Brigade. According to her lively *Recollections* (1909) the two men looked extraordinarily alike.
[2] Ross.

position of fiancée to Max Beerbohm is rather a ridiculous position, after poor Miss Conover's experience, and I don't want Constance to be placed in it publicly. So we mean to be married quite suddenly (so far as the public is concerned). If anyone asks about Miss Conover and me, then you can say that we have agreed to dissolve our engagement, and if anyone asks whether Miss Collier has any-thing to do with it, of course say "no." But don't *volunteer* the information.

I am just home from the Court Theatre,[1] frozen through.

Your affectionate MAX

Sunday [Postmark 3 January 1904]*   *Granville Hotel, Ramsgate*

My dearest Reg,

I stay here over tomorrow. I am so very sorry not to have let you know earlier. I tried to wire this morning: but the telegraph office was shut: it had closed at 10.0. I hope you won't be angry and inconvenienced. This letter will reach you by the first post. I am staying for my body's and nerves' sake; not because the place is charming. It is very un-charming indeed; and I begin to regret that I was not included this year in the Chatsworth party. The hotel is just like the Metropole at Brighton, only on a small scale, and with only a handful of inmates. There is nothing to do except to sit in the hall on a saddle-back chair under an artificial palm-tree, ex-changing haughty and disgusted glances with the occupants of other saddle-back chairs.

This morning I walked over to Broadstairs, along the cliff, in my new coat. There were few people about to see me. But a seal rose from the waves and called me "brother." I unfastened the coat, to shew the lining; and the creature swam away wondering. At the same moment, there came scampering through the stubble of the field three musquashes. They made odious propositions to me, and I had some difficulty in getting rid of them. I thought of Cotsford

[1] Where *Snowdrop and the Seven Little Men*, a fairy play for children by Philip Carr, had been produced on 26 December. In the *Saturday Review* of 2 January 1904 Max described it as "prettily and ingeniously wrought from the original Grimm."

Dick[1] on the Embankment and of *his* fur-coat. Broadstairs turned out better; for the townspeople were having a sort of Church Parade, and were very respectful. And at the Albion Hotel, where I lunched, I was (until I ordered a pint of the cheapest wine on the list) mistaken by some of the waiters for the Grand Duke Alexis, and by others for the Grand Duke Vladimir. I shall be home on Wednesday; so do come to lunch or dinner any day after that.

Your affectionate   MAX

1 March 1904*   *48 Upper Berkeley Street*

My dearest Reg,

Thank you, thank you, for your wholly delightful letters. I wish I had written to you before; only there has been no news, and I was so afraid of writing dully in reply to your own exuberance of news and humour. So please forgive me; and I vow solemnly I will write once a week, at any rate, during the rest of your absence. And how long is your absence going to last, happy little creature? I suppose you are having lots of sunshine still, and not doing a stroke of work. How lovely it all must be! Here the weather has been very bitter-cold—snow—rain—wind—all the usual things. But I have my fur-coat, which is a real friend to me, though already there are signs that it will turn out badly: one of the "frogs" is fraying, and the musquash in the right sleeve has come unsewn. Constance is already acting on the tour, but only at Deptford. She is still at Blenheim Mansions. She starts for Edinburgh next Sunday. It will be very lonely and awful for me when she goes away. I don't suppose she will miss *me* much, having so much excitement and constant change. We shall (*unberufen*) be married as soon as the tour is over. Herbert has given up his part in *The Darling of the Gods*[2] and is going to be on tour most of the time. . . .

I am still waiting eagerly for *Castles in Kensington*.[3] Why does

[1] Charles George Cotsford Dick (1846–1911), author of *The Model and other Poems* (1886), *The Baroness*, a comic opera (1892), *The Ways of the World*, *vers de Société* (1896) and *Society Snapshots* (1901).
[2] A melodrama set in old Japan by David Belasco and J. Luther Long, which Tree had produced at His Majesty's on 28 December 1903.
[3] Reggie's fourth novel (1904).

Greening delay it? Soon we may be dragged into this beastly war,[1] and then there will be no chance of a sale for any book for a long time to come. And that is serious for me as well as for you. For Heinemann is publishing my *Poets* (in May probably, when there will be also an exhibition of them *chez* Carfax) as a popular five-shilling volume.[2] The things will be reproduced in colour. . . .

Marie Lennox is returning already from America—"very angry," I expect. I suppose the panic about fires in theatres out there is the reason why she has done badly, and curtailed the tour. It was to have lasted six months, wasn't it? By the way, I have turned my *mot* about Cosmo into an epitaph for him.

> Here lies Cosmo, and by him
> Not Alma, but Maria:
> He lived twelve years with the frying-pan,
> And finally married the fire.[3]

Nobody seems to like *Captain Dieppe*,[4] and Hal Rhodes has got very little glory out of it. The *Referee* talked of the play "by Mr Anthony Hope and another." (I shall always think of Hal Rhodes as "another"; and so must you.) And Archer attributed the whole failure to the influence of the collaborator. . . .

I had an article in the *Mail* the other day—one I wrote some time ago, about the young man flirting with the barmaid in the Buffet at Newhaven, and with a realistic description of the kind of food one gets there.[5] The caterers are "very angry"—one never can get away from that phrase—and have sent a long lawyer's letter to the *Mail*, demanding a retraction. The *Mail* tells me it doesn't mean to retract. I suppose the matter will drop; but perhaps it

[1] The Russo-Japanese War had broken out on 8 February.
[2] *The Poets' Corner*, Max's second book of drawings, was published by Heinemann on 2 May 1904 at 5s. The drawings were shown at the Carfax Gallery during the same month. D. S. MacColl reviewed book and exhibition together in the *Saturday Review* of 28 May.
[3] Before marrying the actress Marie Tempest (who was known to her friends as Maria) Cosmo Gordon-Lennox had lived for some time with the actress and singer Alma Stanley (1853–1931).
[4] A play by Anthony Hope and Harrison Rhodes, produced at the Duke of York's Theatre on 15 February 1904.
[5] Published as "A Memory" in the *Daily Mail* of 20 February 1904. Revised as "A Home-Coming" in *Yet Again* (1909).

won't. Rather exciting. And—and—but that is really *all* the news I can think of. So good-bye for the present, dear Reg; and do write to   Your affectionate   MAX

Wednesday [*Postmark 16 March 1904*]   *48 Upper Berkeley Street*

My dearest Reg,

Our letters must have almost, or quite, crossed. I had found out your new address from Bobbie. I cannot remember writing the "22," but I hope the letter reached you all right. No news since I wrote it. I am very busy with the final preparations for the *Poets*.

Constance is in Glasgow. Her letters are few and sparse, and she seems depressed by the tour. I miss her horribly, as you can imagine. It seems very odd to be in London, and she not here. . . .

Do write again.   Your affectionate   MAX

12 April 1904   *48 Upper Berkeley Street*

My dear Regie,

Very many congratulations on the book.[1] It is indeed delightful, and you can't think how I laughed, and how we have all been laughing. I see what you meant about it being careless: it is rather episodic in form, it rather jumps; but that after all does not so much matter—I mean *form* does not so much matter as the substance of humour and observation and all that, of which you pour out such a lot. Some people may not like the book: we do. But I don't suppose any people would be unable to like it. *My* people, as I have said, like it immensely. And the notices that I have seen all seem to crack up the fun of it. I hope it is selling well. But I never expect your books to sell really well so long as Greening publishes them. Have you been working in Florence? . . .

And now for a rather sad and beastly piece of news: Constance and I are not going to be married after all. I had thought before she went on tour that she seemed rather different, but I put it down to her rehearsals and hard work. Then when she went away, her letters were different from what they used to be—colder and fewer. And

1 *Castles in Kensington.*

158

last Saturday I had a letter from her saying she had been so wretched and had not known how to tell me that she felt it would never do, after all, for us to marry—neither of us being the sort of people for the serious responsibilities of life. It was a very sweet letter indeed, and *of course* I don't blame her the very least. Indeed, long ago I had always been telling her that it would be madness from the common-sense point of view for her to marry me. I thought I was right then; and I think she is right now. But of course it is sad—being without her, breaking off so many ties of love. She says she cares for me as much as ever; and so do I for her; but that of course only makes it worse. It *is* a pity I was not born either rich or the sort of solid man who could be trusted and who could trust himself to make his way solidly in the world.

Of course I am a success in a way, and may continue to be so for some time; but that is in virtue of certain qualities in my defects: it is in virtue of a sort of nimble fantastic irresponsibility; for solid worldly success this is no good at all. And I now, for the first time clearly, see myself as on the whole a failure. I have never coveted the *solid* quality till now, when I find that without it I cannot get, and don't deserve, Constance.

Don't mention a *word* of this news to a soul. And I know you and your sense of proportion and character and things too well to imagine that you will feel the slightest inclination to blame Constance. I never shall feel anything but gladness for all the happiness I have had since I met her that year in Dieppe. Of course, too, she and I will go on being perfectly good friends.

I have had a slight attack of influenza, and am going to Ramsgate for a few days. Do write to me here.

Your affectionate MAX

Wednesday [*13 April 1904*] *48 Upper Berkeley Street*

My dearest Reg,

Our letters crossed, at the angle described in this diagram.[1] Yours arrived at dinner-time, after I had caught the six o'clock post (and I find my letter went with a penny stamp: many apologies

[1] Two crossing lines labelled Max and Reggie.

for the mistake). I enter into this explanation, and *swear solemnly* that it is true, in case you should suspect that I had written, with an air of spontaneity, only on receipt of your letter. That would be rather like me, I know; but I repeat my oath, and I am not unscrupulous about such things, as I used to be.[1]

I have heard again from Constance—another very sweet letter. I hated yesterday to take up, in writing to you, a sort of apologetic attitude for her. She really needs no apology at all from me to anyone. Circumstances and I myself are such an ample explanation, and I am sure you agree with me about that.

Dear Reg, I was so sorry not to have written to you about the book before—procrastination, not thoughtlessness, and not the absence of daily intention and desire. You will have received *The Napoleon*[2] before my first letter. I think it awfully good. I wonder if you will relent about the author. You told me he lacked "heart." I think there is plenty of that organ mixed up in the book. As to

[1] On 10 April Reggie had written from Florence: "It would be affectation in me to say that I wasn't just a little hurt at no word from you about my rotten little story, which you must have received a month ago. I hope you didn't think the idea too badly treated for comment."

[2] *The Napoleon of Notting Hill* by G. K. Chesterton, which had been published by John Lane on 22 March. In his letter of 10 April Reggie had written:

"I have seen your name mentioned in connection with it, but as far as I can make out you are only taken as the central figure from a pictorial point of view; it is not an attempt at drawing your personality, and saying what you would do under certain circumstances. But I am looking forward to reading the book."

The illustrator, W. Graham Robertson, had drawn all his pictures of Auberon Quin, the King of England chosen by lot, in the likeness of Max, but the character itself is much more Chesterton than Beerbohm. Mrs Chesterton recorded in her diary:

"A delightful dinner party at the Lanes. . . . The talk was mostly about *Napoleon*. Max took me in to dinner and was really nice. He is a good fellow. His costume was extraordinary. Why should an evening waistcoat have four large white pearl buttons and why should he look that peculiar shape? He seems only pleased at the way he has been identified with King Auberon. 'All right, my dear chap,' he said to G, who was trying to apologize. 'Mr Lane and I settled it all at a lunch.' I think he was a little put out at finding no red carpet put down for his royal feet and we had quite a discussion as to whether he ought to precede me into the dining-room."

Paris, I am afraid I can't come. I should immensely like to; *but* I gather that your return will be just about the time of my exhibition, and I shall have to be here for the parturition of that. But there is this chance. Heinemann insists on publishing the book at the end of this month. The exhibition cannot come on till May 11. Bobbie wanted the two things to synchronise. He wrote to me yesterday saying that previous *publication* would make the *exhibition* fall flat. And it was today that Heinemann refused to budge. And I have just written to Bobbie offering to let the exhibition slide altogether. I don't suppose he will accept the offer; but he may; in which case I would be in Paris to meet you.

I might come by the Dieppe route, because it is cheapest; but I think that is all I shall see of Dieppe this year, much as I love the place. For it means to me Constance, more than anything else. And I don't think I could stay in it this summer. I couldn't quite bear that little place on the terrace where they make the electric light, and where we used to sit together at night, and the English Church where she wanted to marry me "next Tuesday," and the dining-room of Lefèvre's, of which the abiding and most distinct of all memories is that birthday dinner at which she sat between you and me, and had from you a laurel-crown, like mine, and a cake with ROMA on it. All this sounds very "literary" and sentimentalistic, but it is real enough to me. I shan't take my holiday on "our sunny south-coast:" somewhere in France; but not Dieppe.

I do so look forward to hearing from you. Till then goodbye, dear Reg.   Affectionately   MAX

Thursday [*21 April 1904. Postmark 22 April*]

48 *Upper Berkeley Street*

My dearest Reg,

Very very many thanks for your letter. It is indeed much to me to have a friend like you, and a letter like that. Constance is in Dublin, and will be there till the end of next week. Do write to her (not mentioning that you know about the breaking-off of the engagement; for I haven't told her that I have told you). She is at the

Shelbourne Hotel. Fenn's and Pryce's play[1] is very poor stuff—Oscar badly de-oscarised. Murray Carson has had a real acting success at the Apollo.[2] I have been staying at the Bull and Bush on Hampstead Heath, as I had had an attack of influenza. It is a dear little place, with a Belgian proprietor and Belgian servants: a kind of Lefèvre's, only with English peasants drinking beer in the bar all day.

I saw a lot of the Rothensteins. Very plain living and very high thinking, and Will very happy therein; but Alice and I hankering after richer food and poorer cerebration.

About Paris: I needn't be here for the exhibition at Carfax's. *But* I promised some time ago to spend Whitsuntide at the Walkinshaws';[3] and I can't get out of that. Whitsuntide begins about May 14. What date should you arrive in Paris? Don't hurry back so that we could be in Paris together; for of course we could go over there later on. Just do whatever fits in with your plans. Do write again.

Affectionately MAX

14 February 1906   *48 Upper Berkeley Street*

My dearest Reg,

Thank you so much for your delightful letter. You know that my silence has not been due to forgetfulness: only to my ineradicable modesty about letter-writing. I always feel that I write such awfully dull letters unless I have a lot of actual news to give. And of actual news there is, as usual, a dearth. I wish I were with you in Nice: it must be very charming indeed there. Next year, perhaps, I really *shall* be able to manage it.

Did you see anything of Boulestin in Paris? I had a letter from him, a few days ago, announcing that he had made his *début* at some

---

[1] *Saturday to Monday* by Frederick Fenn and Richard Pryce, first produced at the St James's Theatre on 14 April 1904, and reviewed by Max in the *Saturday Review* on 23 April.

[2] In *The Wheat King*, adapted from Frank Norris's novel *The Pit*, by Elliott Page and Mrs Ashton Jonson, produced at the Apollo Theatre on 16 April, and reviewed by Max on 23 April.

[3] Unidentified.

theatre with Mme Willy.[1] "And of course all the people do talk a lot about it," says Boulestin; "well! it went off well."

Street and I went to *Nero*[2] lately: he was very unfavourably impressed with the play, and in a cold courteous way rather bullied Herbert, in the dressing-room, for not having the names pronounced in the Italian way. Herbert, however, did not knuckle under. "Agripp*i*na," he said, "seems to me a grand name; but" (changing his tone from a majestic baritone to a sneaking tenor) "Agripp*ee*na is miserable." Street said "Agripp*ee*na" (in his nearest approach to rotundity) "is magnificent." I was appealed to, and felt rather awkward. Street had been upset all day, because Chesterton, in the *Illustrated London News*, replying to some article of Street's, had spoken of "that brilliant and delightful writer, Mr Street." Street objected strongly to this, for some complex behaviourish reason of his own.

I wished you had been with Lydia[3] and myself at the Chelsea Palace last week. The overture was entitled "Darkie Boatmen"— ASHER.[4] And, to my intense surprise and pleasure, Angelo himself, facing the audience with an air of modest pride, *sang the words* while he conducted. A husky but never-to-be-forgotten performance. Also, the "star" of the evening was our dear old friend and master, Harry Freeman,[5] exactly as ever, with just two or three spoken words between each stanza of a song with the refrain "That's him, that's him, that's him!" No, not *exactly* the same is Freeman: he has changed his politics, and he welcomed the approaching

[1] Sidonie-Gabrielle Colette (1873–1954), the French writer, had in 1893 married Henri Gauthier-Villars, beneath whose pen-name Willy her first three books appeared. This marriage was just breaking up and Colette began a stage and music-hall career of eight years. Boulestin had been working as Willy's secretary, and Colette got him and herself parts in *Le Désir, la Chimère et l'Amour*, a pantomime by Francis de Croisset, which was produced at the Théâtre des Mathurins.
[2] A verse tragedy by Stephen Phillips, produced by Tree at His Majesty's on 25 January 1906.
[3] Lydia Burton (d. 1944) married (1900) Walter Westley Russell (1867–1949), painter, who taught at the Slade School 1895–1927 (R.A. 1926. Knighted 1935). Lydia sat for Wilson Steer's portrait "Aminta" (1899).
[4] Max noted that he was the musical conductor at the Tivoli and habitually wore two buttonholes at once.
[5] Comic vocalist of the music-halls (1858–1922).

moment when C.B.[1] would put a stop to Chinese Labour and grant Home Rule to Ireland—the audience tremendously enthusiastic, evidently sharing our feeling that Harry Freeman is right: he was always right.

Yesterday I had a note from Lady Desborough (*mariée* Grenfell)[2] asking me to dine on Friday week: "the de Greys,[3] Soveral, Mr Balfour, Lord Rosebery,[4] the Edgar Vincents,[5] Evan,[6] and a few others." I think I shall try and go. It is the "first London dinnerparty" they have ever given, she says, by way of inducement. Since Lord Cowper's[7] death they have taken a house in Grosvenor Square. I do hope they'll have a list of the guests in the *Morning Post* on the following morning—"and Mr Max Beerbohm" would look so nice, and would make Barry Pain and Charles Goetz[8] very angry. Why I enjoy my periodical plunges into Society is that Society is a sort of substitute for an Academy of Letters— "Mr Max Beerbohm's recent articles in the *Saturday Review* have

[1] Sir Henry Campbell-Bannerman (1836–1908), Liberal Prime Minister, 1905–8.
[2] Ethel Fane (1867–1952), grand-daughter of the eleventh Earl of Westmorland, married (1887) William Henry Grenfell (1855–1945), who was created Lord Desborough 1905.
[3] Frederick Oliver Robinson, Earl de Grey (1852–1923) married (1885) Constance Gladys (1859–1917), daughter of the first Baron Herbert of Lea, sister of the thirteenth Earl of Pembroke, and widow of the fourth Earl of Lonsdale. Lord de Grey succeeded his father as second Marquess of Ripon, 1909.
[4] Archibald Philip, fifth Earl of Rosebery (1847–1929), Liberal Prime Minister, 1894–95.
[5] Sir Edgar Vincent, Bart (1857–1941), Financial Adviser to Egyptian Government 1883–89; Governor of Imperial Ottoman Bank, Constantinople 1889–97; Conservative M.P. for Exeter, 1899–1906; British Ambassador at Berlin, 1920–26; married (1890) Lady Helen Duncombe, daughter of the first Earl of Feversham. He was created Lord D'Abernon 1914, raised to Viscount 1926.
[6] The Hon Evan Charteris (1864–1940), sixth son of the tenth Earl of Wemyss. Barrister (K.C. 1919). Published lives of J. S. Sargent (1927) and Edmund Gosse (1931). Knighted 1932.
[7] The seventh Earl Cowper (1834–1905). Lady Desborough was co-heir to one of his minor titles, the Barony of Butler.
[8] Charles Edward Goetz (1872–1938) had been a Balliol undergraduate 1891–94. He was later called to the Bar and worked as a journalist. He was a nephew of Edward Lawson and brother-in-law to Barry Pain.

been 'crowned' by Lord and Lady Desborough:" that is what the list in the *Morning Post* would amount to, and my gray hairs would be gladdened by the recognition of my integrity and purity of taste.

By the way, I do hope you'll be back in time to see *His House in Order*.[1] You would love it: I never saw anything so *du théâtre*; and even I enjoyed it enormously. Do please write to me, and tell me all about everything. I am looking forward to *Uncle Peaceable*,[2] which I fancy will be a great success. Are you writing much in Nice? Why don't you start on *Portossington*? You remember, you won the toss, at Constance's supper—of which I am glad; for I couldn't have done the play alone (as *you* most certainly *can*); and I believe collaboration to be the very devil.

Well, dear Reg, goodbye. Mind you write to your affectionate

MAX

Saturday [Postmark 28 April 1906]   *48 Upper Berkeley Street*

My dearest Reg,

Very many thanks indeed for your letter of sympathy. I knew you would be so sorry that poor Julius is dead, and I wished you could have been here to say goodbye to him before he died.[3] He was so fond of you, admired your wit so much, used so often to quote your *mots* and *aperçus*, and to say that you were like the people he had known when he was a young man—people more *fin* than exist today. You will be glad to know that he died in no pain. He *seemed* to be suffering—the drawing of breath *seemed* so difficult and painful; but the nurses and doctors all agreed that he was not *feeling* anything, for a long time before the actual end.

I ought to have written to you long ago. I had so hoped I could meet you in Paris: it would have been lovely to have a week or so with you there. Let us do it next year. Also I ought to have written

[1] A comedy in four acts by Arthur W. Pinero, first produced at the St James's Theatre on 1 February 1906, with George Alexander, Irene Vanbrugh and Herbert Waring in the leading parts.
[2] Reggie's seventh novel, published in 1906 and dedicated to Robert Ross.
[3] Max's half-brother Julius Beerbohm had died of pneumonia on 21 April 1906, aged fifty-two.

to say how very much I enjoyed *U.P.*[1] which, I am glad to "note,"
is in its second edition. Such a lot of delightful things in it—most
especially the pianola party, and the performing animals scene, I
thought.

I suppose you will be home almost at once now. Your return is
always a red letter day in the Beerbohm calendar, and in the Max
calendar most of all.　　　　　　　　　　Your affectionate　MAX

Sunday [*10 June 1906. Postmark 11 June*]

　　　　　　　　　　　　　　　　　48 Upper Berkeley Street

My dearest Reg,

Wasn't Farquharson absolutely marvellous?[2] I'm a bad correspondent. But sometimes enthusiasm puts the pen into my hand,
insisting on being shared with you, who are the person I would
always soonest share it with.　　　　　Yours affectionately　MAX

Monday [*23 July 1906. Postmark 24 July*]　　　　*Tidworth House*
　　　　　　　　　　　　　　　　　　　　　　　　　Andover

My dearest Reg,

If you are not dining anywhere next Thursday, do come in and
dine at 48. I shall be home by then. My thoughts turn towards you,
my old friend, as I sit in this large and unfriendly bedroom, to
which I have retired early, accompanied to the threshold by my
host (Sir I. Hamilton[3]) who is sleepy after his military duties. The
whole country round, as I saw it from the window of my railway
carriage, is an armed camp; and this house (a much larger one, I
feel, than the H's can afford) is full of majors, captains, subalterns,
etc., who talk deferentially to me about Bernard Shaw. And the

---

1 *Uncle Peaceable.*
2 Oscar Wilde's *Salome* was revived at the King's Hall, Covent Garden,
on 10 June 1906, with Robert Farquharson as Herod.
3 Major-General Sir Ian Hamilton, soldier and writer (1853–1947), was
G.O.C. Southern Command 1905–9. He was promoted General 1907,
and commanded the Expeditionary Force to Gallipoli 1915. He married
(1887) Jean Miller (d. 1941), daughter of Sir John Muir, Bart.

General has asked me whether I have my "riding kit" with me, as he would like to show me some manoeuvres which are taking place near here tomorrow. In the flurry of the moment, I merely murmured something about *not* having my riding-kit with me. Heaven help me if, tomorrow, he offers to lend me his boots and spurs!

My position in regard to Lady Hamilton is scarcely less false. For she talks to me all the time about modern French literature, I occasionally, for a change, saying "No! *That* I *haven't* read—though I have been *meaning* to—I can imagine it's just the sort of thing I should like."

At my time of life, I really ought to be able to rely on myself to say "I don't read French; and I have never ridden a horse." I suppose my duplicity is a sign of preserved youth—"some late lark singing"[1]—and therefore not wholly lamentable?

Your affectionate MAX

8 September 1906   *48 Upper Berkeley Street*

My dearest Reg,

No news at all here. I have been going on with my parodies, and next week shall try them on the *Tribune*.[2] Today I am going down to Chiswick with Miss Kahn[3] to lunch *chez* Tree and see the Harvard race.[4] *The Winter's Tale* has had good notices; but *oh* what a deadly stupid play—except for snatches of poetry here and there which are done no justice to by Viola & Co. Somerset is a sad stodger as Autolycus.[5]

---

[1] From W. E. Henley's poem "Margaritae Sorori, I.M.," published in his first volume, *A Book of Verses* (1888).

[2] Of the seventeen parodies gathered together in *A Christmas Garland* (1912) seven (those of Henry James, Rudyard Kipling, H. G. Wells, G. K. Chesterton, Bernard Shaw, Maurice Hewlett and George Moore) appeared in the *Saturday Review* between 8 and 29 December 1906.

[3] Florence Kahn (1878–1950) was born in Memphis, Tennessee, had been on the American stage since 1897 and was already a leading lady on Broadway. Max first met her in 1904.

[4] On 8 September the Cambridge VIII beat Harvard University by two lengths over the Putney-to-Mortlake course on the Thames.

[5] A revival of *A Winter's Tale*, arranged by Tree, had opened at His Majesty's on 1 September, with Ellen Terry as Hermione, Viola Tree as Perdita, and C. W. Somerset as Autolycus.

I think I shall start for Italy about the twentieth.[1] I should love to stay a day or two in Paris or at Barbizon;[2] but I rather doubt whether I can: I will let you know.

The bag goes on being as beautiful as ever. I am not sure that it doesn't grow more so: anyway it puts quite a different complexion on my journey: it will be a great stand-by in my agonised solitudes of sight-seeing and literary composition. I imagine Barbizon must be very delightful. You haven't been there before, have you? Though you have been everywhere. Do write to me again.

Your affectionate MAX

Thursday [Postmark 20 September 1906] 48 Upper Berkeley Street

My dearest Reg,

I am starting for Venice on Sunday morning—Paris that evening —Orient Express the next morning. So do meet me at the Gare du Nord (if you are free on Sunday evening) or await me (having engaged a bedroom for me) at the Castille.[3] It will be such great fun and pleasure to see you on the eve of my pilgrimage. I go via Vienna—may stay a day there or not. Do you remember my long yellow overcoat that I first wore for my second visit to Mme d'Oliveira? It has been cleaned, looks as beautiful as ever, and will "knock 'em" on the Grand Canal. Venice—Padua—Verona— Mantua—Florence—Siena—Perugia—Assisi—that is my syllabus: I cut Rome and Naples.

I am so looking forward to the new novel, and am delighted you are pleased with it. Miss Kahn was much amused by your opinion of her opinion of you, which I recounted to her;[4] and on the contrary has a great sentiment and admiration for you; but that is of course.

Please look forward to seeing me and my dressing-case.

Your affectionate MAX

[1] Alfred Harmsworth had commissioned Max to write for the *Daily Mail* ten articles on Italy, which he had never before visited.
[2] Where Reggie was staying.
[3] The Hôtel de Castille in the Rue Cambon, where Reggie was staying.
[4] Reggie had written from Barbizon: "Please remember me to Miss Kahn. I fear she doesn't like me—and, quite wrongly, thinks me vulgar. However, I like her, and must not expect more than that."

Thursday [*20 September 1906. Postmark 21 September*]
48 *Upper Berkeley Street*
Second Letter

My dearest Reg,

Slight change of plan: I start Saturday night, leaving Paris on Monday evening, so shall come and see you in your bed on Sunday morning.

Also, Agnes and Miss Kahn are coming over with me. They will stay probably at the Grand Hotel. Great haste

Your affectionate MAX

Monday [*8 October 1906. Postmark 9 October*]   *Verona*

My dearest Reg,

Years ago it seems since I saw you, and Paris does not seem at all like a real city. Nor does Verona; nor does Padua: nothing seems real after Venice.

"While other cities mutually vie, Venezia is *sui generis*." These are the last two lines of a sonnet from an American magazine— invented by myself for quotation in the *Daily Mail*.[1] I wonder how you, being free to go, can ever go anywhere else. Tonight I go to your beloved Florence, and shall take a room at the Grand Hotel, afterwards presenting myself at the Palazzo Horne, and asking if he knows of a good *room* somewhere. I don't want to stay with him, even if he were kind enough to ask me. For I must write—must develop something from the chaos of little notes that I have made; and this cosmicising process will need solitude. I think I shall make a little book on the whole journey—a little continuous narrative. But the present necessity is to make ten articles, each as separate as possible, for the *D.M.*—a much more difficult task than it would be to write the narrative straight off.[2]

[1] They duly appeared, slightly amended, in the sixth of Max's Italian articles on 27 November.
[2] Max's ten articles appeared in the *Daily Mail* between 8 November and 27 December, but he never published them in a book, though he got as far as producing a revised draft of a dedicatory epistle to Alfred Harmsworth. Later he used some of the material to form the essay called "A Stranger in Venice," which appeared in *A Variety of Things* (1928 and 1953).

I wonder how I shall like Florence. I expect it will go the way of Padua, and of this place, and of all other places I have seen in this world: Venice will cancel it. For the first time in my life, I wish I were a poet, so as to do some sort of justice to Venice. I feel it so impossible to *describe* beautiful things. Not even such a poet as Ruskin can really describe them (I have been reading *Stones of Venice* with much delight and surprised reverence for Ruskin); but he can give *something* of them; and I shall only be able to give pretty little personal-fantastic irrelevancies. However—I shall take a melancholy pleasure in giving these as best I can. Packing and unpacking the dressing-case, whenever I arrive or depart, is a pleasure un-dulled as yet, and the fittings, arranged on the latest dressing-table, are (as Douglas Ainslie[1] would say) a thread of ivory and silver on which the various cities string themselves. As regards the actual packing of clothes, books, etc., I find that in Paris I wasted a great deal of space; and now despite the various objects of antique art which I have bought as presents for friends in England, the bag gives forth an almost hollow sound when I tap it.

Do write to me—say at the *Poste Restante*, Florence.

Your affectionate MAX

Sunday [*14 October 1906. Receipt Postmark 16 October*]
22 Lung'Arno Acciaioli, Firenze

My dearest Reg,

What do you think of that for an address? And your very own room, too, so Herbert Horne tells me. I "descended" at the New York Hotel, on the Lung'Arno, but they were such a nuisance—rows of American-speaking, frock-coated, white-shirt-fronted Italian major-domos forming an avenue in the hall whenever I went in or out, and asking me whether I was comfortable or not, and whether I was going to take my next meal *in* the hotel, and seeming so wounded when I said I had promised to take the meal with some old Florentine friends, that finally I decided to "flit," and H.H. showed me the way to the rooms hallowed by your tenancy—rooms with a

[1] Poet, translator of Benedetto Croce, and sometime diplomat (1865–1948).

ceiling crudely painted over with flowers, and with small human faces which have, I feel, looked down on scenes which I should not have approved of. I am there till the end of this week. Then I do Siena. Then, I think, I do "home." I shan't go to Rome, thank you. I must end up on a quiet note—a pure and gentle Italian note.

I love Florence, but somewhat in the sense in which the late Sir Henry Irving loved M. Renan[1]—and in saying to you that I love her I feel that I am putting you somewhat in the position of the late (how old we are growing!) Mr Haweis.[2] I see that she has a charm. I feel sure that if I had come straight through to Rome and worked back, *via* her, I should have *really* delighted in her. But a man who has loved a fairy must find the women of this earth coarse and stupid. And I have met and loved, and love, the fairy named Venice; and, though it is unjust to compare any other city with her, I can't rid myself of the comparison. Venice, Venice, Venice—with "decimal point recurring:" that is the sum of my journey. I hope we shall, some day, be there together: it would be a delight to show

[1] In Bram Stoker's *Personal Reminiscences of Henry Irving*, first published in two volumes in October 1906 (Max "improved" the illustrations in his copy), occurs this passage:
"On April 3, 1880, when we were playing *The Merchant of Venice*, Ernest Renan came to the Lyceum; the Rev. H. R. Haweis was with him. At the end of the third act they both came round to Irving's dressing-room. It was interesting to note the progress through the long Royal passage of that strangely assorted pair. Haweis was diminutive, and had an extraordinary head of black hair. Renan was ponderously fat and bald as a billiard ball. The historian waddled along with an odd rolling gait, whilst the preacher, who was lame, hopped along like a sort of jackdaw. The conversation between Irving and Renan was a strange one to listen to. Neither knew the other's language; but each kept talking his own with, strange to say, the result that they really understood something of what was said. When I was alone with Irving and remarked on it he said:
" 'If you don't know the other person's language, keep on speaking your own. Do not get hurried or flustered, but keep as natural as you can; your intonation, being natural, will convey something. You have a far better chance of being understood than if you try to talk a language you don't know!' "
At this time Max spoke no Italian.
[2] The Rev Hugh Reginald Haweis (1838–1901) was for many years incumbent of St James's, Marylebone. In his youth he fought under Garibaldi in the war of Italian independence. A great lecturer and author of many books on religious and musical subjects.

you things there: I saw few enough, being no sight-seer; but I saw a few, and was happy in them.

I am so glad you admired *The Guarded Flame*.[1] I wonder whether you agree with me (it is the sort of technical-novelistic point that would occur to you rather than to me) that the author was wrong in making the pivot of the tragedy the death of the fiancée: I see no true artistic reason for the fiancée being there at all: she and her death were simply an unnecessary addition—a blacking of the chimney: the tragedy would have come just as effectively, and much more naturally, out of the conjugal infidelity. You see—I am in Florence. I couldn't have written about this sort of thing in Venice.

Do write to me again. There will be just time before I go to Siena.   Yours affectionately MAX

Tuesday [30 October 1906. Postmark 31 October]
48 Upper Berkeley Street

My dearest Reg,

How I wish I could come; but I simply can't and mustn't. I *must* do the articles, as the *Daily Mail* is probably anxious to have them —has probably been expecting them for some time. I feel rather guilty in not having yet sent anything; and I must put my shoulder to the wheel. Please thank Frank very much, and explain to him. If I were like other writers, I could go on with my work down there; but, as you know, I have to do *all* or *nothing*. I have just arrived here, and did not write from Paris today because the letter would not have reached you any sooner. When shall I see you? Do come and lunch one day—say Thursday? I have done the initial article, and hope to finish the second tomorrow. Paris—yes— seemed very loathsome after Italy; and anyhow, surely, it isn't what it was.   Your affectionate MAX

[1] A novel by W. B. Maxwell, first published in August 1906.

Friday [*9 November 1906. Postmark 10 November*]

48 Upper Berkeley Street

Dearest Reg,

I do so look forward to the novel,[1] and have already "instructed" Webb.[2] How wonderfully lucrative the *D.T.* is! Lucky rogue.

[1] Reggie's eighth novel, *Davray's Affairs* (1906). The British Museum copy is stamped 30 November.

[2] Messrs George and William Webb were Max's solicitors, as they had been his father's. Probably Reggie had warned Max that he was to appear, thinly disguised, in *Davray's Affairs*, and Max was pretending to take legal advice. The passage runs as follows:

"Hans Branders was by no means averse from playing a part in the comedy of life himself, but he was quite as pleased to watch the comedy going on, and his eyes were keener than most people's. His eyes, which were the best part of his face, were given to troubling men and women alike. When they looked at women it was difficult to say whether they were being used for love-making, or for prying into the heart of the person on whom they gazed; and when they fell on men, especially men who had a good opinion of themselves, they seemed to be lighting, in kindly fashion, on a weak point. Even Davray, who was least of all men given to self-consciousness, sometimes felt a little confused as he saw Hans gazing at him. The eyes, big blue eyes surrounded by long lashes, seemed glimmering with amusement. Everyone who knew Hans Branders —and everyone either knew or wanted to know him—called him Hans. He signed his articles 'Hans,' he signed his caricatures 'Hans,' and his friends and acquaintances called him 'Hans.' The name possessed a portmanteau of meaning. On different occasions it expressed intimacy, dignity, affection, or official recognition. His great success in life was due far more to his personality than to his achievements. He did not, as a matter of fact, do very much compared with other producers, but everything he did was first-class, everything was distinguished; very seldom, though it had happened, was Hans to be caught tripping in judgement or in execution. And, when that did happen, his sturdy refusal to recognise his weakness caused others to forget it, or to think they must have been mistaken. People said he was one of the most interesting and engaging figures in London life, and, like so many other distinguished Englishmen, he was English neither by blood nor temperament. His popularity was amazing. He was not a sportsman, nor a Bohemian; as a very young man superficial people had pronounced him effeminate, but sportsmen, artists, fools and wise men, and women of all ages and conditions, had a real affection for him. He never made any apparent effort either to push his work, or to make a friend; he never altered his attitude, but he brought everyone to him. More matured years had given him a distinguished appearance; the intimates of his early days gradually realised that he looked like 'somebody.' The head was already showing signs of becoming one

173

The *D.M.'s* starring of me *is* a sort of compliment, I suppose. I hope nobody will think *I* invented that title.[1] They put it without consulting me. It rather oppresses me, throwing my writing out of "value:" every time I write "I" it becomes "I." However——

At any rate it brought me a telegram (followed by a visit) from Bobbie, this afternoon. I am so sorry, I can't dine on Wednesday; for I have promised to dine with W. Toynbee[2] that night.

Your affectionate   MAX

26 November 1907   *Castell San Giorgio, Portofino, Liguria*

My dearest Reg,

Three delightful letters from you, in as many days; and from me very many thanks. I am so glad you think the book[3] comes out

---

day 'magnificent.' As Vivian Chitters said, 'he was rapidly developing for the picture postcards.' In dress he inclined to an eccentricity of old-fashioned fashion, and street urchins sometimes looked on him with a wonder which might easily have developed into a grin or an exclamation: but people did not easily take a liberty with Hans. The secret of his popularity—for it did not spring from those obvious causes which give the victory to the good-looking, good-humoured fellow—was himself; that personality which influenced people who met him. He had not the curly locks and fresh complexion which win so many hearts; he was not a man who would good-naturedly stand any amount of chaff; he was not given to making himself useful, or putting himself out for other people; and for all his amiability, he was sometimes imperturbable to the verge of irritation. There was a strain of cruelty in him, not harshness nor brutality, but cruelty simple and isolated. But there was no malice in him, no pettiness, and he had the kindest of hearts. Two qualities, bad and unpleasant in mediocre men, vanity and selfishness, were in him as in all great personalities, however they may be disguised, or unseen by the crowd; and he did not attempt, as fortunately do most smaller and weaker men, to conceal them. Finally, he had that quality in common with nearly all really great men—he had an appreciation of all people and all things, big and little. There was nothing and no one he could not draw satisfaction from. Where meaner people condemned, he smiled or was silent; where narrower people were blind, he saw the light."

[1] "Max Beerbohm in Italy."
[2] Poet and writer (1849–1942), elder brother of the economist Arnold Toynbee (1852–83) and the Dante scholar Paget Toynbee (1855–1932); uncle of the historian. Edited W. C. Macready's *Diaries* (2 vols., 1912).
[3] *A Book of Caricatures*, published by Methuen in November 1907.

nicely. (I think so too: it reached me this morning.) But what bosh about your being pleased and surprised at receiving a copy. You would of course always be the first male person to go down on the list of receivers of any book of mine. Also, I am so glad of your praise of "The Fire."[1] I haven't yet had a copy of the *New Quarterly* and am looking eagerly forward to getting it, as I now know (I hadn't been at all sure) that the article is a good one. Pray don't expect me to sympathise with any depression produced in you by criticisms of your work from "Robert Ross."[2] You know my opinion of his opinion on any subject under the sun—especially of any opinion by which he can count on making an intimate friend uncomfortable for the moment. You really ought to be able to discount that sort of thing by this time. And I have no doubt your novel is going on perfectly well, despite your own doubts.

Meanwhile, I send you my love, and also that of the Nicholsons.[3] We are enjoying ourselves very much here. It is a really beautiful life here—very free and sunshiny and sea-airy, with a great deal of nonsense talked, and nap and poker played, and pictures and books discussed, and going to bed in the small hours and getting up in the big ones. The Baroness[4] turns out to be a charming creature, and so does the Baron, whose mother, aged seventy-seven, and brought up exclusively in Court circles of the dullest and smallest kind in Germany, is enjoying immensely her sudden immersion into English Bohemian society. She is very anxious to go down with us into the village of Portofino and share our daily vermouth; but this rapture will have to be postponed, I fear, as she is suffering from a bilious attack brought on by over-excitement.

Mabel began rather badly here, with a constantly deepening

[1] This essay, first published in the *New Quarterly* for November 1907, was included in *Yet Again* (1909).
[2] Both Max and Reggie seem to have turned against Ross at this time. The exact reason is not known, but probably Ross tried to involve Reggie in his long feud with Lord Alfred Douglas.
[3] William Newzam Prior Nicholson, English painter (1872–1949), and his wife Mabel, sister of the painter James Pryde. Max was a close friend of Nicholson and drew many caricatures of him. His portrait of Max, painted in 1901, is in the National Portrait Gallery.
[4] The Baroness von Hutten (1874–1957). Born in Pennsylvania of Irish-American parents, she came to Europe in 1891 and married the Baron in 1897. Author of many popular novels.

silence and sallowness as she smoked and smoked without ceasing—
the gloom of the process being accentuated for us by her holding the
cigarette clipped between the prongs of one of those dressing-case
instruments made for extracting thorns from fingers. This was to
prevent nicotine-stains on the fingers. .... However, she is much
better now; and she limits herself strictly to twelve cigarettes a day,
and all goes well. The Kid[1] is delightful here—much more amusing
than even he ever was; and so fertile in grotesque invention that he
sometimes rivals *you*, than which no higher compliment could be
paid. It is not, however, *Italy* that has caused him to blossom. I
think it is only the circumstances of irresponsibility. He does not
seem to imbibe the *atmosphere*, remains thoroughly English and
himself, and in Portofino is Mecklenburgh Square via Hampstead
and Woodstock,[2] and resolutely says "Thanks" and "Come in"
where I say "Gra*h*-tia" and "Av*ah*nnn-ti" with an enormous stress
on the division of syllables. And the fishermen on the quay seldom fail
to draw the comment "*There* they go—jolly fellows—there'll be
holes in the snow tonight, *I* know. Why is not Christian here?"[3]
etc. etc. Also, his passion for low tones in painting is unaffected by
the local climate; and his picture of the Capello San Giorgio, with
sea and sky effects, though it was a bright enough affair at first, is
rapidly being toned down to the aspect of St Martin in the Fields.
It remains, however, a beautiful picture; and the Kid himself is one
of the dearest and most delightful of men. I think I shall be going
hence to Florence next Saturday—shall be there not longer than a
week, and so home. And I am so looking forward to seeing you.

Your loving friend MAX

Wednesday [Postmark 8 April 1908]   *48 Upper Berkeley Street*

My dearest Reg,

I only got your letter (April 1) yesterday; as it had been sent on
misaddressed to the Reeces[4] with whom I had been staying. I *am* so

1 William Nicholson's nickname among his family and close friends.
2 Nicholson had lived in all three.
3 The despairing cry of Mathias in Act III of *The Bells*, adapted from the
French of Erckmann-Chatrian by Leopold Lewis, and first performed by
Irving at the Lyceum in 1871.
4 Nancy and Harry Reece were old friends who lived at Sevenoaks.

Mr Reginald
Turner

MAX

A photograph taken by Alvin Langdon Coburn in London on
15 January 1908

sorry you have been "let in" in that unfortunate manner, and I need hardly say that my sorrow is not complicated with regret for self, as the idea of your "pre-decease" had never occurred to me as a possible contingency; and *had* it so occurred would not have been made less unpleasant by your kind intentions. My regret is that you hadn't spent on yourself the money that you had wonderfully saved. You say you won't guarantee M. Gilbert[1] any more; and of course, if you were any one else, you wouldn't. But you being you, I have a horrible suspicion that a few really piteous appeals would make you waver. *Don't* waver. And don't disburse, except on your own deserving self, a penny of the many hundred pounds which I hope you will make out of your play. I do hope you are progressing with that. Of course it is difficult. You have only to leap the difficulties, or rather to climb over them. I am sure you have the genuine vocation for play-writing, and need only the proper confidence in yourself.

I have done forty-seven of my caricatures now, and the show opens towards the end of the month.[2] Do write to me again and tell me all about yourself and your doings. My mother is quite well again. And Aggie is much better for her long rest.

Your affectionate   M A X

22 *December 1908*   *48 Upper Berkeley Street*

My dearest Reg,

How are you enjoying Paris? I rather envy you with your little balcony in the sky, and the lady at the bureau who loves you, and the man in the hall who calls you Master. Also the climate, and the food. Not much news here. We shall as usual be here for Christmas. Aggie's party will be rather dull without you. George Street will also be away. It is almost certain that he will be made bankrupt in January—at the suit of a deceased creditor, named Clapp, whose dying wish ("which we are bound to respect," said his solicitors in

---

[1] Almost certainly Maurice Gilbert, the friend of Oscar Wilde's last days, about whom almost nothing is known. In 1898 Reggie had put him up at Clement's Inn.

[2] This, Max's fourth and last exhibition at the Carfax Gallery, opened in April 1908 and ran into May. It contained fifty-three drawings.

their letter to George) was that George should be made bankrupt. Poor George seems rather distressed, and I try to cheer him up by calling him Portugal Street[1] and offering to lend him, as being an old pal, my Colt revolver, if he will just leave a line for his landlord, telling him to send the revolver along to me afterwards.

I could not resist writing to Henry James, about "The Jolly Corner" and about his writings in general, and I have had such a *very* lovely letter from him.[2] When shall you be back? Frank Richardson's[3] mother has died; and he tells a story at the Garrick about an editor asking him to do 2000 words on Death from the

[1] Adjacent to the Bankruptcy Court.
[2] James's story first appeared in the December 1908 issue of the *English Review*. Max's caricature based on it is now in the possession of Mr Siegfried Sassoon. James's *"very* lovely letter" is here printed by courtesy of Mr John James:

19 December 1908   Lamb House, Rye
My dear Max Beerbohm,

I won't say in acknowledgment of your beautiful letter that it's exactly the sort of letter I like best to receive, because that would sound as if I had *data* for generalizing—which I haven't; and therefore I can only go so far as to say that if it belonged to a class, or weren't a mere remarkable individual, I *should* rank it with the type supremely gratifying. On its mere lonely independent merits it appeals to me intimately and exquisitely, and I can only gather myself in and up, arching and presenting my not inconsiderable back—a back, as who should say, offered for any further stray scratching and patting of that delightful kind. I can bear wounds and fell smitings (so far as I have been ever honoured with such— and indeed life smites us on the whole enough, taking one thing with another,) better than expressive gentleness of touch; so you must imagine me for a little while quite prostrate and overcome with the force of your good words. But I shall recover, when they have really sunk in—and then be not only the "better," but the more nimble and artful and alert by what they will have done for me. You had, and you obeyed, a very generous and humane inspiration; it charms me to think—or rather so authentically to know, that my (I confess) ambitious Muse does work upon you; it really helps me to believe in her the more myself—by which I am very gratefully yours   HENRY JAMES

[3] Frank Collins Richardson (1871–1917), playwright and novelist. Author of *Bunkum, Whiskers and Soda* and many other books. He recorded that at Oxford York Powell said to him: "Richardson, you will always be a fool, but your sense of humour may prevent you from being a damned fool."

Comic Standpoint. Characteristic of him, is it not? I saw yesterday the *Who's Who* for next year. Robert Ross has spared no pains, and gives an extraordinarily vivid and exhaustive account of himself.

Florence[1] sailed for America, and arrived on Sunday. An awful voyage, according to the papers. She returns in the spring or summer, after staying with her brothers. All my people are well. *Pinkie*[2] a huge commercial success. Herbert going to Egypt, on the proceeds, to stay with Hall Caine. How is the novel going? *Well*, I hope.

Affectionately   MAX

23 December 1908   *48 Upper Berkeley Street*

My dearest Reg,

What *can* I say? It is *very* wrong of you; *much* too generous and sweet of you. And my first (and better) instinct was to send the cheque back defaced, and to ask you to knock off £15 and write another. However (I began to think) if you *will* do that sort of thing —after all, you are not "a minor"—I am not my brother's keeper, etc. etc.

And so I am going to pay the lovely £20 into my bank—under protest—and shall devote it to some definite purpose that will (I am not sure *what* it is) give me true solid pleasure. I don't feel I can devote the money to personal adornment: I am, for the moment, excessively "broke;" and it would be a mockery to hang myself with jewels. In due time I shall be able to come to some decision what to do with the money. Meanwhile I am not telling anyone about it, except my banker! And then the handkerchiefs—how very beautiful *they* are! You are much too good—so are they—and the ones you have sent to my sisters: the whole household is re-echoing with gratitude. You will have received the letter from me which crossed yours. I am delighted to hear that you have been hard at work, and I hope you will have a *regular popular* success with your novel.[3] Also, *do* write a play.

[1] Florence Kahn.
[2] *Pinkie and the Fairies*, a play for children by W. Graham Robertson, with music by Frederick Norton, produced by Tree at His Majesty's on 19 December 1908, with Ellen Terry in the cast. Max wrote about it in the *Saturday Review* of 2 January 1909.
[3] Reggie's tenth novel, *Samson Unshorn*, published in 1909.

I agree so much with what you say about the difference between the French and English languages as vehicles for the spoken word. And then, of course, there is the pendant-fact that the Latins are born actors, while the Saxons have to train themselves up to the scratch. Ever so many thanks again, dear friend (using both these words in their extreme literal sense), from yours affectionately MAX

Friday [8 October 1909. Postmark 9 October]
48 Upper Berkeley Street

My dearest Reg,

I cannot at all get near to expressing how much your letter delighted me and warmed my soul. I can only say, like the Queen of Morleville, *"Merci, merci, et toujours merci!"* [1]

I think you over-rate the book; [2] but that only makes your opinion the dearer to me, as giving the measure of our dear and never-altering friendship.   Your affectionate MAX

Monday [8 November 1909. Postmark 9 November]
48 Upper Berkeley Street

My dearest Reg,

I am so awfully sorry: I can't come to tea tomorrow. The reason is that I have to be working at top-speed on caricatures for the New English. [3] I have to go to Chelsea tomorrow morning, to look at Hugh Lane, [4] then dash back and draw him, and put finishing-touches to some other caricatures, and send the lot down to Chap-

[1] Quotation untraced.
[2] *Yet Again*, Max's third volume of essays, had been published on 5 October.
[3] Max was now a member of the New English Art Club and had shown fifteen caricatures at its Summer 1909 exhibition. He contributed a further nine to the Winter 1909 exhibition.
[4] Hugh Percy Lane (1875–1915), Irish art expert and collector. Knighted 1909. Drowned in *Lusitania*. This caricature is entitled "Sir Hugh Lane, producing masterpieces for Dublin."

man[1] to be mounted in time for "sending-in-day"—a great bore for me. Please be sorry for me, and forgive me too. . . .

You will be glad to hear that they have been re-printing *Yet Again*. Second impression ready within a few days. Pom-pom-pom. And if that is sold out, my gains will run into tens of shillings.

Your affectionate MAX

[*Postmark 22 November 1909*] *48 U.B.S.*

My dearest Reg,

A thousand thanks for your very delightful letter. . . .

Massingham[2] thinks the country ought to be plastered with "The Horny Hand."[3] But I rather doubt the advisability! No one would feel he could vote on either side, and the money spent in fitting up polling-booths would be all thrown away.

I am off to Paris tonight, and so cannot come to tea on Wednesday.

I wish you were I, for my mission is one that you would really revel in: to present myself, in ceremonious attire and just a hint of half-mourning, and in company with Bancroft,[4] Hare,[5] Wyndham, and Bourchier[6] (I representing Herbert[7]) at the *Théâtre Français* on Wednesday at noon, there to offer to Claretie[8] and all the *sociétaires* a bronze medallion of dear old Coquelin[9] (executed from a design by Forbes-Robertson!!).[10] I feel you would rise to the occasion,

[1] Chapman Brothers, frame-makers and picture-cleaners in King's Road, Chelsea.

[2] Henry William Massingham (1860–1924) was editor of the *Daily Chronicle* (1895–99) and of the *Nation* (1907–23).

[3] One of Max's caricatures shown in the New English Art Club's Winter exhibition 1909.

[4] Squire Bancroft, English actor-manager (1841–1926). Knighted 1897.

[5] John Hare, English actor-manager (1844–1921). Knighted 1907.

[6] Arthur Bourchier, English actor-manager (1864–1927).

[7] Who had been knighted in the summer.

[8] Jules Claretie (1840–1913), French dramatist, critic, and manager of the Comédie Française from 1885.

[9] Constant-Benoît Coquelin *aîné*, French actor (1841–1909), had died on 27 January.

[10] Johnston Forbes-Robertson (1853–1937), the actor-manager, had been an art-student before he was on the stage, and painted a number of portraits and other pictures.

with Gallic gusto and solemnity, whereas I shall probably lose command of my features—as at Freeling's funeral.[1] . . .

Your affectionate MAX

Monday night [*7 February 1910. Postmark 8 February*]
Café Tourtel, Paris

My dearest Reg,

Chantecler[2] is *magnificent*. So, at least, I gathered from the hints about the rehearsal, in the London papers this morning. I hope to get in somehow and somewhere tomorrow evening. I am going to call on Jean Coquelin, to see what can be done.

Meanwhile, sitting here after dinner (or rather supper) I feel impelled to write to the old Parisian, of whom Paris so much reminds me always, though I have only twice been here at the same time as you—the first time only for one night, when I came here from Boulogne. I never feel that you are English, or see you as anything but a brilliant *visitor* to London. *I* am not English, am something vague, whereas you are so definitely Parisian, in your views of life and art and everything; and the Savile becomes the Café Savile when you come into it; and even Merton is, in retrospect, the barracks in which you did your conscript service.

Paris, I am bound to say, smells horrible, and 'orrid, tonight; and I feel that typhoid may rear its head at any moment—and I shall be glad to get back as soon as duty lets me.

Your affectionate MAX

I have "descended" at the Castille, where they seemed neither glad nor surprised to see me. Their only emotion seemed to be pride in the electric light and the hot water, both of which have been restored after the *inondations*. The lift is still deranged.[3]

[1] Canon Freeling died in his rooms in Merton on 10 January 1892, and the funeral service was almost certainly in the college Chapel.

[2] A verse-play in four acts by Edmond Rostand, first produced at the Théâtre de la Porte Saint-Martin on 7 February 1910, with Lucien Guitry as Chantecler and Jean Coquelin as Patou. Max wrote about it in the *Saturday Review* of 12 February.

[3] In January 1910 France suffered its worst floods for centuries, and on 25 January *The Times* reported that "nearly one half of France is under water." The Seine burst its banks, and a great part of Paris was out of action for days or weeks.

My dearest Reg,

This time I have not merely the excuse of being a bad correspondent—a person who *wants* to write and puts off the writing because he feels his letter will be dull. I have the good excuse that I
did not wish to write without giving you a piece of news about
myself which you of all people ought to hear—a piece of news
which, from day to day, I thought I might be in a position to
divulge, but which till now I have had to keep secret.

And this news (as perhaps you are already guessing) is that I am
going to be married! Whether in a church or in a registry-office, is
not settled. Nor is it settled on *which* day of next week the ceremony
will be. Probably Wednesday. I am very happy in the prospect of it.
Florence is the one woman with whom I could be always and wholly
happy, and the one woman apart from whom I could not be happy.
I count myself extraordinarily fortunate in having, after my various
driftings and pleasantries and narrow escapes, had Florence vouch-
safed to me. To me she represents the achievement of happiness,
happiness for good and all. We shall be rather poor, financially,
but able to live without discomfort or anxiety: neither of us has
"expensive tastes." Very likely we shall live in Italy. In tomorrow's
Saturday appears my valedictory article.[1] I have some money "in
hand"—some of it from (this is a dead secret. Don't breathe it to
Carfax or to anyone) "Leicester Brown"[2] on the strength of a
retrospective exhibition of my caricatures, to be held next year.
And other money is in prospect (Kegan Paul, per Frederick Whyte,[3]
wants the right of pre-emption of "Meanwhile"[4]—which will
amount to a tidy sum). Florence and I will be all right, in point of
bread and butter. I think I shall be able to do a good deal of work,
now that I am quit of dramatic criticism. I shall first devote myself
to the Alexander play.[5] My mother and Con and Aggie are all very

---

[1] "Habit" (*Saturday Review*, 16 April 1910), reprinted in *Around Theatres*.
[2] Ernest Brown, joint-proprietor of the Leicester Galleries.
[3] Author, journalist and publishers' scout (1867–1941). His *A Bachelor's
London* (1931) was one of the most savagely annotated and "improved"
books in Max's library.
[4] Presumably a book which Max projected but never wrote.
[5] See note, p. 220.

much delighted, though I suppose they will miss me. Dearest Reg, dearest of all my friends, I am sure you will be glad at my happiness.

Your affectionate MAX

All this is to you alone. Except you and my family, no one is to know till after the event.

Monday [Postmark 18 April 1910]   *Savile Club*

My dearest Reg,

What can I say to thank you? You will have had my wire: "overwhelmed." I very truly am. It is *much* too good of you. I don't feel I ought to take it; and at the same time I am afraid to send it back. Nobody but you would have thought of giving me a present like that, and not even from you should I ever have expected a present like that. I have not seen Florence yet today: she will be as staggered as I am (and as my people are!). I wired "date Monday." And on Monday the marriage will be.[1] I do hope you will be there: I did not like to *ask* you to come, because I thought you might not want to be hauled out of your beloved Paris. But without your presence the marriage would seem hardly valid. Meanwhile, don't breathe it to a soul: I am telling *no one* outside the family. I shall just have an announcement in *The Times* or somewhere, a day or two after. Florence and I equally hate anything in the nature of a to-do. Also, don't mention that we *may* live in Italy. One thing is certain: we shan't live in *London*, but somewhere that is uncomplicated and pleasant and easy and un-fussy and lets one be oneself. And wherever it is, there must be a great deal of my dearest Reg. Just what you say of Florence, she has often said of you—almost in the same words. Of all my charming and un-charming acquaintances I want to get rid: they are a charming or un-charming nuisance, taking up one's time—clogs and drags. Henceforth I am going to be as exclusive as the Duchess of Buccleuch.[2] There will be no

[1] Max was married to Florence Kahn at the Paddington Registry Office on 4 May 1910. His mother and Reggie were the witnesses.
[2] Louisa Jane Hamilton (d. 1912), daughter of the first Duke of Abercorn, married (1859) William Henry Walter Montagu-Douglas-Scott (1831–1914), who succeeded his father as sixth Duke of Buccleuch 1884. The

184

FLORENCE KAHN

one but Florence, and my people, and *you*—one or two others *perhaps*, such as the Nicholsons, but I am not sure. I shall always keep your beautiful letter, dearest Reg.

Your loving friend MAX

Sunday [Postmark 15 May 1910]   *The White Cottage, Hythe*

My dearest Reg,

It is delightful here basking in the garden, with what we fondly pretend is a good view of the sea, though we don't really look much at anything but each other, and are as happy as the day is long (and this though June 21st is almost come).

Florence cooked a beautiful luncheon, and I ate so much that she thinks me greedy. Do write to us, please. We send you our fondest love, and all our thanks for all that you have been to us at the time of our marrying.

Your affectionate and loving MAX

Narrowly though I watch Florence, I detect in her no touch of Anne Hathaway.

24 June 1910   *Grand Hotel Regina Elena, Santa Margherita*

My dearest Reg,

Florence was so delighted with your letter—and so was I; and this letter is primarily a bait to catch another one from you. Please "rise" promptly! Also, please do cause the new book[1] to be posted here, so soon as copies of it are sent to you. All best wishes for a great success. Florence (you will be glad to hear) continues to justify the confidence I reposed in her; and altogether she is—there is no other word for it—divine, and seems all the time like a thing too good to be true, and I doubt whether I shall ever become used to being with her. Even Paris, which I had never liked or got the

---

Duchess was Mistress of the Robes to Queen Victoria and Queen Alexandra, and was described by *The Times* obituarist as "a lady—and a very great lady—of the old school."

[1] Reggie's eleventh and penultimate novel, *Count Florio and Phyllis K.* (1910).

hang of, was delightful to me by reason of my being there with
Florence, and I look back on it with affection. This is a not bad
hotel, and not dear, and the great point is that our bedroom has a
balcony "bang on to" the sea. (I am writing on this balcony to you.)
We generally bathe in the mornings, from our bedroom, and the
water is more than tepid, but I can't say that we cut much of a dash
in it: three strokes is the utmost one can swim in it, as it is filled to
the brim with rocks and crags which arrest one on every side.

Prévost[1] would be very grave about our exploits, and Lindemann
would toss his beard. On land we have more chance of impressing
the peasants—Florence by the studied simplicity and appropriate-
ness of her costumes, I by a wild and orchidaceous elaboration,
which includes the wearing of three of Florence's diamond rings
on the little finger of my left hand. I suppose these would look all
wrong at the Savile; but here they are quite the thing. I am also
growing a *barbiche*. Yesterday I inadvertently shaved off one half
of it, so have to begin all over again.

I have seen not a single English person here, except, one day,
"Dodo" Benson, who looked extraordinarily out of the setting, in
a blue flannel blazer and white canvas shirt and tennis shoes, all
fresh from the banks of the Cam. He was hurrying along, seemingly
on his way from playing fives with the Bursar of Caius, and going
to have tea with Bobbie Mainwaring of Peterhouse. The only
other known person whom I have seen since England was Rostand.[2]
Him I saw in the Rue de la Paix, dashing out of a motor into a
hosier's, followed by a satellite to whom he was talking over his
shoulder with intense nervous vitality. He looked very ill, and was
as overdressed for Paris as I am for Santa Margherita. I waited
outside the shop to see him again, and occasionally peered through
the window where I could see him choosing ties with immense
anxiety and gesticulation and "patter"; and there he still is, for
aught I know, for after a while I decided I could wait no longer.
His likeness to poor Clyde is as amazing in figure and movement as

[1] Camille Prévost, a retired army officer and fencing-master who had
taught Maupassant. See Appendix D, pp. 303–04.
[2] Edmond Rostand (1868–1918), French dramatist whose plays *La
Princesse Lointaine* (1895), *Cyrano de Bergerac* (1897) and *L'Aiglon*
(1900) had taken Paris by storm.

it is in face: the two men (barring Rostand's thinness) are doubles, and must have been born under the same star. Seeing Rostand was really painful, in that respect: I wished so much it was he who had died, and dear old Clyde who had been spared to flutter and shine, and to write new plays and buy new ties.

This letter seems to have drifted away from local news; but there is nothing to write about except Florence, who can't be put into words; the aforesaid epithet "divine" is all that can be done in that way. She has, however, a constant succession of nicknames, such as the Gazy-Bo Girl, the Houri-Housewife, Graminivorous Gertie, the Pittsburg Virago, and many others. And one of our eternal topics is you.

Your loving friend   MAX

Sunday [21] *August 1910.* [*Postmark 22 August*]   Grand Hôtel
Rapallo

My dearest Reg,

You can't think how I revelled in your letter and all its Dieppe news. The unbeardedness of the host of the Tribunaux is certainly a grave blow. Also the idea of his becoming a croupier! "Ὦ δώματ' Ἀδμήτει', ἐν οἷς ἔτλην ἐγώ,"[1] etc. But how, exactly, has the Olympian's slavery come about? I should have thought the Tribunaux was a great "property." Please explain. Also, tell me how it is *chez* Lefèvre. How is the food this year? And is Prévost keeping his eye on Frank Richardson? (Please give him my affectionate regards.) And is Rivard[2] liking everything you say "immensely"? And how are Ada and Violet?[3]—to whom my love. Do write, and tell me how you are, and how your new novel is getting on. I long to receive the *Autumn* novel. I have been doing a lot of work here— or rather *working a lot*, for progress is slow. I wish Nature would

[1] "O hall of Admetus, where I suffered" (Euripides, *Alcestis*, line 1). The next line (θῆσσαν τράπεζαν αἰνέσαι θεός περ ὤν) means "To be content with a servant's table, though a god." The pun is on τράπεζα, which means both a table and a gaming-table.
[2] Except that he was a French resident of Dieppe, I have failed to discover anything about him.
[3] Ada Leverson and her daughter.

sometimes "take the pen and write for me";[1] but this she steadily refuses to do; and I get along at the old rate of ten to fifteen words an hour. Rather more than this, really; and anyhow it is a great relief not to have *Thursday*[2] cutting in, to leave one prostrate, and then looming up again before one has quite recovered. I hope you'll like what I've done. I *think* you will.

It has been a delightful time here, with my darling Florence. Rapallo is not in itself so sympathetic a place as Santa Margherita. One can imagine Charles Goetz in it. And Clement Shorter, in all the hideousness of his holiday mood, and with Mrs Clement Shorter, might almost, on days when the sun shines not, be somewhere round the corner. It is very *hotel-y*. But still very pretty. And we have a charming room, with a huge window looking down on to a huge palm tree and out to sea; and for some reason the mosquitoes are very much less "owdacious" than they were in Santa Margherita; and I fancy there will be no mosquitoes at all up at the place to which we are presently going. Florence wrote to you a week or more ago, and told you of our plan. Here are some details. We are taking the place for a while, and might perhaps stay there for a long while if the air suits us. Rapallo itself, I think, is rather relaxing; but our place is much higher up. It is on the road between here and Zoagli—about twenty-five minutes walk *up*, and twenty *down*. On one side of the road is the cliff, very olive-ish, going sheer down to the sea. On the other side of the road is the cliff again, going up into the sky; and our place is on this side. The ground floor is high, having been built by the landlord as a garage, and except as a garage could be of no use to anyone but to us, to whom it is useful as a sort of pedestal, raising us above the road and giving us a good view across to the sea. The landlord's idea was to let the garage and the flat over it separately. However, we don't want to have motors living under us; so we have taken the garage with the flat. It makes hardly any difference in the rent; and Florence

[1] "Nature herself seems . . . to take the pen out of his hand, and to write for him with her own bare, sheer, penetrating power." (Matthew Arnold on Wordsworth, originally as introduction to the Golden Treasury selection of Wordsworth's poems, 1879, reprinted in *Essays in Criticism*, Second Series, 1888.)

[2] When, for twelve years, Max had had to hand in his weekly article to the *Saturday Review*.

says it will be very useful for keeping an ice-chest in; so that is all right. The flat above has four rooms on the sea-side—and on the other side a bathroom and a dressing-room and a kitchen; all small, but just about the right size. And the roof itself is built as a terrace, with a balustrade all around, and a heavenly view out to sea. And

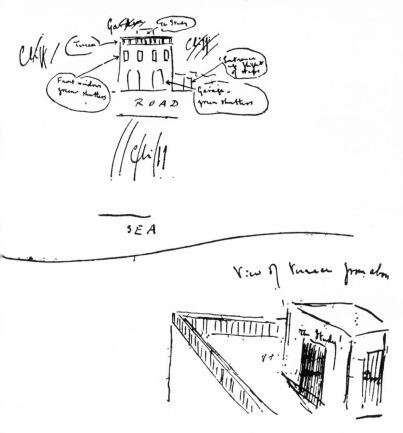

in the middle of the terrace stands a small room, which will be my "study." And behind the terrace—on the side remote from the sea —is the garden; a small and rough garden up the side of the cliff. It looks rather dried up, but seems to be luxuriant, all the same; and we have a fig-tree and a vine, and an orange-tree and an almond-tree, and a lemon-tree. There are also tomatoes.

So now you know all about it! Florence and I think the place is really delightful (it is brand-new, by the way: plaster hardly dry). But I am afraid that you, as having devoted so much earnest thought to the subject of flats in general, will find many drawbacks in this one in particular. When will you come and find them, please? There is a spare bedroom awaiting you.

Love from us both.

Your loving friend   MAX

I have, of course, been much immersed in the Crippen case.[1] The Paris *Daily Mail* was a great daily excitement throughout the week of Crippen's flight. Florence at first disapproved of my great enjoyment of the whole matter; but was gradually drawn in to the vortex; and surprised me somewhat, one day, by starting the subject of the *Dickman* case, quite of her own accord![2] I always insisted to her that the people staying in this hotel had strong suspicions that I was Dr Crippen and that she was Miss Le Neve. And whatever we did seemed to lend colour to the suspicion. "They seemed animated and cheerful at meals"—"they kept themselves to themselves"—"they used to go out daily to buy the Paris edition of the *Daily Mail*"—etc. etc.

Tuesday [*15 November 1910. Postmark 16 November*]
Villino Chiaro, Rapallo

My dearest Reg,

No excuse, except the usual one: that I am such a wretched correspondent—always meaning to write and *wanting* to write, but

[1] Hawley Harvey Crippen (b. 1862) was an American doctor, who had come to England in 1900. At the end of January 1910 his wife disappeared from their London home. When the police began to investigate, Crippen fled to America with his mistress, Ethel Le Neve. The remains of Mrs Crippen were found under her own cellar floor, and on 31 July Crippen was arrested on board ship off the coast of Canada. This was the first time wireless telegraphy had been used for the interception of a criminal. Crippen's trial opened at the Old Bailey on 18 October; three days later he was found guilty, and on 23 November executed at Pentonville.
[2] On 6 July 1910 at Newcastle-on-Tyne John Alexander Dickman was found guilty of murdering John Innes Nisbet in a railway carriage on 18 March. Despite an appeal and a widely supported petition for his reprieve, he was executed on 10 August.

always brought up short by the prospect of sending a dull and inane letter in return for an amusing one full of news. Lack of news—you see I am making excuses after all! It is no news merely to say that I am consciously happy during sixteen hours out of the daily twenty-four, and unconsciously happy during the other eight; and yet that is the only news I have. What goes to constitute that happiness would make a poor recital. Absolutely nothing "happens." Florence and I "see" nobody: there is no one to see—except a good many German tourists who all look exactly alike. There are Italian peasants and tradesmen, to whom I say "*Buon Giorno*" with a singularly pure accent; but I haven't conversed with a single human being except Florence since we left England. Stay! I *did* see Edmund Davis,[1] who was driving a motor-car into Rapallo and stopped to greet me, about two weeks ago; and in Paris I met a man with whom I had been at Charterhouse. Otherwise Florence has had the exclusive privilege of hearing my remarks during the past six months. The sun shines, and the sea shines under it, and I eat a good deal twice a day, and the camellias are just beginning to bloom, and the oranges and lemons are ripe, and I do a great deal of work, and everything goes on from day to day with a heavenly sameness of peace and happiness.

I read more here than I used to in London, and one of the great delights in this kind has been *Count Florio and Phyllis K.* Florence and I roared with laughter over so many things in it. I explained to her the nature of Herbert Horne and of Punch Hodgkinson,[2] so as to accentuate for her the fun of the presentments of them; not that there was any need of that; for the two re-created figures are perfect in themselves—really lovely. I wonder if P.H. or H.H. has "had his attention drawn" to the book. The former would be quite pleased, I am sure; but the latter would be wounded to the core. The whole book is in your very best light vein, I think, and capital as a story, so neat in construction from beginning to end. I hope it has been *selling* well? "Come with me to a little place I know of, and have a final *méringue*" is of many passages the one that outstands for me most gloriously. I love also the Ladies White, Brown,

[1] Wealthy patron of art and artists (d. 1939). Knighted 1927.
[2] Possibly Thomas Hodgkinson (d. 1933), who contributed light verse to *Punch* from 1909 to 1933.

etc. I seem to see Hichens[1] in the midst of them—their pet and trump-card. Some day you *must* make a figure of Hichens: you would give him so exquisitely, starting from the Buckingham-Palace-Road-and-*Gentlewoman* period of him and pursuing him throughout his motor-tour with the late Duchess of Manchester.[2] His mourning for that great lady would make a good chapter in itself, I am sure.

This reminds me that he is one of the people I have just been caricaturing: I have had and am having a great bout of caricature, and am glad to think this latest batch is the best I have done. I was rather afraid that, not being on the spot, I might not be able to work up the sense of intimacy and *au-courant*-ism that is needful for caricaturing. But all is well. I suppose the exhibition will be at the end of April.[3] That was the date that Leicester Brown desired. And according to that date will be my presence in London. Don't mention the exhibition to Bobbie; because I am not sure that I be-haved quite well in not giving Arthur Clifton[4] the refusal of the exhibition; and I would like A.C. to know first through *me* that I have deserted him. However, I daresay A.C. knows already. And after all it will be a different sort of exhibition from what they could have at Carfax: a *retrospective* and rummage-sale affair, with the new caricatures thrown in to give point and be a bait for the rest. (Hichens I have done in the desert, with a tremendous sunset effect, dictating to a rather plain typist, who, we may be sure, is in love with him, and to whom, when the long day's work is over, he talks with a marvellous insight into what she takes to be the secrets of her starved soul.)[5]

---

[1] Robert Smythe Hichens (1864–1950) had followed *The Green Carnation* (1894) and *The Londoners* (1897) with immensely popular novels such as *The Garden of Allah* (1905) and *Bella Donna* (1909).
[2] Consuelo Yznaga del Valle, an American of Cuban extraction, married the eighth Duke of Manchester in 1876. She died in November 1909. For an account of her motor-tour, see Hichens's autobiography, *Yesterday*, (1947).
[3] Max's first exhibition at the Leicester Galleries opened on 24 April 1911, after a Private View on 22 April.
[4] Arthur Bellamy Clifton (1862–1932) was a solicitor who gradually be-came an art-dealer. In 1898 he was one of the founders of the Carfax Gallery in Ryder Street, where Max's first four exhibitions of caricatures were held.
[5] This drawing, entitled "Dawn (and Mr Robert Hichens, not less punctual) in the Desert," was shown in the 1911 exhibition.

Zuleika has had to stand aside for the caricatures; but within a few days, when I shall have finished the essentials of the caricatures, *Zuleika* will be gone on with and at last completed. I do hope you'll like her. It does seem such a pity to Florence and me that you cannot go further afield than Paris. *When will* you be able to? We both long for you to stay here, and we are sure we would make you happy and comfortable. I am glad dear old George's new book[1] is so good. *The Finer Grain*[2] has been a great delight here. That and *Count Florio* are all the fiction I have read (no, I forget Arnold Bennett's new long novel—rather a pale reflex of the *Old Wives*, but interesting).[3] I thought G.K.C.'s *What's Wrong with the World?* very cheap and *sloppy*, though with gleams—gleams of gas-lamps in Fleet Street mud and slush. Your letter to Florence was so amusing, and made us laugh so much. Do write again, and I will write (even though this sort of letter is all I have to offer) more promptly. Florence sends you her best love, and she will write to you tomorrow.   Always your loving old friend   MAX

22 *December 1910*   *Villino Chiaro*

My dearest Reg,

A very happy Christmas and New Year to you. The New Year here seems quite a conceivable thing; but *Christmas* seems very odd indeed, what with the sunshine and the foreign language and the absence of shops with Christmas cards, etc. . . .

I am so glad George's book has been selling well. Do write to me soon, please, though it has been almost a luxury lately to feel that *you* owed *me* a letter, instead of the other way round.

Florence and I are just as happy as ever. We always talk much about you, and long for the time when you will visit us. I hope you will like my new caricatures: there are more than thirty of them now. Florence sends her best love and wishes to you and so do I.

Ever your affectionate   MAX

[1] *People and Questions* (1910), a book of essays by G. S. Street.
[2] Henry James's last book of short stories, published in October 1910.
[3] *Clayhanger*, published in September 1910.

Wednesday [*15 February 1911. Postmark 16 February*]
Villino Chiaro

My dearest Reg,

Thank you for two delightful letters; and also for three delightful books. And very soon I shall be able to thank you in person; for I shall be coming to London on—well, I don't know what date yet; but just about March 20th, and shall be at Upper Berkeley Street for a month. Florence will not be coming, because we cannot quite afford the expense. (Not that we are "hard-up" at all: only we haven't money left over for extra things.) So I must come alone. My exhibition opens on April 22nd. A few of the caricatures I cannot put the finishing touches to until I have paid a flying-visit to the House of Commons! I shall also have to see Arnold Bennett (who, I suppose, is at Fontainebleau; so that I shall catch him on my way through Paris). I also want to do Garvin.[1] I have been having the same perfectly and unsurpassably happy time here with my darling Florence. The flat is now complete to the last detail. All very simple, but very nice indeed, and not at all "New-Englishy." We long for you to come and stay in it, for as long as you can, and as soon as you can. The winter is now over, it seems, and during the past month I have spent many whole days basking on the terrace. And the winter itself was very mild. It is an adorable climate—for people who don't care about violent pick-me-up air.

I have been having great artistic pleasure in *Zuleika*. She is now over sixty-six thousand words long; and will be just about seventy-one thousand altogether. I am glad now I didn't go on with her when I first began her; because I am sure she wouldn't have been as good as she is now. The early part is good; but the later is better —stronger and suppler (*unberufen!*). How really delightful G.S.S.'s essays are—quite his very best.

Belloc's *Verses*[2] also have been a great treat: a lot of absolute chaotic rot, as in all the work of that gifted young writer, but splendid things abounding too. I love the address to the Balliol men in the war; don't you? Chesterton doesn't wear well at all,

[1] "Mr J. L. Garvin, giving ideas to the Tory Party" was shown in the April exhibition at the Leicester Galleries.
[2] Hilaire Belloc's second volume of poems, published in December 1910.

though I'm not sure whether it is that he has lost his quality or merely that he hasn't acquired a new quality to keep me interested. You don't say anything about your new novel. See how much I have said about mine; and follow my example, if you please.

Many thanks for the *Academy*, and the amusing inscription in it. I heard in every line of F.H.'s letter the fruity splendours of his well-remembered voice; always music to me.[1] But it made me feel very Rip-Van-Winkleish to find no Alfred Douglas and no Crosland.[2] When did they go? And why? Do let me know. The new editor seems to be "no scholard": I was much amused by the review of Maurice Baring's book, in which the writer said what a delightful and characteristic touch of Mr Baring's it was to represent Socrates as married to a shrew!![3]

I have been made to feel R-V-W-ish in another way by the arrival of a long-miscarried copy of the *Saturday*, dating from the early days of the recent General Election.[4] I am told that "the results so far are not unsatisfactory," and "we hazard the conjecture that the Government will once more have recourse to a Conference;" also "we are convinced that many of the Radical victories in London have been won by personation." It is extraordinarily fascinating reading. And I think that to get at the heart of journalism, and to savour the full sweet essence of it, one should never see a newspaper till it is about three months old, perhaps even a

[1] "Shaw on Shakespeare," an Open Letter to Bernard Shaw from Frank Harris, which appeared in the *Academy* of 11 February. It was an answer to Shaw's long and adverse review of Harris's play *Shakespeare and His Love* in the *Nation* of 24 December 1910 (reprinted in Shaw's *Pen Portraits and Reviews*, 1931).
[2] Douglas edited the weekly *Academy*, 1907–10, and owned it 1908–10. During that time he and his unsavoury henchman, T. W. H. Crosland (1868–1924), were involved in considerable litigation. In 1910 they brought an unsuccessful libel action against R. F. Horton and the *Daily News* for saying the *Academy* had passed into "Roman hands," and soon afterwards Douglas sold the paper.
[3] One of the scenes in Maurice Baring's *Diminutive Dramas* (published December 1910) is between Socrates and Xantippe.
[4] As a result of the General Election of December 1910 the Liberals (Asquith) had 272 seats, the Unionists (Balfour) 272, Labour 42, and the Irish 84.

trifle older. I gather that Hugh Walpole has had a success with his new book.[1] Do you see him sometimes?

Well, goodbye, dearest Reg. Florence sends you her best, and so do I.   Your loving friend   MAX

Wednesday [*19 April 1911*]   *48 Upper Berkeley Street*

My dearest Reg,

How very sorry for you I am! And how sorry we all are! To-morrow's dinner is robbed of all its glory.

The great bore is that I must not come and visit you. As I said before (when you *hadn't* influenza), I shouldn't at all mind the risk of infection for myself; only I should be so afraid of giving it to my mother, for whom of course it would be dangerous. I am off on Sunday morning, and it is hateful to think I shan't be able to see you again. You certainly must not *think* of going to the Private View. The pictures won't run away: you can see them all just as well when you are entitled to be out and about. And you certainly won't be entitled next Saturday. Influenza is a dangerous thing if it isn't taken seriously. You have to stay indoors and keep warm till you are really rid of it. But all this you know as well as I do. I will call "to inquire" tomorrow morning. I post you a copy of the *Sketch*. It contains a photograph of me. I don't mean that this is a sovereign remedy for influenza. Good night.   Your loving friend   MAX

[*Postmark 21 April 1911*]   [*London*]

Dearest Reg,

Thank you for your very charming letter. You must indeed be better to be able to write such a letter. I was glad this morning to hear you were better. I left you a couple of papers. Good heavens, what a scrawl this is! I write in a Bedford Street post-office, with an umbrella under my arm, and with gloves on. You were *very* much missed last night. Three quarters of the fun was gone. Don't happen to mention *Zuleika* (I mean my negotiations about the book)

[1] *Mr Perrin and Mr Traill*, Walpole's third novel, published on 25 January 1911.

to any one. Sydney Pawling[1] is immensely keen. But, for reasons which (as Bobbie would say) I will explain to you another time, I don't want any one to know as yet that I am Heinemannising. I will write to you again tonight, and will bring you round some daily papers which will give you a sort of Private View after all.

Your loving friend   MAX

Saturday [*22 April 1911*]   *48 Upper Berkeley Street*

Dearest Reg,

Here are three evening papers, and many thoughts for you from me. You and the telegraph girls between you have produced a monument of Latinity, which has delighted me (though what Mr Tidd,[2] a Draco in just these matters, would have said, I tremble to think!). And Mamma has been delighted with the beautiful tulips and carnations. She will write and thank you. It was very charming of you to send them. *Une bonne presse* altogether, isn't it? I went in for a minute or so before luncheon, not into the actual room, but outside. Shaw, Colvins, Gosses, Laurence Irving,[3] were "among those present." I do hope the show will do well and won't have been killed by the more-than-usual fanfaronade. I shall go in again before closing-time, to hear how things have gone. Meanwhile *packing*. And tomorrow the high seas. It is a real grief to be going away without seeing you, dearest of all friends. I will write to you as soon as I arrive at Rapallo.   Your loving friend   MAX

Saturday night [*22 April 1911*]   *48 Upper Berkeley Street*

My dearest Reg,

What a letter![4] And what joy it has given me! I rejoice in your

[1] William Heinemann's partner.
[2] Reggie's old tutor, according to Max, but I cannot find his name in the Merton or Oxford records.
[3] Laurence Sydney Brodribb (1871–1914), younger son of Sir Henry Irving, was actor, author and manager.
[4] On receipt of the reviews of the exhibition in the evening papers Reggie had written:

April 22 [1911]   13 Little Grosvenor Street
My dearest Max,

The papers have sent up my temperature and I am trembling with excitement. I suppose my Influenza has made me very susceptible to rejoicing. It certainly is, *unberufen*, very pleasant and jolly to have made this sort of wild public success—newspaper success, I mean. It remains to be seen whether this means a definite *commercial* success. I don't think the sales depend much on the public prints, though these probably help. Fourteen of the drawings are sold—most of them "important" ones; and this I think very satisfactory. B and P[1] had hoped to sell more today. But my experience is that the first day or so is not the most important. Wasn't Bobbie's

---

emotion, for I feel as weak as—well—I can think of nothing better than a cat. I asked "the doctor" if I could go to the private view after all, and he said I had better not, but I might if I wanted to very much—and now I feel too weak to do so. So I shall think of you instead and go on Monday with the hoi polloi. It is a terrible grief to me, but as writing people draw on their own experiences, it will give me copy for the story I told you about, the old man who gets his pleasures and excitements vicariously while sitting in a chair at home.

You are going to have a *great* success, perhaps the greatest of your life so far as public recognition is concerned, though of you it may be said—what is not a safe axiom—the artist revolves in a cycle of masterpieces. Though I make bold to say that not all your *likenesses* are equal. You have made a position which no one else has in England, a position which only the favourites of Paris get. It must be lovely. I like to see also that they are beginning to acknowledge your "biting" power. A caricaturist such as you, a satirist of the first and purest water, is not properly treated when people say that "his work can never give offence." "Amiability" is not your most outstanding quality in your work, any more than "gentleness" was in Napoleon's. And I see signs now that "the old country" is waking up to the danger of having you about. I rejoice, I rejoice, I rejoice.

And now you are going back to your vineyard and your wife, and your little paved terrace. You will cool your head by the Mediterranean after setting the Thames on fire. What a life!!

Send me news of *Zuleika*. I always fancied Heinemann for you, and I hope you will publish with them. It should come out while we are still sizzling (or whatever the word is) with the Leicester Gallery.

My dear love to Florence and to you. May you make great sums of money and come and spend some of it in the old country. But, really, I feel that it is better to spend it in other places. But it will make flying visits possible. I should have liked to have sent something back with you "for the house." But not going out has prevented that, and—after all—where you are there is not much need of other furniture or decoration.

Your loving friend   REG

[1] Brown and Phillips, the proprietors of the Leicester Galleries.

notice good and witty?[1] I was also much pleased by having a *leader* in the *E. Standard*. No other exhibition of pictures has been so pampered assuredly as this. And so I go "to cool my head in the Mediterranean" very well pleased.

It is lovely to think of Florence being there when I step down from the train. She is meeting me in Genoa. And oh the happiness of being with her again and of being with her all the time.

Our "Stranger's Room" stands neatly furnished—small, but bright and pretty and comfortable, awaiting you always.

Your loving friend   MAX

Tuesday [*25 April 1911*]   *Villino Chiaro*

My dearest Reg,

How are you? Almost quite well, I do hope? Florence says you ought to spend your convalescence here. I wish you would. This seems to be just *the* moment for Rapallo. I arrived here last night. Florence met me in Genoa. Re-union with her is very lovely. I suppose I am not really happier than I have been any time in the past year here. Only, having been away for a month, I *realise* how intensely happy I am. Florence, for the past fortnight, has not been well—has been feeling weak, and not up to anything. But she is all right again now. She never told me she wasn't well, while I was away, because she didn't want to worry me. This was as wrong as it was sweet of her, and she has of course been reprimanded. But it is her excuse to you for not having answered your letter when she received it. She found that the necessary letters to me were all she could achieve in the way of writing. She is going to write to you tomorrow. The Villino looks so fresh and fair; and the sun and the sea are surpassing themselves; and lemon-blossom is the loveliest of scents, I find. And the Leicester Gallery seems even further away than it is. I wonder if you have been there. Do tell me how you think the whole show looks, and whether the new things there are "up to standard."

[1] The *Morning Post* printed a column review of the exhibition on 22 April, and the *Morning Leader* half a column on the same day. One was certainly by Robert Ross, and possibly both were.

Thank you again for the beautiful letter I had from you on Saturday.   Your loving friend MAX

Wednesday [*10 May 1911. Postmark 11 May*]   *Villino Chiaro*

My dearest Reg,

We were so happy at having the wedding-day telegram. I think you are the only person who remembered the date of the ceremony, for there was no message from U.B.S. It seems impossible that I have really been married for a whole year; for every day is a new delight and surprise to me.

Do tell me about Walter Greaves.[1] I am glad his show didn't open at the same time as mine—glad I had a full fortnight's start of this most sensational of septuagenarians. I simply cannot guess how it is that nobody seems to have known anything about him. Do explain this, and tell me details. I fancy Whistler comes very badly out of it. Is this so? You certainly ought to meet and cultivate Greaves, for the sake of your new novel: there is a distinct analogy for you to study from the life.[2]

Talking of novelists, what did you think of Arnold Bennett on

[1] Reggie had written from London on 8 May:
"Have you heard of the artist of seventy, Greaves, who was a pupil of Whistler and who did not exhibit because 'the Master' made him promise not to do so without his permission? Now he is having a boom and his pictures are selling like hot cakes." Max was much amused by the sudden appearance of Greaves (1846–1930), and there is in Merton a spoof oil-painting by Max, signed Walter Greaves.
[2] On 21 May Reggie reported:
"The Greaves bubble seems burst. Robbie says they are very bad and all a fraud, though I don't quite see how, as he says that four are obviously by Whistler and left in Greaves's studio, and he says that Greaves has altered the dates to make them seem painted before Whistler's time. *I* don't know, they seem to me very pleasing and even remarkable. They were all bought by the Goupil for a trifling sum from some shop-keeper, but they are giving Greaves a good sum as a present. Now Marchand is wondering if he has not sold them too cheap—*if* they are Whistlers. It is the fashion now to decry them. Anyway, Greaves has had his splash—a short one—and I suppose he will not be heard of again. Robbie's stern attitude is, I think, partly because Clutton Brock boomed them, and he was determined not to lose his head lest he should be found to have been hoaxed. It is a pity you have not seen them."

further acquaintance? And also tell me—this letter is very full of Miss-Dartle-isms[1]—how you thought the caricatures looked. The "sales"* have been very good—over £700 last Monday morning; and I expect there will be more before the close. I am pleased and surprised that a good many of the old and previously exhibited and neglected drawings have "gone off." Desmond MacCarthy had a capital article in the *Nation*. I haven't yet seen Filson Young's in the *Saturday*; but I hear it was very good.[2] Florence sends you her love. She wrote to you the other day, and hopes you will write to us, and so do I.   Ever your loving friend   MAX

* Putting this word in inverted commas is rather an affectation, surely.

Thursday [Postmark 25 May 1911]   *Grand Hotel, Venice*

My dearest Reg,

Good news indeed about the exhibition! Commercial success at length stares me in the face, and she is not so ugly as I had supposed from the descriptions of her.

I daresay the sales now actually exceed £1000; as the Editor of the *New Age*[3] wants to buy the John Bull series for £50, and to publish it; and I imagine that Brown would not have counted in this offer among the accomplished sales. I have written to the Editor saying he can publish the series if he makes it quite clear to the public that they are *old* drawings—historical curiosities, and nothing to do with the present moment. I suppose he will agree. I had already had from the Galleries an advance of £200; but, even allowing for this, I shall now be rather rich. So far as I had speculated on the chances of the exhibition, my main hope was that the Galleries would recoup themselves on the advance: it would have been so humiliating if they had kept the unsold drawings as security! It had never certainly struck me (I mean, of course, before the exhibition

[1] Rosa Dartle in *David Copperfield* was always asking tiresome questions "for information."
[2] Both these reviews appeared on 29 April. Desmond MacCarthy wrote: "Max's talent is the finest and most intellectual in English caricature." Filson Young (1876–1938), author, journalist and lifelong friend of Max, was editor of the *Saturday Review* 1921–24.
[3] Alfred Richard Orage (1873–1934) founded the *New Age* 1894.

opened) that the sales would exceed £400 or £500. Nor, after the opening, had I expected more than £600 at most.

By the way, £400 was the advance on *Zuleika* that I stipulated for to Pawling; and this sum Heinemann (who has now returned to England) is going to pay me on publication. So that there is no chance that the book won't be well advertised, at any rate. I get a royalty of twenty per cent in England. . . .

The *Bookman* is going to bring out a special *Max Beerbohm Number*—on the strength of the Leicester Galleries success, I suppose. (Robertson Nicoll was one of the purchasers there.)[1]

Here again is commercial success. R.N. and his kind are guided by no consideration but the amount of money a person earns. As I began this letter by talking about the exhibition, I have gone straight on, to exhaust the subject, without explaining the address of this note-paper. Our servant had to go back to an ailing father; and so, as there was no immediate prospect of another servant, Florence and I came to Venice. The delight of revisiting Venice is quintupled by Florence's seeing it for the first time.

The first day was rainy, and we were both tantalised and miserable; but since then the weather has been quite all right; and the place is as lovely as ever. Today is the feast of the Virgin; and accordingly, when the hour strikes in the clock-tower of the Piazza, large mechanical figures of the three Magi appear in file through a door under the clock and do a stiff homage to the figure of the Virgin, and then disappear through another door. This ceremony is performed hourly throughout the coming week, and is most touching and entrancing; and we shan't fail to see it as often as possible while we can—two days more: we start for home on Sunday morning.

We have not seen one single soul here that we know, though the place is very full. Some of the pigeons in the Piazza look vaguely familiar to me. Otherwise we have had our usual and delightful independence.

[1] In August 1911 the *Bookman*, of which Sir William Robertson Nicoll (1851–1923) was editor, published a long article, "Max Beerbohm; or, Art and Semolina," by George Somes Layard, together with reproductions of nineteen of Max's caricatures and three portraits of him.

Poor Frank[1] going to Switzerland with a nurse! It sounds as if he must be *seriously* ill. Is he? And is it a temporary illness, or lasting? I am so sorry.

Florence and I send you our best love, and are always looking forward to your arrival, and hoping it will be sooner than you think. *Any* time, at shortest notice, for us.

Your loving friend MAX

---

10 July 1911   *Villino Chiaro*

My dearest Reg,

I am very truly grieved by the news of Mrs Frank's death.[2] I am afraid she must have had a frightful amount of suffering in the brief span of the illness. But I am glad for her that it wasn't a long and lingering illness: she would have hated more than anyone to be an invalid with a prospect of many years of empty existence. Poor thing, though—I do so wish she were alive and well. I always enjoyed seeing her: she was always very charming and kind to me; and (it seems incredible) I had known her for more than twenty years. The first time I saw her was at breakfast in Hill Street, in my first Christmas vacation from Oxford; and I can still exactly visualise her as she came into the room behind the dining-room, looking even prettier than I had always been told she was. I have written to Bertie.[3] It would be rather too difficult to write to Frank, of course.[4] But, if you think fit, please manage to convey my sympathy.

I wonder how long you will be staying with him; and I hope you will soon be in Dieppe: it is cosy to think of you being there, at your post—reading the *D.T.* at the Tribunaux in the late afternoon, with many muttered comments on the literary and the political tendencies of that journal, and telling some friend that you are not going to the Casino tonight, but going all the same.

There is a café in Rapallo, too. I hope you will presently patronise it. It has its points, though the most salient of these is a large gilt

[1] Lawson.
[2] Mrs Frank Lawson had died of peritonitis on 1 July.
[3] Bertie Benedict, Mrs Frank Lawson's son by her first husband.
[4] Frank Lawson and his wife had been separated for some time.

inscription on the wall, recording in German that the Emperor Frederick once came there. It is very exciting to know that your novel is finished, and another begun. I am daily expecting the first proofs of *Zuleika*. Heinemann is a charming person to deal with, and (though there are commercial reasons against the idea) has consented that the book be issued in a form more like that of essays than of a novel—square-ish octavo, wide margins, etc. Such an odd feeling it is to have really finished the book (it comes to 79,000 words, some ten of which are otiose). Florence and I are both very glad. We send you our best love and thoughts.

Your loving friend   MAX

Monday [*2 October 1911. Postmark 3 October*]   *Villino Chiaro*

My dearest Reg,

Fancy your being at dear old 19 Manchester Street![1] I am so glad you are *there*, though very sorry indeed that you *are* there. I hope to hear from my people that all went, and is going, well with you—as I am very sure is the case. Had you felt there was anything the matter for long? Or was it a sudden discovery? Anyhow, it must be pleasant to have had the operation over and done with, and to be taken a lot of care of. Please give my affectionate remembrances to Sister Loveridge. Also to Nurse Sharp. I wonder if she is your nurse? And is Nurse King your night-nurse? If so, give her too all best messages from me. I wish you would tell Sister Loveridge how sorry I was to leave England this spring without having visited her, and that I was so "rushed" that I had not time to go and see anybody, and only saw *you* twice for a few minutes! I wish I could send you something for the sick-room, but there is absolutely nothing to send, except pebbles and sea-water and olives—and my love and Florence's you already have.

How *very* delightful indeed was your essay on *Books I Shall Never Read*.[2] You assuredly ought to do a whole volume of essays. You have the authentic touch—very much so. As soon as you are

[1] A nursing home, in which Max had once been a patient.
[2] Untraced.

rid of the tentacles of the *D.T.* you will, I feel sure, be inclined to write lots of essays, in the intervals of novels. I was much amused by what you told me about Bobbie and the Connaughts. I expect he will presently find that his interests in Canada necessitate a flying visit.[1]

I am much irritated by the interminable delays of the Ballantyne Press (Heinemann's printers). It is very necessary that *Zuleika* should be out not later than early October. And I haven't yet had the whole of the "terrified revise"—a revise all the more terrified because the corrections I made in the first proofs have been printed in a very slovenly way and have to be all gone over again. Heinemann says something about there having been "a printers' strike" which has thrown everything out of gear. I think the fellows ought to be shot down, as Charles Goetz would say.

How we long for your visit! Do give us some idea of when it will be. Oughtn't you to make your convalescence *here*—*D.T.* or no *D.T.*—forthwith?   Your loving friend   M A X

Saturday [7 October 1911. Postmark 8 October]   *Villino Chiaro*
                                                      Rap. It.

My dearest Reg,

How delighted are Florence and I by your very amusing and long letter. Delighted, too, that you have been doing so well and are so comfortable and happy. I remember Nurse Bailey so very well—very kind and charming she was; and please give her my best messages. We wish you were coming here at once, but will patiently await you. I hope the weather will be good when you come. January is supposed to be a good month, as a rule. There has been thunder and lightning for the past three days and nights! But this is unusual, I assure you, and is now over.

[1] On 26 July Reggie had written from London:
"Robbie, by the way, has been lunching *twice* (unlike Frank Harris) with the Duchess of Connaught, and has selected for her the books she is to take to Government House when she goes to Canada. Needless to say the works of Max Beerbohm and the entire library of fiction of Reginald Turner are going, while Hichens, who was suggested, is not on the list, as 'not nice'!'"
The Duke of Connaught was Governor-General of Canada 1911–16.

Since I wrote to you, I have had all the rest of the *Zuleika* proofs; and I gather that the book will be out promptly enough now. I hope it won't be a dead frost; but even if it *is* I shan't lose my satisfaction in having really done it just as well as it possibly *could* be done by *me*.

Please imagine a very graceful and affectionate inscription from me in the copy which you will receive direct from Bedford Street.[1] And please write again and tell us how you are.

> Love from us both.
>
> Your affectionate MAX

First Review

Messrs William Heinemann and Sydney S. Pawling, those ripe judges, write:

AUTUMN FICTION

Each Volume Crown 8vo, price 6s.

HOW Zuleika Dobson went to Oxford and became the Helen of an Undergraduate Troy is described with all the piquant wit and light, subtle, cunning satire that in his caricatures and dainty essays have made "Max" the joy of the most fastidious public. From the Duke of —— to the commonest commoner all succumb to her fatal charm, and the final universal suicide of all Oxford, headed by the Duke in all his Garter robes, is one of the most delightful pieces of extravagant comedy in the world. And there is not a misplaced word in the whole exquisite book.

ZULEIKA DOBSON
By MAX BEERBOHM

The first ten large editions have been exhausted before publication.

The book has been "crowned" in advance by the English Academy of Letters, and banned by all the Circulating Libraries.

A book for all who care for the future of the Empire.

Have YOU ordered it of your bookseller?

An Empire-Building Book.

24 October 1911   *Villino Chiaro*

My dearest Reg,

Florence and I rejoiced in your letter, and I hope you have been enjoying Brighton—a place where it is always cosy to think of anyone being, though I have never liked being there myself. Great

[1] Where Heinemann had his office.

excitement here today, because there was a deluge of rain last night, and Rapallo was more or less under water: boats in the streets—quite Venetian—but of course where *we* are, up here, no inconvenience.

I hope you are now *absolutely* recovered and have quite forgotten you ever had the operation?

Here follows a strange request: would you please tell me the colour of D'Annunzio's hair? I think you saw him in Florence. Is the effect of him *blond?* [1] I rather think his beard and moustache are a pale brown. I want to know as soon as possible, because I have to send over some caricatures (D'Annunzio figuring in one of them) for the New English. [2] *Don't* mention to anyone that I have asked you this, because of course I want the caricature to be taken as a "document"—as one of the first-fruits of residence in Italy. I expect you will have received *Zuleika* by the time this letter arrives, and I long to know what you think of her. Tell me "candidly" of course. The day of publication is *Thursday*, and *my* copies are to be sent out the day before. [3] I am afraid that a general railway strike would not send up the sales, and the news of the possibility of one is rather depressing. I hope for the best. Anyhow, there *Zuleika* is!

Ever your loving friend   MAX

[1] Reggie answered from London on 27 October:
"It is years since I saw D'Annunzio, but my recollection is that his hair was black, though not markedly so. It was thin and not fierce. He looked rather like a grave and malicious Walkley, nothing jolly or twinkly about him. And rather smaller than Walkley, and a little thinner. His beard was quite short and trimmed close."
Two days later, reinforced by an Italian friend, he wrote:
"D'Annunzio is very nearly bald and has a small pointed beard which is dark brown—or so my friend thinks—but as he is not *quite* sure I fancy the poet must dye his hair from time to time. I wish I could have been more certain. Certainly the effect of him is not blond."

[2] Max showed eight caricatures at the Winter 1911 exhibition of the New English Art Club, including one of D'Annunzio (see note, p. 281), meeting Edmond Rostand, now in the possession of Mrs Alan Bott. D'Annunzio's hair and beard are a greyish-brown.

[3] *Zuleika Dobson* was published on 26 October.

My dearest Reg,

Your news about Lydia[1] and the collar-throwing cyclist produces in me very much the sort of effect that *Zuleika* produces in *you*: horror and laughter battling in me. I don't think the news can be true, or at least it must be *distorted*. Do verify it. Find out the actual facts, and let me know. If she *has* really left Walter with anybody—on a trick-cycle or otherwise—I am awfully sorry for Walter, who was deeply devoted to her; and awfully sorry for her too, for I can't imagine her not being very much more discontented than she was in Cheyne Walk. Do tell me *la verité vraie*: Albert[2] or Tonks[3] would be sure to know.

And now for the almost impossible task of thanking you *enough* for your splendid letter, and telling you what a joy it was to Florence and me. What you say is so much more worth having, so much more interesting, than if you had said "delightful from beginning to end" or " the essence of Max" or anything of that sort. For it throws a (for me) new light on the book—a light in which *I*, however, find myself blinking and doubtful.[4] I certainly had not

---

[1] Lydia Russell (see note, p. 163). She and her husband lived at 107 Cheyne Walk, Chelsea.

[2] Albert Rutherston (1881–1953), artist, younger brother of Will Rothenstein.

[3] Henry Tonks (1862–1937), painter and teacher, was a colleague of Walter Russell at the Slade School, and was Slade Professor 1917–30.

[4] Reggie had written from London on 29 October:

"It is not so much a masterpiece as made up of masterpieces. The joy and pleasure one has in it are inexhaustible and one can dip into it anywhere and find delight. It is an astonishing piece of virtuosity, with Max in every line, and no one else capable of doing it. I do not say that it is— as a whole—an unalloyed joy to me as your work usually is, and for this reason. The exquisite reality of some of it occasionally makes the exquisite fantasy of the tragedy too poignant, so that my feelings are genuinely hurt. I *feel* the tragedy and I don't like to feel it. I can't take it as fantastic, and I weep at Katie, so wonderfully real that she might have stepped out of the pages of a purified George Moore. This is indeed a tribute to your power. I wonder if you feel this yourself in reading it. The scheme of the story does not prepare one to feel tearful or horrified, and yet one does. I can't help taking it seriously. I can't laugh, and resent the awful drowning, *till* I come to it, and then you have manipulated it sublimely, so that one gets all the sensations proper to a fantasy. After

realised that Katie and those others were at all real; and it won't be until a year or so has elapsed, to let me look at them with a fresh eye, that I shall be able to agree that they *are* real and that you haven't merely injected some of your own over-flowing humanity into them. Certainly I wanted them to *behave like* real people, within the limits of the absurdity conditioned. I wanted to forge the links of logic correctly *from my premises*; because it seemed to me that thereby— that is, by taking the characters solemnly—the fun of the absurdity would be by contrast the greater. But it never occurred to me that while I was trying to do this I was giving to the characters anything in the nature of a *real*, as opposed to a fantastical-humorous, reality. And if I have done this without knowing it—well, I have over-shot the mark; but am rather pleased at having done so; for assuredly the achievement, though it must mar the "form" of the book, makes the book more curious and interesting, and gives it the more chance of abiding in people's minds, as something to be worried about, something rather baffling.

When I say "people's" I mean of course only a few people's. I don't see how the book—whether it be what you think it, or be merely what I set myself to make it—can be anything like a popular success. But I do think it has a good chance of surviving, in either case, as a treasure for experts in fine literature, and especially for such of those experts as are, or have been, or shall have been Oxford men.

I can well imagine two literary undergraduates, fifty or more

---

reading it, and while reading it, I feel that you would do a serious story magnificently, and I don't know whether one ought to feel that just at the moment; it complicates one's emotions too much. I couldn't begin to tell you what touched or struck me most, for it all teems with strokes of genius, and to give you my favourite passages would be to present you with the book. One thing is certain. It is a classic. One can quote Zuleika and the Warden and Katie and Mrs Batch and all of them, and compare people with them and by them. It will be even better to re-read because during the first reading one is too anxious. Being master of it, one can open it at once and sink into a purple passage as on a carpet wherever the feet tread. It remains. One can imagine it being read with delight and astonishment 100 years hence. Apart from the style, it is marvellous how you present a picture in a phrase, as where 'a sudden white vertical streak slid down the sky,' and the lines which follow. What would not any novelist give to be able to do that as you do it?"

years hence, standing under the Emperors,[1] looking across the road, discussing with some heat which house was Mrs Batch's.

Yes, I think the book will survive by reason of the very beautiful writing of it, even if you aren't right about the discordant human note which would make its survival more sure.

Meanwhile, I have had press-notices good, bad, and indifferent; and am indifferent to the indifferent ones and the bad ones, because the book has its quality, invulnerable. And as for the good ones, they have none of them given me nearly as much pleasure as your good and stirring letter.

Your singling-out of that phrase about the streak of lightning is a proof that Rothenstein and Ruskin are right about reverence for nature. For the phrase was written after seeing a thunderstorm from our terrace, and was an attempt at accurate notation! The word "slid" was in the first draft "slithered" which, though more accurate really, looked rather *cherché*, and so was jettisoned. I am afraid that from a strictly meteorological point of view the weather *preceding* the storm may leave something to be desired: I don't think the thunder-clouds would have "ponderously massed themselves" at 8 a.m. and sat tight till 6 p.m. I must keep a weather-eye from the terrace, with a view to alterations in some possible new edition. I do trust Roberts[2] will put on his coat soon and fall into a senile doze, thus enabling Heinemann and Pawling to steal out on tip-toe and insert an advertisement somewhere or other.

Love from Florence and from your affectionate MAX

[1] The busts of the Roman Emperors outside the Sheldonian Theatre in Broad Street, Oxford. At first sight of Zuleika Dobson "sweat started from their brows."

"'Let that incline us to think more gently of them. In their lives, we know, they were infamous, some of them—'nihil non commiserunt stupri, saevitiae, impietatis.' But are they too little punished, after all? Here in Oxford, exposed eternally and inexorably to heat and frost, to the four winds that lash them and the rains that wear them away, they are expiating, in effigy, the abominations of their pride and cruelty and lust. Who were lechers, they are without bodies; who were tyrants, they are crowned never but with crowns of snow; who made themselves even with the gods, they are by American visitors frequently mistaken for the Twelve Apostles."

[2] Henry Chalmers (usually known as Joker) Roberts (1866–1949) was an American who had been a war-correspondent before 1903, when he joined Heinemann to edit a magazine called *The World's Work*.

P.S. As to what you say about "dramatic power"—yes, I *was* conscious that there were really dramatic scenes; for one *can* get dramatic effect without humanity (though I never would have admitted this in the *Saturday*)!

Wednesday [*Postmark 6 December 1911*]   *Villino Chiaro*

My dearest Reg,

I am longing for more news of *Orpheus*;[1] and I am so very glad you have been doing the work—you who are so very *du théâtre* and love being behind the scenes among T-lights and properties and acting-managers. Also I am glad that the difficulty about the original author has evidently been smoothed over, and that you are once more in possession. I hope you are being *paid* well? Did you make any agreement with Dana[2] at the outset? Or are you just going to receive a vague cheque from Herbert later on? I was amused at seeing in the *Daily News* a few days ago a very complacent and self-important interview granted by Mr Alfred Noyes—all about the spirit in which he had approached his task, with compliments to Sir Herbert, couched in the spirit that here was a manager with whom a great poet could work in harmony. Do you see A.N. at the theatre? I suppose he is a very ridiculous person. I wish I were in London for a day to *see Orpheus*, and Florence wishes herself there too. We must content ourselves with the now-so-near

---

[1] *Orpheus in the Underground*, a version of Offenbach's comic opera *Orphée aux Enfers*, which Tree produced at His Majesty's on 20 December 1911, with Courtice Pounds, Eleanor Parry and Lottie Venne in the chief parts. The music was by Frederic Norton, who five years later was to make his fame and fortune with the music of *Chu Chin Chow*. The libretto was ostensibly by the poet Alfred Noyes (1880–1958) and Tree, but Reggie had been called in to brighten up the lyrics and dialogue. On Christmas Day he wrote to Max from London:

"Noyes's lyrics are rather dreadful, and the best are two by *me*, which are the *only* ones which get an encore, though that of course is not my fault but that of the music."

[2] Henry Dana (1855–1921) had been general manager of His Majesty's Theatre since its opening.

prospect of seeing the saviour of *Orpheus* out here. That will be lovely indeed.

Do let us know just when you can be here. We will have great fun. You will be our first visitor except Dora (who was here in the summer) and possibly Heinemann (!) who is probably going to Capri for Christmas, in which case he is going to break his journey in Rapallo to see me. I have been doing a *rather* beautiful illustrated and grangerised copy of *Zuleika*—medallions, illustrating this and that character and incident, pasted into the margins or at the beginnings of chapters. It isn't quite finished yet, and I don't quite know what I shall do with it when it *is* finished, but sooner or later, I expect, I shall sell it. Meanwhile I shall dazzle Heinemann with it. I think he is very pleased with the reception of *Zuleika*, and so am I. There was "a sharp recovery" (as they say on the Stock Exchange) in the reviews; all the later reviews have been really fine, though none of the dithyrambs have been quite so discerning as the *Manchester Guardian's*, which I don't suppose you saw.[1] Of course I've had a lot of letters from individuals too. . . .

One rather amusing result of *Zuleika* will be a sort of little Christmas pamphlet privately printed by the Ballantyne Press, and containing two or three letters of mine to the firm—the first of these letters a furious diatribe about some misprints in *Zuleika*.[2] At

[1] A column by Dixon Scott in the issue of 1 November, headed BEAU BEERBOHM, and including these words:

"It bears the same relation to realism that music does to noise or dancing to pedestrian exercise. It is as formal as Mozart and as irresponsible as a fairy tale; fine literature it is, and yet a lark."

[2] I can find no evidence that this pamphlet ever appeared, but Max preserved copies (now at Merton) of two letters he had written to Heinemann's partner Sidney Pawling. In the first, which is dated 16 November 1911, he wrote:

"As to that word 'inexpell*a*ble,' and Messrs Ballantyne's impressive invocation of half-a-dozen dictionaries and 'the custom of 120 years' against me: I know very well how the word is spelt in dictionaries, and I further assume that Messrs Ballantyne's proof-readers have instructions (also 120 years old) to correct *in proof* any obvious mis-spelling and to query *in proof* any doubtful spelling. Of *Zuleika Dobson* I had two proofs, and in neither of them was 'inexpellible' queried. Had it been so, I should have written *stet*, and (as my nature is keen and communicative in such matters) have explained that for good reasons of Latinity 'inexpell*a*ble' is as vile a word as would be 'inelig*a*ble' or 'inaud*a*ble.' The

first the Ballantynes meant to consult their solicitors, but they calmed down, and so did I; and the end of the storm was that they thought my letters such beautiful compositions that they proposed this pamphlet. I, of course, am to receive some copies (there will be fifty printed in all) and you of course shall have one from me.

I suppose all intellectual London is tearing its hair out by the roots and throwing it in the bland blank face of Charley Brookfield.[1] He, I suppose, will just sit tight. There he is, and I don't see how they are going to get rid of him. He and Lord Spencer,[2] by the way, were born in the same year, and were both at Trinity Coll., Cambridge. Spencer, I know, was in the A.D.C.; and I assume that C.B. was also a member, and that anyhow they were "pals"—hence, after all these years and vicissitudes, the beautiful appointment. I am glad poor Hankin[3] was not spared to know of it.

I am delighted that you liked the N.E.A.C. drawings (of which, OF COURSE, Lord Morley is by far the best!). The Courtney one,

---

proof-reader, having been lax, had no possible right to suppose at the last moment that I had been so.

"As to the general typography: I am quite ready and glad to believe that all those swaying lines, those letters bobbing up, those letters slipping down, and other defects over which I had to expend so much time in correcting the proofs, and which have not wholly been purged away from the published edition, were due merely to 'a slight inequality in the alignment of this particular fount.' In all friendliness, then, I implore Messrs Ballantyne to seal up this particular fount (which is evidently our old friend the *fons et origo malorum*) for ever and ever, or to set it playing only on very special occasions—as when they are called on to print *The Confessions of a Dancing Dervish*, for example, or *The Random Memories of a Palsied Hottentot*. And then, if they will do that, I will do a drawing that shall represent them as not less beautiful than the figures on the Parthenon Frieze."

[1] Charles Brookfield (1857–1913), son of Thackeray's friend, author and playwright, had just been appointed Examiner of Plays for the Lord Chamberlain. On 26 November Reggie had written from London: "Really it is too stupid, and I expect that he will have to resign, the outcry will be too great, unless indeed those who cry have not as much power as we think." In *Mainly on the Air* (1957) Max wrote that Brookfield was "the best actor of stories I ever heard."

[2] The sixth Earl Spencer (1857–1922) was Lord Chamberlain 1905–12.

[3] St John Hankin (1869–1909), playwright and journalist.

certainly, was a very deadly thrust, and I knew it would please you, summing up your own opinion of the gentleman.[1]

Arthur Balfour's resignation[2] was rather a bore for me, as I had to cancel a charming cartoon in which he was saying to the Die-Hards "And so, though I dare say you are none of you at all restive really, I have prevailed on dear Gerald to return to public life and lead you in my stead." He was holding the dreary Gerald firmly by the wrist. But of course this drawing was no good after his resignation.[3]

I gather from the newspapers that the publishers of those John Bull cartoons have made a good many misprints.[4] But I don't care, as of course my own inscriptions on the drawings are there to explain my meaning. But from their own point of view, how silly of these publishers to go to all the expense of colour-printing, etc., and then not take the trouble to read the printers' proofs!

The series was bought for £50 by Orage of the *New Age*. He found the reproductions too expensive, and re-sold, at the same

[1] Reggie had written from London on 26 November:
"What *wonderful* caricatures in the New English. That of Courtney is of course especially designed to please me for I know better than anyone how well deserved it is: it is a bitter indictment of a man who has long abused what might have been a powerful position. The others are equally wonderful and delightful with the exception (if I may say so!) of Lord Morley, which doesn't strike me as characteristic. I have no doubt it is really the best, but even so it doesn't appeal to me."
Max's caption to the caricature of W. L. Courtney reads:
"Mr W. L. Courtney, wondering whether it is not too much to say that Mrs Thingumy's latest work ('Through Mire and Mist,' by Elizabeth Thingumy, Trashby, Stodger & Co, six shillings) may unhesitatingly be pronounced in some respects—though not, perhaps, he ventures to think, in all respects—a masterpiece, or a masterly achievement, or something of that sort."
[2] On 8 November 1911 Arthur Balfour resigned from the leadership of the Conservative Party in the House of Commons, which he had held for twenty years. His younger brother Gerald (1853–1945), after holding a number of ministerial posts, had retired to private life. In 1930 he succeeded A.J.B. as second Earl of Balfour.
[3] The drawing survived and was shown at the Leicester Galleries in 1952 at the exhibition called "Max in Retrospect."
[4] *The Second Childhood of John Bull*, Max's fourth book of caricatures, was published by Stephen Swift in November 1911.

price, to Swift. (Don't happen to mention they were sold for £50; as this low price might injure my present "market.")

We both send you our best love, and are longing to see you, and to know how soon this is likely to be. Do send more news of *Orpheus.*   Your loving friend   MAX

[*Postcard*]

[*Postmark 31 March 1912*]   [*Postmark Rapallo*]

You are being greatly missed here, and we are already looking forward to your next visit;[1] also wondering what you are doing "at the moment"—perhaps you are dining at Melini's.[2] I have done caricatures of Rodin and "*il*" D'Annunzio today.[3] The weather has much improved here, and I expect Florence was able to greet you with proper sunshine. The other Florence now takes up the tale: but it is a tale that ends as it began "you are being greatly missed here—and we are looking forward—"[4]

Saturday [*27 July 1912. Postmark 29 July*]   *Villino Chiaro*

My dearest Reg,

Forgive the long delay of this letter. I have been wanting to write, but putting it off on the chance of there being news of some sort to send to you. And now I write with *no* news of any interest to give you. We were so delighted with your letter about Berlin; and Florence said it was so exactly what she had felt when she was there some years ago.[5] When do you at length revisit England? I

---

[1] Reggie had just paid his first visit to the Villino Chiaro.
[2] A restaurant in the Via de' Calzaioli, Florence.
[3] Probably the ones exhibited at the Leicester Galleries in 1913 and published on 9 October of that year in *Fifty Caricatures*.
[4] The last eleven words are in Florence's hand.
[5] On 10 July Reggie had written from Paris:
"I have waited till I left Berlin to tell you what I thought of it. Well! I stopped in a very nice hotel Unter den Linden, the best possible place, and I arrived at the best moment when the wonderful trees hid the town a good deal and the lovely Tiergarten was at its best. But I hated Berlin and its people; it is what I imagine New York to be, a hell on earth. Heavy and monotonous buildings and an unsympathetic lot of folk. Yet it was vastly interesting to see it, and the museums are the best I have seen. The Kaiser Friedrich Museum, arranged by Bode, has the best

suppose you will remain in Dieppe more or less for the "season." It seems odd that this letter will be carried through that so familiar little portal in the Rue de l'Hôtel de Ville—possibly by that same old familiar postman with the pointed beard and the mincing gait. How is Titine? Please give her my best compliments and regards. And let me know of any changes that may be under her roof or elsewhere. What sort of a new *patron* has the Tribunaux? And are you playing baccarat much? If so, winning, I hope. And has the general *monde* in Dieppe gone on deteriorating? Please remember me to Prévost if he is there; and tell him I often think of him.

Ada Leverson has just sent me her book,[1] and it is delightful, I think—especially the Regie Temple[2] in it. We bathe every day here, of course; and I think this place is really nicest of all in the hot weather. We just live between here and the bathing *strada*, never or hardly ever going down into Rap. I have been rather busy finishing and revising my parodies, which Heinemann brings out towards the end of October,[3] and on which he seems keen: he is a very amiable publisher, and our communications are of an exquisite amenity.

Viola sings in Genoa in September. Her wedding seems to have been done in the grand manner, and I wish I had seen the *D.T.'s*

Italian collection I know and most *exquisitely* arranged. Such Donatellos and Desiderios and Verocchios I never saw, and the pictures were almost equally interesting. Potsdam also was pleasing and the gardens and Palace of Sans Souci a real joy. The Palace is a perfect example of rococo at its best, and I never liked it before. There are Lancrets and Watteaus and Paters just as Frederick the Great placed them and dusted as if they had been put there yesterday. It is really a beautiful place. I was also glad to see a bronze of Carlyle in the Town Palace of Potsdam. The whole thing is far nicer than Versailles, which I never much cared about. The street life in Berlin was extraordinary. As busy at 2 a.m. as at 2 p.m. No one seems to think of going to bed. But oh! the relief to be in France. Paris seems light and beautiful and so charming in spite of the heat. I never want to go near Berlin again, but I am glad to have been there. I had a *frisson* in passing through Hanover as I thought of our Georges and how they loved it and what it meant to them. It looked a truly detestable place."

[1] Her fourth novel, *Tenterhooks* (1912), dedicated to Robert Ross.
[2] Reginald Willock Temple (b. 1868) was an old friend of Max, Reggie and Ada Leverson. In *Tenterhooks* he appears as Vincy.
[3] *A Christmas Garland*, published on 12 October 1912.

account of it.[1] Did you know that Lord Ribblesdale[2] had proposed to her? I am thankful she didn't accept him: it would have been so very ridiculous for both of them, and for Herbert and Maud and everyone. My only authority for this news (if news it be) is Con. So for heaven's sake don't mention it to a soul, as it is very possibly quite inaccurate. I hope *The Respectful Memoirs* are going on well. I am sure you will make a splendid thing of them.

Boitano[3] is still bed-ridden; and there is a *festa* to-day at San Pantaleo; and our gardenia plant has yielded more than a hundred gardenias; and—but I fear you will be over-excited if I go on like this. Best love from us both   Your loving friend   MAX

Friday morning [*Postmark 8 November 1912*]   *Savile Club*

My dearest Reg,

The wonderful glasses have arrived.[4] Wonderful they are. I have been spending much time on the little balcony at U.B.S. scanning the horizons along Connaught Street and towards Portman Square —deciphering the mottoes of the crests on the buttons of footmen who themselves are hardly visible to the naked eye. If the glasses are like this in London, what will they not be in the clarity of Rapallo! I long to sweep the sea from the terrace. Florence is as much delighted and excited as I am. A thousand thanks. The thing will be a daily pleasure for ever.

Come in and lunch on Sunday?

Your loving friend   MAX

14 November 1912   *48 Upper Berkeley Street*

My dearest Reg,

Alas, next Wednesday Florence and I have to lunch out. We should so have loved to come. Best remembrances to Guy

[1] Viola Tree, Herbert's eldest daughter, was married to Alan Parsons at St Martin-in-the-Fields on 11 July 1912.
[2] Thomas Lister, fourth Baron Ribblesdale (1854–1925), was thirty years older than Viola Tree.
[3] Max's next-door neighbour at Rapallo.
[4] A pair of Zeiss binoculars.

Rawlence.[1] Meanwhile we look forward to seeing you here on Tuesday evening. Thank you for what you say about the cur who dared not sign his name in the *Evening Standard* but dared to say I should have adorned any age or community.[2] But let these curs yelp and do their worst. I am a little hurt, I confess, but at the same time profoundly unmoved. And if they insist on driving me back to Rapallo, it is their own look-out, and my withers are unwrung, and I merely pity them and spit on them.   Your loving friend   MAX

Wednesday [*20 November 1912. Postmark 21 November*]

48 Upper Berkeley Street

My dearest Reg,

I *am* so sorry about the lumbago. I hope it has gone and that you were able to come back to London all right?

Tomorrow—Thursday—Florence and I are going to *Drake*.[3] We have a box. Are you disengaged? If so, do come and dine here at seven o'clock and accompany us. I forget whether you have seen the play. If you have, don't mind seeing it again.

Your loving friend   MAX

23 December 1912   *48 Upper Berkeley Street*

My dearest Reg,

All best messages and Christmas and New Year wishes from Florence and from me. I am so glad you like your "quarters" and are having a pleasant time.[4] You really do seem to have left London, to all intents and purposes, almost as definitely as I have. It is a pity that the old botherationist Bobbie took those rooms underneath you, thereby leading you such a life of botheration.[5] I am sorry

[1] Novelist (b. 1888).
[2] An anonymous and favourable review of *A Christmas Garland* had appeared in the *Evening Standard* on 13 November, headed AN ORNAMENT OF SOCIETY.
[3] A patriotic play by Louis N. Parker, first produced by Tree at His Majesty's Theatre on 3 September 1912 with Lyn Harding in the chief part.
[4] This letter is addressed to 4 Rue Van Bemmel, Brussels.
[5] From 1909 to 1914 Reggie had rooms at 13 Little Grosvenor Street.

Also, he has no back
to his head — or practically
none — which I suppose
accounts for his many
tactical errors. This
is the
sort of
thing — but
I shall do
better than
this. Do
write again.
I will
write
again: this
is only

a Christmas
note: Love
from us both.
Your affectionate
Max

indeed to hear from you of the way his affairs are going. The out-
look is decidedly bad for him—as we have so often agreed. I hope
that in some unforeseen way the case may yet not come into court.
Meanwhile you are well out of Bobbie's neighbourhood: he could
only worry you and wear you down; and you have done all you
could in his true interests. We dine tomorrow at Agnes's, and will
all drink your health, of course, and shall much miss you.[1]

We go back to Rapallo at the end of next week. I have got a good
amount of subjects and ideas for caricatures in London. I was in the
H. of C. last Friday when Winston made his exciting attack on
Lord Charles Beresford.[2] Everybody seemed so delighted (including the victim, who grinned from ear to ear, but must have writhed
within). "Bonar Law[3] *is* common," but has a strong antiseptic
William-Archerish charm—seems so very *good* and *guid*; and the
way in which his Kino frock-coat rides up over his Hope Bros
collar is a perfect dream. Also, he has no back to his head—or
practically none—which I suppose accounts for his many tactical
errors. This is the *sort* of thing, but I shall do better than this.[4]

Do write again. *I* will write again: this is only a Christmas note.
Love from us both

Your affectionate MAX

Thursday [*23 January 1913. Postmark 24 January*]
48 Upper Berkeley Street
My dearest Reg,

We were hoping to hear from you again (Florence and I both
wrote to you at Brussels). I hope you are having a good time, but I

[1] Max's sister Agnes had first married Ralph Neville. A few months
after his death she married (on 8 April 1917) Edmund Francis Vesey
Knox, K.C. (b. 1865). He died in 1921 and Agnes in 1949.
[2] This occurred on 20 December during a debate on the resignation of
the First Sea Lord, Admiral Sir Francis Bridgeman (1849–1929). The
lively invective of Winston Churchill, the First Lord of the Admiralty,
filled almost a page of next day's *Times*. Admiral Lord Charles Beresford
(1846–1919) had been Commander of both the Channel and Mediterranean Fleets.
[3] Andrew Bonar Law (1858–1923), Conservative politician. Leader of the
Party from 1911. Prime Minister 1922–23.
[4] See illustration opposite.

don't know *where* exactly that good time is: I expect you will have left Brussels. Perhaps you have already pitched your tent in Rome? Do let's hear from you. We talk always so much of you, and we want some material for conversation about you. Are you writing your novel? I do hope you are.

Have you heard that G. Alexander is doing my play at the Palace next Monday?[1] He does it there for four weeks. I hope it will be a success. He is *very* good in it. So are C. M. Lowne (Robbins), Fred Kerr (Amersham) and Kate Cutler (Lady Amersham). The rehearsals are very interesting, and I am more fertile in suggestions and objections than one would have expected of me. Alexander is perfect in relation to the author—so very anxious to do exactly what I want. I get £100 for the four weeks at the Palace (£25 a week). That clears off the "advance sum" received. I am afraid *Turandot*[2] is a failure; otherwise G.A. would probably tour with *my* play (if that is a success) in provincial music-halls. If it *is* a success, I suppose it will be done in those music-halls by somebody. G.A. in the contract makes himself "sole agent" for disposal of rights—he receiving one third of profits, and I two thirds. It is a very fair and good arrangement. All this is rather egoistic, but I think you'd like to hear all about the matter. And I know you'll be glad, as I am, that the thing is *not* a curtain-raiser at the St James's. My only fear is that John Palmer,[3] a one-act play by whom G.A. had under consideration for some months, may be "not glad because of me." I think I must write him a charming letter, pointing out that he is very young and has plenty of time before him, and that his powers will mature, no doubt.

I suppose the Douglas-Ransome case is quite inevitable now.[4]

[1] Max's one-act play *A Social Success* was first produced by George Alexander at the Palace Theatre on 27 January 1913. It was published in *A Variety of Things* (1928).
[2] *Turandot, Princess of China*, a musical play by Karl Vollmoeller and Jethro Bethel. It opened at the St James's on 18 January 1913, but survived only twenty-seven performances and lost George Alexander more than £6000.
[3] John Leslie Palmer (1885–1944), author and journalist, had succeeded Max as dramatic critic of the *Saturday Review* in 1910.
[4] Arthur Ransome had published a biographical and critical work on Oscar Wilde in 1912. Lord Alfred Douglas was not mentioned in it by name, but he nevertheless brought a libel-action against Ransome. The

What a pity! I hope Bobbie will come out of it unscathed. Florence and all the family send you their best love. Do write to your loving friend   MAX

We go back to Rap next week. I have been doing a lot of caricatures here—doing them just in pencil, to be finished at home. I *may* have to come back for a short time to set the exhibition going.[1]

Tuesday [*11 March 1913. Postmark of receipt 14 March*]
Villino Chiaro

My dearest Reg,

I won't make the usual apologies for having put off writing; for they must be so very familiar to you by this time. I will plunge straight away into saying I am truly delighted that you like Syracuse so much. It sounds most lovely, and you must be having a delicious time. I am not sure that you oughtn't to *reside* there. I have never heard you not make so much as *one* reservation about a place. . . .

I myself (as Florence will have told you) collapsed for some days —chill, internal pains, injections of opium, etc. Have much enjoyed my convalescence. You can imagine that Florence made everything run on wheels beautifully. I should have been much worried during the illness if I had not already got well forward with my caricatures. These are now all but finished. Sixty-one unexhibited drawings. Also there will be four or five drawings that *have* been exhibited. *Unberufen*, I think it will be a very good show. I wish you could see it. I will send you as many reproductions as I can, so that you may get some idea of the things. I go to England about the 28th of this month, returning after Private View (April 12th). It seems a long journey for so short a time; but the shortness of the time is the best thing about it—though of course I look forward to seeing my mother and Con and Aggie again.

The play seems to have some chances of bringing in money. I had applications for it from two of the chief Berlin theatres; also

---

case opened before Mr Justice Darling on 18 April 1913 and lasted four days. After some of Douglas's letters to Wilde and the whole of Wilde's *De Profundis* (brought specially from the British Museum) had been read aloud by the Defence, the action was dismissed with costs.
[1] Max's second Leicester Galleries exhibition, which opened on 11 April 1913.

from the National Theatre in Prague. But the German and Austro-Hungarian rights are being handled by an agent, who has paid £75 down on account of fees at £1 a performance (which, I believe, are good terms for Germany). Also, Alexander wired to me the other day that he had a "good" offer from America, if I wouldn't mind the scene of the play being transferred into American life. (New York, I suppose.) I wired that I had no objection, but would like to see the alterations. I haven't yet heard what are the terms offered. Meanwhile, I have a good idea for another one-act play. You don't say that you are forging ahead with your novel. I hope you soon will be.

I have signed a birthday letter to Henry James—a letter to be sent to him on his seventieth birthday by a number of friends and admirers; and I have subscribed two guineas towards a birthday present to him. This present will (it is "earnestly hoped" by the committee which is organising the sending of the letter and the buying of the present) "take the form of a painting of Henry James himself by Mr John Sargent."[1] And among these earnest hopers who send out this appeal is Sargent himself! They earnestly hope to raise the sum of £500; after which "up goes the donkey," I suppose. Poor Sargent, most sensitive and most correct of men, can't have known that his name was going to be included among the names of this committee. But anyway, as he is such a devoted old friend of H.J., I think he might have done the thing gratis—else better not do it at all. However, I hope he will buy himself something nice with my two guineas. H.J. arriving at J.S.'s studio to have a sitting would be a lovely theme for a caricature—with appropriate dialogue; but this I must forgo as the circular was marked "private and confidential," and the birthday is only a few days before my show opens.[2]

The Zeiss glasses are a daily delight from the terrace. . . .

And now do write again to your loving friend   MAX

[1] John Singer Sargent (1856–1925), American painter who lived mostly in France and England.   R.A. 1897.
[2] On James's seventieth birthday, 15 April 1913, he was presented with a golden bowl and a letter from 269 friends, of whom Max was one. The Sargent portrait was privately shown to subscribers in the artist's studio in December. Later, when it was on exhibition in the Royal Academy, it was slashed by a suffragette. Now, invisibly repaired, it can be seen in the National Portrait Gallery.

Tuesday [*15 April 1913*]   *48 Upper Berkeley Street*

My dearest Reg,

I hope these cuttings will reach you. I am sending them by messenger to Little Grosvenor Street—thence to be projected towards you.

This isn't a letter, but a scrawl done with Con's stylograph (which leaves much to be desired). The cuttings are a selection. All the other papers were equally excited. Of course I'm especially pleased with *The Times*. Also touched by F.C.G. in *Westminster*.[1] The printing of the catalogue in *The Times* must have been Northcliffe's own idea: nobody else would have dared this strange innovation.[2] Altogether a great success. Already 610 guineas-worth have been sold from the walls. Show remains open a month. I was going back to Florence yesterday, but had very bad cold and postponed departure. Was in bed all yesterday. Right enough today. Off tomorrow.

When do you return? Florence told me she had had a letter from you the other day. It would be lovely if you could descend on the way. There at Rap we shall be *all the time*, and there is the spare-room, and you know how Florence and I should *love* to see you. Do write. I will write again from Rap—or rather not "again," for this isn't a letter.   Your affectionate MAX

Tuesday [*Postmark 22 April 1913*]   *Villino Chiaro*

My dearest Reg,

I arrived here on Friday. Florence met me at Genoa. It is lovely to be here with her again. Two delightful letters from you since I came (at least, one *since*, and one was awaiting me). It is good of you to be so interested in the show. I send you a cutting from the

[1] Francis Carruthers Gould, caricaturist and writer (1844–1925), devoted more than a column to Max's exhibition in the *Westminster Gazette* of 15 April.
[2] *The Times* of 12 April had devoted half a column to a favourable review of Max's exhibition ("We therefore make bold to say that we think Mr Beerbohm the greatest of English comic artists"), followed by the complete catalogue of the exhibition, which occupied a full column. Lord Northcliffe had become chief proprietor of *The Times* in 1908.

Manchester Guardian, which gives the composition of the Bennett drawing.

And here are the numbers of the sold (according to "advices" received yesterday): 1, 3, 7, 9, 10, 11, 12, 13, 14, 16, 21, 22, 23, 28, 29, 30, 31, 33, 35, 38, 41, 42, 44, 47, 48, 50, 52, 53, 54, 57, 58, 59, 62, 63, 64, 65, 66, 67, 68.

That is, in all, thirty-nine sold from the walls. There are also four sold from drawer or portfolio. The total is more than £843. (I have, alas! included the shillings of the guineas in this princely sum.) As to the purchasers, I know little. I know that Edgar Speyer[1] and Eddie Marsh[2] and F. E. Smith[3] bought themselves. *John Bull* bought Bottomley[4] (with copyright), Clutton Brock[5] bought the Servants' Hall, Edmund Davis bought Claude Phillips[6] (and probably will buy *himself* when he does get his *bouton rouge*), Gosse bought Courtney-Morley, Bennett (I suppose, for he wrote from the country asking to have it reserved) bought himself.[7] Speyer bought also Edward Grey.[8] The rest is darkness. It is extraordinarily much more fun to watch the progress of the show from here than on the spot. The distance gives a peculiar thrill.

Everybody in London, by the way, seemed to wonder how I, living in Italy, contrived to be so abreast of the times; and the one and only new metropolitan development which they were able to

[1] Financier of German extraction (1862–1932), one of the founders of the Whitechapel Art Gallery. Made a baronet 1906.
[2] Edward Marsh (1872–1953), civil servant, patron of the arts, friend and editor of Rupert Brooke. Edited five volumes of *Georgian Poetry* (1912–22), translated Horace and La Fontaine. Knighted 1937.
[3] Frederick Edwin Smith (1872–1930), barrister and Conservative politician. Lord Chancellor 1919–22, Secretary of State for India 1924–28. Knighted 1915, created Lord Birkenhead 1919, raised to Earl 1922.
[4] Horatio William Bottomley (1860–1933), journalist and financier. Twice a Member of Parliament, from which he was finally expelled in 1922 on being sentenced to seven years' penal servitude for fraudulent conversion.
[5] Arthur Clutton-Brock (1868–1924), art-critic of *The Times*.
[6] 1846–1924. Keeper of the Wallace Collection 1897–1911, art-critic of the *Daily Telegraph* and other papers. Knighted 1911.
[7] "A Milestone," in which Hilda Lessways chides her creator, Arnold Bennett.
[8] Liberal politician (1862–1933). Secretary of State for Foreign Affairs 1905–16. K.G. 1912. Viscount 1916.

announce to me was that William Archer had become a dramatic critic: he has been engaged by the *Star*.[1] The Servants' Hall drawing hasn't been reproduced anywhere, because of journalistic etiquette, but the design is simple enough to be described in few words:— Above the mantelpiece hangs a little oleograph of John Bull. Facing it stands the house-keeper, a middle-aged, sad, smug "treasure" (the *Spectator*), gazed at by a *very* old and decrepit footman (*Punch*), while between them, leaning against the mantelpiece, haughtily, is the large and wildly Semitic butler (*Daily Telegraph*).

Bobbie's "selections"[2] are not bad from the *literary* standpoint. The drawings he likes best are the most amusing in meaning, certainly. But from the artistic standpoint, I should say that 33[3] is merely a bit of laborious cartoon-mongering, and 13[4] likewise (though it is a pretty thing in its way), and 29[5] rather feeble. Whereas the "very poor" Burnham and the "silly" Teixeira[6] happen unfortunately to be just the two gems of the whole collection (two of the *three*, rather—the other one being the Balfour frieze).

These are caricature in its finest purity—caricature brought to a pitch of such simplicity and of beauty as you won't find except in very good Japanese prints. What a terrible thing to be an art-critic and not an artist! But don't, for heaven's sake, repeat to him what I have written. If he wants to know what I said, say that I thought his selections very good (as I *have* said) *from the literary standpoint*.

What awful egoism this letter is, isn't it? I will write again. Meanwhile, I am so delighted to hear that you have done a lot of work, and I do so look forward to another book of yours. The

[1] Archer, having been dramatic critic almost continuously since 1879 (on the London *Figaro*, the *World*, the *Tribune* and the *Nation*), had not written regularly about the theatre for two years when in February 1913 he joined the *Star*. He stayed with it till 1920 and then retired.
[2] In a three-quarter-column review in the *Morning Post* of 11 April, headed A GREAT CARICATURIST.
[3] "Dons of Magdalen at great pains to incur no imputation of flunkeyism" [on account of the Prince of Wales's arrival as an undergraduate].
[4] "Sir Edward Grey wondering whether, after all, he is so wise as he looks and sounds in the House of Commons."
[5] "Mr William Rothenstein warns Mr Tagore against being spoilt by Occidental Success."
[6] Alexander Louis Teixeira de Mattos (1865–1921) translated into English works by Maeterlinck, Fabre and Couperus.

Zeiss glasses go on adding much to the amenities of Florence's and my life. . . .

Alfred Douglas does not seem to have come well out of the witness-box. The Boitanos have a fox-terrier puppy, which they asked us to name, and we have named it *James* (after the septuagenarian)—pronounced Ya-mes.

Your loving friend MAX

Tuesday [3 June 1913. Postmark 4 June]   *Villino Chiaro*

My dearest Reg,

You will have had a wire from Florence and me on the morning of your birthday; and here again are all our very best wishes for many happy returns and for all the best things that can be wished. In Rapallo I find nothing worthy of your acceptance. The picture postcards are the least ineligible things in the shops, and I feel you might not like even them. I must therefore postpone my present—not indefinitely, but until I am within reach of proper shops.

How long are you staying in Florence? We do so hope, as I said in my last letter, that we shall see you here. (Dora is due here on the 12th and will be occupying the "Visitors' Room," but if you synchronised with her you could have meals etc. with us.) There is no news of much interest. The exhibition of drawings did splendidly. Altogether £1218 worth were sold—fifty-one drawings of the sixty-eight on the walls "went," and some others from portfolio, all at very good prices. £1218!—more than the price of a portrait by Sargent! How very rich Sargent would be if he had my industry and application! Heinemann is bringing out a book of fifty or so of my caricatures, about thirty of which were in the present exhibition.[1] Meanwhile I have been doing a lot of drawings of Florence, "from the life." I must do you. It is great fun.

You will be amused to hear that I have been "nominated for a seat on the Academic Committee."[2] I heard from the Secretary

---

[1] *Fifty Caricatures*, published by Heinemann on 9 October 1913.
[2] In 1910 the Royal Society of Literature decided to institute an Academic Committee of not more than forty members, "to maintain the purity of the English language" and in general act like the Académie Française. The original twenty-seven members (1910) were Alfred Austin, Laurence

yesterday. I gather that this means I am a Member, practically (barring the chance of my refusing to be so—a chance which hasn't come off), and that all that remains is for my name to be put forward at the next meeting of the R.S.L. itself, for election as an Hon. Fellow. I am rather surprised at this affair. Aren't you? I don't see what place I have in any sort of an Academy—especially one of which I drew a rude picture recently.[1] I am sure Barry Pain will echo this opinion. Living so far away, I fear my voice won't be raised very high in the councils of the Committee, but I shall try to encourage a strong forward policy.

I suppose Alfred Douglas won't succeed in getting a new trial on the ground of misdirection. And I hope Bobbie Ross won't be bothered by him in other ways. The case seems to me very cleverly conducted by Ransome's counsel.[2] But, as the main part of this cleverness was in keeping Bobbie Ross out of the witness-box, certainly the victory was not of a glorious kind. Evelyn Beerbohm was here, en route for Australia, for a couple

---

Binyon, A. C. Bradley, Robert Bridges, S. H. Butcher, Joseph Conrad, W. J. Courthope, Austin Dobson, J. G. Frazer, Edmund Gosse, R. B. Haldane, Thomas Hardy, Henry James, W. P. Ker, Andrew Lang, Sir Alfred Lyall, J. W. Mackail, Lord Morley, Gilbert Murray, Henry Newbolt, E. H. Pember, Sir Arthur Pinero, G. W. Prothero, Walter Raleigh, G. M. Trevelyan, A. W. Verrall and W. B. Yeats. In 1911 were added A. C. Benson, Edward Dowden, Maurice Hewlett, T. Sturge Moore and George Wyndham; in 1912 J. M. Barrie, John Galsworthy, Lady Ritchie and Bernard Shaw; in 1913 W. H. Hudson and Sir Arthur Quiller-Couch; and in 1914 Max Beerbohm, W. R. Inge, John Masefield and Mrs M. L. Woods. George Moore was proposed by Gosse in 1914 but was not elected.

[1] "Members of the Academic Committee discussing whether at future meetings an Agenda Paper shall be provided, and, if so, what on earth to put into it." Shown at the Leicester Galleries in 1913 and reproduced in *Fifty Caricatures*. The drawing includes nineteen men, of whom three (Frederic Harrison, Anthony Hope Hawkins and Rudyard Kipling) appear never to have been members of the Committee.

[2] J. H. M. Campbell (1851–1931, Lord Chief Justice of Ireland 1916–18, Lord Chancellor of Ireland 1918–21, created Lord Glenavy 1921) and H. A. McCardie (1869–1933, Judge of the High Court from 1916, when he was knighted). They skilfully prevented Robert Ross from being called as a witness.

of days last week; and he told me that Walter Emanuel[1] had a great success at the Chelsea Arts Club annual dinner, reading a sheaf of bogus telegrams, one of them from Mr Justice Darling:[2] "Regret dare not venture out. Much worried by letter from Lord A. Douglas beginning 'My dear Darling.'"

Bobbie Ross, by the way, in writing to me before I left London, to thank me for writing to him, said "I daresay you know that for some seven or eight years I have been offended with you." I suppose he expected me to write and ask how I had offended him. But really I can't profess to feel any curiosity about, or any sympathy with, a grievance that hasn't prevented him from showing the most unctuous cordiality whenever we have met.

Well, my dear Reg, here is an end to a long and tedious letter. Again, very many happy returns.

Ever your loving friend   MAX

[Postmark 8] October 1913   Villino Chiaro

My dearest Reg,

I owe you *two* letters. Here is one of them at any rate. I laughed greatly over your description of the house-party. I suppose (though I send this to Little G. Street) that you are still in Scotland; and I hope for your sake the guests have not remained stationary. I had no idea that the Faudel-Phillipses were either of them still living.[3] I thought he died on the expiration of his Lord-Mayoralty, and she

[1] Humorous writer (1869–1915). Wrote a great deal about dogs.
[2] Charles John Darling (1849–1936) was a Judge of the King's Bench Division 1897–1923. He had clashed with Douglas in the Ransome case, and was to do so even more violently in the Pemberton Billing trial (1918), when he had Douglas ejected from the court. He was fond (many thought too fond) of making jokes on the bench, and Max's caricature of him (1913) shows him handing the Black Cap to his Marshal and saying: "Oh, and get some bells sewn on this cap, will you?"
[3] George Faudel-Phillips (1840–1922) married (1867) Helen Levy, sister of Edward Levy (later Lawson) and therefore Reggie's putative cousin. Faudel-Phillips was Lord Mayor of London, 1896–97, when he was made a Baronet.

after her portrait by Sargent. That is what it is to live in Italy. No doubt you yourself will find, when you live here, that you believe the Faudel-Phillipses, like Pan, are dead. I do hope you *won't* live in the Viale. There must surely be some good rooms available in Florence (of which I do not recognise the Viale as a part: it is a part of the salubrious north-western residential district of Huddersfield—or, say, of *Bursley*: yes, Bursley; and Arnold Bennett was born there. It is an utterly impossible place to live in). I wonder if you have yet disposed of your London rooms? It will be pleasant for you to feel that you are no longer a fellow-lodger of Robert Ross. I am sorry he has been behaving so badly to you. But, as you were already sick of him and his ways, it is just as well that there should be a definite rupture.

I rather think I shall not be in London before the third week of December. And it is possible that Florence may not go with me, but go straight from Genoa to New York, to see her brothers. We had hoped one or both of her brothers could come *here* to see *us*; but they haven't been able to; and Florence feels that she must go and see *them*. In that case, I shall go to see *my* people meanwhile; and Florence will join me in London for our return to Italy. But it is just possible she mayn't have to go to America at all; in which case we shall both go to U.B.S. for Christmas.

I am sending you half-a-dozen photographs (Brownie No 2) of her. I have taken a great many. The whole fun of photographing is the developing and printing—this is really exciting, every time. Florence guided my faltering steps at the outset. She is wonderful at understanding the "directions" given with the various paraphernalia, and at remaining quite calm and cool in crises among acids in the dark. I have now become quite expert on my own account.

I gather from Romeike that my book of caricatures was to be published last Thursday, but have not yet received my copies of it: I will of course post one to you as soon as they arrive. Except commercially, I don't feel much interest in the book. Compton Mackenzie came and was a great success. I like him for being such an "actor-r." All that part of him is delightful, and quite atones for the veneer of Oxford. Have you read his new book yet?[1] In writing to

[1] The first volume of *Sinister Street*, published 1 September 1913.

Florence, he said he had just heard from you; and I expect it was about his book that you wrote to him. . . .

You don't say whether you have been writing. I do hope you have. Please give me news.

Love from us both.

Ever your loving friend   MAX

Villino Chiaro

14 April 1914

My dearest Reg,

It is awful, the length of time since I wrote; but, as you know, not writing doesn't mean not thinking, on my part. Also, if the will could be taken for the deed, you would have received a score of letters from me by this time; for I have been in a constant state of *going to* write—withheld always by the knowledge that the letter would be so dull and stupid. Such a letter, written to an acquaintance round the corner, is well enough; but to one's greatest friend at a great distance one wants to write something better than that, and, well, there it is.

How jolly for you to be in Tunis! It sounds delightful. I wonder if you will have seen there "Franky Schu,"[1] who was lunching here the other day and was en route for Algiers and said (I think, but I am not sure) that he should be going also to Tunis. He was very cosy and pleasant, as always, and seemed to be enjoying himself very much in a large motor-car with all sorts of things in it—rather like Napoleon's travelling-coach, which you may remember, at Madame Tussaud's. I saw (this reminds me) the waxen effigy of G.B.S. when I was in London. I thought it might form a good basis for a caricature. Some days later I was lunching at his place, and mentioned the effigy to him; at which he flushed slightly, and waved his hands, and said he had *had* to give Tussaud a sitting, as "it would have seemed so *snobbish* to refuse"! Considering that it had been the proudest day in his life, I was rather touched by this account of the matter. I am afraid he is afraid of me. I met him also

---

[1] Frank Schuster (see note, p. 141).

dining at Philip Sassoon's,[1] and he seemed decidedly uncomfortable at being caught by me there. Also, poor man, he got almost nothing to eat. No special dish had been ordered for him. The eyes of Mrs Shaw (who was next to me) kept wandering up and down the menu, in fearful anxiety for him. It was only towards the end of dinner that he did get a potato and some beans. Of course, meanwhile, I talked a lot to Mrs Shaw about him, as always, and with much affection and admiration, but also, at one point, with considerable frankness. "He is *not*," I said, "an artist." At this her face beamed suddenly more than ever. "Oh," she exclaimed, "how glad I am to hear you say that! That is what *I* always tell him. He's a REFORMER."

But these are details, and if I go on in that way my letter will never be over. Enough that Florence and I were at Upper Berkeley Street together for about six weeks, and enjoyed very much being with my people, and enjoyed more or less the seeing of a lot of other people. Then Florence went to New York, and was with her two brothers there; then to Memphis, and was with her other brother *there*; then was in New York again, and sailed thence direct to Genoa, to avoid the rougher Northern crossing, and at Genoa landed on March 14th. It was lovely to be re-united with her on the quay, and is lovely to be here once more. Towards the end of my time in London I began to feel as strong a hatred of London as I used to have when I lived there. When first we arrived in London, the place only seemed to me ridiculous and (having to be tolerated only for a couple of months or so) tolerable; but presently it began to oppress me, and the relief of being away from it is immense. All the chatter and clatter and hustle and guzzle—not one single person having a good time, and not one single person thinking of anything *but* the having of a good time. What I enjoyed most was a visit of three days paid by us to Bognor, soon after our arrival, in order to get rid of the two bad colds we had caught.

Florence has not been well during the past week here, but is now getting all right again, and I think will be perfectly well in a few days. She had got overtired, and she had a sudden shock in

[1] Philip Albert Gustave David Sassoon (1888–1939) succeeded his father as third Baronet 1912. Under-Secretary of State for Air 1924–29 and 1931–37.

hearing that her brother Silas had died suddenly. This was not one of her favourite brothers; but still, she liked him, and had seen him a good deal in America this time, so that the news of his death was naturally painful.

I have been drawing a good deal—have made the rough drafts for almost forty cartoons. My next exhibition will be just after Easter of next year;[1] so I have plenty of time really; but it is pleasant to feel that the thing is already well under way.

I suppose you will have seen Henry James's articles about Wells, Conrad, etc?[2] I haven't yet, for the wretched *Times* people didn't understand that a cheque I sent them was to include a subscription for the *Supplement*. But the back-numbers of this will arrive in a few days now.[3] I met old Henry himself several times: he has become one of the stock ornaments of dinner-tables, uniform with Sargent, Claude Phillips, etc.—though he insists on being regarded as a recluse; and, wherever he is, nobody is *supposed* to see him there. All the same, he is in great form, really delightful to be with—though he hasn't a good word to say for anyone. I particularly want to read him on the subject of Arnold Bennett, of whose *Hilda Lessways* he said (but will not perhaps put in writing) that it was "like the slow squeezing-out of a big, dirty sponge." He was splendid about a production of *Hamlet* by William Poel at the Little Theatre.[4] Somebody had taken him to see it, and I asked him what it was like. "Like? Like? It was like Morning Prayers in a work-house!" George Moore is in the Holy Land, staying in a monastery, to get local colour for a play about Christ. A curious picture! It seems that, on his way, he wrote from Algiers to Gosse,

[1] This exhibition never took place.
[2] "The Younger Generation," which appeared in the *Times Literary Supplement* of 19 March and 2 April 1914. Revised and amplified, it was reprinted as "The New Novel" in James's *Notes on Novelists* (1914).
[3] Hitherto the *Literary Supplement* had been distributed free with *The Times*. The issue of 19 March 1914 was the first to be sold separately, price one penny. In the previous issue (12 March) the front page had been occupied by Max's essay "Books within Books," which was reprinted in *And Even Now* (1920).
[4] William Poel (1852–1934), the pioneer of Elizabethan stage revivals, produced a version of the Second Quarto *Hamlet* at the Little Theatre on 27, 29 and 30 January 1914, with Esme Percy as Hamlet and Edith Evans as the Queen.

saying "Will you send me a copy of *Tristan Shandy* or *Tristrum Shandy*, which I have never read? A *cheap* copy. Send it to me, care of Cook, Jerusalem." At Tonks's, one night, I said a thing that rather worried him. He had begun suddenly to talk of Carlyle. He said "He was a nasty old man. He was never nice about his friends. He was not nice about *Emerson*. He was not nice about *Herbert Spencer*. He was not nice about *Tennyson*. He was not—" "Was he not nice," I interrupted, "about Yeats and Lady Gregory?"[1]

You don't say whether you are writing, and you don't give any further news about what you have written. I do hope you and your Muse have been getting on well, and that there will be a new book very soon? Con and Aggie are very well, and my mother, though her memory is still less good than it was a year ago, is also very well —*physically* much stronger than she was. I hope you will make some sudden and splendid *trouvaille* in your quest of rooms in Florence. All best love from us both.   Your affectionate MAX

[*Postmark 27 April 1914*]   *Villino Chiaro*

Many thanks for delightful letter. So glad you have been writing, and am sure you—and the world—will presently be satisfied with the outcome. Florence is much better, almost well, and sends her love. Hugely delighted with the postcards. The likenesses are exact, spiritually. . . .

Also you are wrong in your prophecies of George Cornwallis-West's future.[2] His heart has been given once and for all now. His

[1] Of whom Moore had made fun in his autobiographical trilogy: *Ave* (1911), *Salve* (1912) and *Vale* (1914).
[2] George Frederick Myddleton Cornwallis-West (1874–1951), brother of Daisy, Princess of Pless, married (1) in 1900 Lady Randolph Churchill; (2) in 1914 Mrs Patrick Campbell; (3) in 1940 Mrs Georgette Hirsch. On 12 April 1914 Reggie had written from Tunis:
"I suppose the third Mrs West will be Miss Carlotta Addison, the lady who played the part of the mother in Hankin's *Return of the Prodigal*. How he must regret that Helen of Troy and Ninon de l'Enclos were not spared a little longer. But after all, when he has finished with the Campbell and the Addison, Millicent Duchess of Sutherland will be ripening for him."

wife, a few days after the wedding, became suspicious because he began to absent himself from home throughout the whole day—going out early in the morning and not returning till nightfall. She had him watched by detectives. They report that he goes straight to Kensal Green (pausing on the way to buy a bunch of violets) and spends the whole day beside the tomb of the late Baroness Burdett-Coutts.[1]　　　　　　　　　　　Your affectionate MAX

The Arnold Bennetts—very dusty and scrutty[2] but nice—alighted from a motor-car here yesterday, on the way to Genoa, and had tea on the terrace. He is going to do his *Lessways* sequel as soon as he gets home.[3]

6 September 1914　　　　　　　　　　　　　　*Villino Chiaro*

My dearest Reg,

What a world! What a period to have been born into! It is very epical and all that; but the horror and sadness and absurdity of it! The horror duly horrifies me, and the sadness saddens, whereas by the absurdity "we are," like Queen Victoria, "not amused." If the whole thing were a sort of *purge* for the human race, if presently the human race were going to feel, and be, *better*, I shouldn't so much mind. But, so far as one can foresee, the thing is not so much a purge as an additional poison: there will be more hatred and bitterness and unrest after the war than there was before; more sulks and scowls, and preparations for other wars, than ever. It is all very well

[1] Wealthy English philanthropist (1814–1906). King Edward VII said that she was "after my mother the most remarkable woman in the Kingdom." Like Lady Randolph Churchill and Mrs Patrick Campbell, she had married a man considerably younger than herself.
[2] "Scruts" was the title of Max's parody of Arnold Bennett in *A Christmas Garland* (1912). The word was invented by Max to describe the broken pieces of pottery which, according to him, the inhabitants of the Five Towns mix into Christmas puddings instead of sixpences.
[3] Arnold Bennett wrote in his journal on 25 April:
"Max in whites, no waistcoat, and a calico sort of jacket. Fine tiled terrace. He was engaged in altering a portrait of George Moore in *Century* in order to tease Moore. Fine tea. Good servant. Picked a lemon off tree for tea."

to talk about beating Germany to her knees, freeing Europe from the dread of an insolent hegemony, and so forth. But not the most bloodthirsty person proposes that Germany shall be altogether crushed out of existence; and I am sure that whatever is left of her will have even more recuperative power than France had after 1870, and a more urgent spirit; so that either she will have to be crushed all over again (as Bismarck wanted to crush France in '75), which wouldn't be a very pretty thing to do, nor an epical thing; or we shall in the not very remote future have the epical business all over again.

All this is assuming that Germany will this time go under. I live, from day to day and hour to hour, on tenterhooks of hope that Germany will in the end be beaten this time. My breadth and delicacy of mind, and my far-sighted misgivings, come out only when I set pen to paper. They are but a part of my literary style. In myself I yield to no one—not to the most rabid of non-combatants—in the bitterness of my feelings against Germany, in depression at her triumphs, and in joy at the least of her reverses; and I seriously believe (though pen-in-hand I can't believe) that Russia is a beautiful and admirable power for the world's good. But the appalling thing is that, as yet, the German reverses have been so few and slight and so quickly counterbalanced. Liége was cheering, and one began to think that perhaps, after all, the German army etc. etc.[1] But ever since Liége, alas! The French seem to have fought splendidly, but this fact does only accentuate the German triumphs. I live in hopes that the new phase, the Parisian phase, of the war will go better for us. Of course it wouldn't so much matter if one were sure of Russia. I wish I hadn't the ever-present dread that Russia will once more turn out to be a handless giant. Gigantic and brave one knows her to be. But has she, this time, got the necessary food and ammunition? And the brains? At the moment when I write there has been no explanation given of the ghastly surrender of 90,000 unwounded men.[2] Shortage of ammunition, I suppose. Not a very nice augury for the future. However, Russia does seem to have done splendidly

[1] The heroic Belgian defence of the fortress of Liége held up the Germans from 5 to 17 August and cost them 40,000 casualties.
[2] In fact the Germans took some 120,000 Russian prisoners after the Battle of Tannenberg on 26–27 August.

at Leopoli[1] (and you can imagine the joy of the Italians at this—the size of the headlines in the newspapers mocking the correct air of neutrality maintained).

Dear England has behaved with all the fineness one expects of her; and I love to think of her fleet and its magnificent success the world over, and its superb little raid on the Heligoland ships.[2] She deserves the good fortune she has in being an island and safe. But, just as I haven't the slightest fear that any attempt at invasion would not be an immediate and ludicrous fizzle, so do I not see how, *if* Russia and France fail, she, with the best will in the world, and with all her Colonies doing all they can, and with America sympathising to the utmost, can hope to beat Germany on land. Of course, if Germany could be starved by the fleet, then—but I don't see how Germany can be prevented from getting enough food through various channels. Perhaps Germany *can* be prevented. I am very ignorant. Anyhow the *spirit* of England is beautiful. Ever since I have lived away from England I have been growing more and more fond and proud of England as an *idea*. As such, there never has been or will be anything to touch her. Florence has always loved her—loved her at first sight. As soon as I got away from England, and began to see England with a fresh, a stranger's eye, I began to share and understand Florence's love of her. As you can imagine, Florence has been much horrified and appalled by the war; all the same, we are two Jingoes together, tearing open the *Capparo* in the early morning, devouring the *Corriere* and *Stampa* in the afternoon, walking down into Rapallo every evening to be exalted or downcast by the telegrams posted up in the Piazza.

The war is very bad, of course, for my little finances and for my mother's and sisters'. Do go and see Aggie at Connaught Street, and she will tell you what has been happening and how things stand. Letters take such an interminable time to reach here that I don't know how things stand at the present moment nor just what arrangements are being made about my people's affairs. I wired to

[1] The Italian name (from the Latin Leopolis) of Lemberg (or Lwow), the capital of Galicia and fourth largest city of the Austro-Hungarian Empire, which was captured by the Russians on 3 September.
[2] On 28 August a British force commanded by Vice-Admiral Sir David Beatty made a surprise attack on the German fleet in the Heligoland Bight, sinking three light cruisers and a destroyer.

Aggie some days ago, giving my views of the situation. It was a great delight to have your letter with all its news.

I am glad you didn't stay in Brussels, for you would have had to clear out so soon (the Germans having threatened to shoot any newspaper-correspondent found there) and the getting-back to England might have been very difficult. Also, though you would be now, as ever, very much in your element in Paris, I am glad you weren't able to get there. Every time I saw an account of a bomb thrown from an aeroplane I should have been afraid that *il galante e simpatico corrispondente del Dily Telegrap*, Lord Turna, might have been one of the injured. I suppose you, with your great interest in the Church, have even now been keeping an eye on the events at the Vatican.[1] These have been, in the midst of the horrors of the war, rather a relief to me, too. "It is pleasant to turn to," etc. etc. as the art-critics say. It has soothed me to think of the Cardinals coming like locusts and swarming over Rome, all peaceful and seemly—so unlike the German army, in all but numbers. *Habet mundus Episcopum* —the initiation and adoration—the fisherman's ring—all very cosy and eternal these things seem; a narcotic for the fevered brain. The newspapers here seemed as if they never would recover from the blow of Pius X's death, because Pius X had been so simple and so pious and (wonder of wonders!) a peasant. Now they are quite frankly in the seventh heaven because Benedict XV is an intellectual and a subtlist and a politician and (best and most marvellous of all!) an aristocrat. The doctrine of Infallibility still holds its own, at any rate in the Press. It is said that Benedict's first act will be the issue of a Bull against the war. What a chance the man has! If he would bluntly hold Austria and Germany responsible for the war, denounce German ill-faith and German atrocities, and so on, he would, I do believe, immensely strengthen the Catholic Church all over the world—even (at a long view) in Germany and Austria. Anyhow what a splendid thing to do, if he had the wit to do it! But I suppose the document will be the ordinary sort of snuffy, drowsy rigmarole that nobody will have patience to read: a vague regret that the doctrines of the Sermon on the Mount—but no, not that: the Sermon on the Mount is only mentioned in Protestant circles.

[1] Pope Pius X had died on 20 August, aged seventy-nine. He had been Pope since 1903. His successor, Benedict XV, was elected on 3 September.

The vague regret will be that the doctrines of Holy Church have not in any part of the world sufficed to etc. etc. And yet I can't help hoping against hope that Benedict *may* have a touch of sporting instinct in him. I like to think that his first step will be, *tout nettement*, to excommunicate the Emperor of Austria. My belief in the evil star of that Emperor upholds me in my dream. I don't believe he has *yet* drained the cup of his sorrows. I feel we shall *yet* see him deprived of the Sacrament. Those phrases which in every London newspaper office are kept permanently set up in type will for the thousandth time come in handy: "The hearts of all will go out in sympathy to the venerable Emperor Francis Joseph in this, the latest and perhaps most cruel affliction that has befallen him since he ascended the tragic throne of the Hapsburgs. It would seem as if" and all the rest of it.

Do write to me again, dear Reg, when you get this letter and tell me your views of whatever will then (I don't know how long this letter will take on its journey) be the situation of Europe.

Love from Florence and from   MAX

Sunday [*27 December 1914. Postmark 28 December*]
Villino Chiaro

My dearest Reg,

I send you all my sincerest sympathy and sorrow. I know how devoted you were to your nephew, and he to you.[1] I had not seen him since he was quite a little boy, but you had told me much about him in recent years; so that I almost seemed to know him. And I mourn him as much as I should mourn somebody known to me really well, because I realise how grievous and terrible to my dearest friend the loss of him must be. I wish I could think of something comforting to say to you. But a death such as this leaves one with only a sense of the seeming blindness and stupidity of Fate. There seems to be nothing to say that would not be utterly barren of comfort. All the more, for that reason, is one full of *inward*

[1] Frank Lawson's eldest surviving son, Second Lieutenant Frank Harry Reginald Lawson, had committed suicide in his army billet.

sympathy. And so, though sympathy is no good, be sure that my heart is full of it for you, dearest Reg.

We wish very much you would come here. Is there a chance that you would? We shall be here for a month at any rate, and perhaps longer. I have been wanting to go over to England with Florence to see my people and also to feel that I shall not have been away from England during the *whole* of England's hour of need. The delightfulness of being here at home has seemed to Florence and me almost oppressive while so many millions of people in England and elsewhere are having such a bad time. And so to England we shall be going, I fancy, early in February, for a while. You yourself have already done "the correct thing" to England, and have *earned* Italy; but we haven't. And it would be lovely for us if, before we go, you could come and stay with us.

Love from us both.

Your loving friend   MAX

Tuesday [*19 January 1915. Postmark 20 January*]   *Villino Chiaro*

My dearest Reg,

We are so disappointed at not seeing you yet, but of course we quite understand, and we do so look forward to seeing you presently —seeing you in Feb *if* we still are here. I am not yet sure whether or not we *shall* be. It depends on lots of things—expense of journey, etc.—also *difficulty* and *duration* of journey. If I were going alone, I shouldn't mind slow travelling. But I don't want Florence to have to be endlessly in waiting trains. How long did it take *you* to get through from London?[1] Please tell me. It seems absurd to want to go to London at all; but in a way I do want to be there for a little while—quite apart from wanting of course to see my mother and the others. I hope meanwhile your chill has quite gone. I can sympathise, having had one on my own account (says the egoist) a year ago. Take care of the beastly *tramontana*. Dress warmly. I laughed so much, in the midst of my sympathy, at your extracts from the letters of your nephew about "the whitest woman." I should think

[1] To Florence, where Reggie was now living.

the whole affair may blow over when once the boy is here, with Frank playing the not-too-heavy father, stern but understanding.

> "For ah, the sight recalled too plainly
> The half-forgotten time when he,
> A boy of nine, had worshipped vainly
> A governess of forty-three."

If the worst came to the worst, and if the boy did actually insist on marrying the lady, the mischief couldn't be long-lasting. He would so soon be sick of her, and she isn't the sort of lady whose behaviour wouldn't very soon make a divorce easy, leaving not a wrack behind. However, let us hope it won't come to anything at all.

I am so very glad you liked my "James Pethel."[1] It appeared also in the *Century* in America, with surprising and delightful illustrations: James Pethel and myself in the motor-car, both of us extraordinarily keen, noble, square-jawed Amurrican men, simply vying with each other in strenuousness and vim and grit.[2]

Yes: you were quite right, by the way: it *was* Hannay whose driving suggested the idea to me.[3] I have been writing another and longer essayish story, called "Enoch Soames: A Memory of the Nineties," which I hope you'll like later on.[4]

We both send our fondest love.

Ever your loving friend   MAX

Thursday [Postmark 25 February 1915]   *Villino Chiaro*

My dearest Reg,

So very sorry, such a very great disappointment for Florence and me; but we cannot have the joy of looking forward to seeing you next week. Florence hasn't been at all well. She is "run down." I had been hoping she might "pick up," but she hasn't. And it seems to me the only thing to take her away somewhere for a change of air. She has been here for a whole year, you see; and,

---

[1] First published in the *English Review*, December 1914. Included in *Seven Men* (1919).

[2] "James Pethel" appeared in the January 1915 issue of the *Century Magazine*, with two full-page illustrations by Dalton Stevens.

[3] Arnold Hannay (see note, p. 145) was an early motoring enthusiast.

[4] First published in the *Century Magazine*, May 1916 and in the *Cornhill*, June 1916. Included in *Seven Men* (1919).

beautiful though the air in itself is, I think she needs a change into something more bracing—something, also, away from the sea, and on a higher level—for a little time. She, of course, wanted me not to say she wasn't quite well enough to be here and to receive you here next week. But I have "insisted." We are both so very sorry, but we know you will forgive us and come to us later on, at any time that may suit you for coming. I don't quite know where we shall go. Perhaps to Monte Catini (I am not sure of the spelling). It has, *mutatis mutandis*, the sort of reputation that *Margate* has in England! Please send us a line to say that this necessary postponement will not have really inconvenienced you and upset your plans. The apartment sounds exciting, and I hope it will be all that an apartment should be.

I have just been reading again Gordon Craig's *Art of the Theatre*,[1] and have come to the conclusion that he is, amongst other things, one of the three or four best living writers of English. It is an amazingly beautiful "style," his. Really like a flower—and "no flowers" at all; nothing of *my* kind or Maurice Hewlett's.[2] Another recent discovery of mine, in the way of sheer excellent *writing* power, is Repington.[3] Rather a far cry—and a descent to a far lower plane. But Repington on his plane is as good a writer as can be, I think. The rest of *The Times* has been appallingly North-cliffised—everything cut up into snippets, with idiotic head-lines. Do you read it, or the *D.T.*?

In your letter of the other day you told me about the Bobbie Ross Fund, and how your name had been put in without your knowledge.[4] A week or so earlier MacColl[5] had sent me the circular, etc.,

---

[1] First published 1905.
[2] Maurice Henry Hewlett (1861–1923), novelist, poet and essayist. His historical novel *The Forest Lovers* (1898) was an immense success.
[3] Lieut-Col. Charles A'Court Repington (1858–1925), after a distinguished military career, was appointed military correspondent to *The Times* 1905. His *Diary* of the war (1920) caused something of a sensation.
[4] In November 1914, after extreme provocation, Ross had brought a libel action against Lord Alfred Douglas. The jury disagreed, and Ross withdrew his action. As a mark of sympathy and affection his friends presented him with an address and £760, of which Ross gave £700 to found a scholarship at the Slade School of Fine Art. Both Max and Reggie were among the 310 signatories to the address.
[5] Dugald Sutherland MacColl (1859–1948), art-critic and author, was

and I had sent a "small" subscription. I wouldn't have done this if I had known that you were standing aside. As it was, I contributed, not having ever "officially" or directly quarrelled with Bobbie, and supposing that a refusal on my part would be taken as a sign that I disapproved of the whole scheme. I take it that the scheme is not so much to honour Bobbie's magnificent services to British Art as to back him up against Douglas, Crosland, and Co. All the same, I would certainly not have bothered to send in my name if I had known you were withholding yours. Anyhow, the whole affair is of the last unimportance. And I hope you won't let yourself be bothered with Bobbie or any of his concerns. He has been a nuisance in your existence, and you can well afford to let him pass. He has his good points; but to you he seems to have shown always his worst; and you are well quit of him.

Well, dearest Reg, again all apologies and regrets for the postponement of the visit, and all lookings-forward to later on.

Best love from us both.   Your affectionate   MAX

[*Postmark 20 February 1920*][1]   *Villino Chiaro*

My dearest Reg,

I have been meaning to write to you for a long time. Here is a letter at last. Evidently the mild air of Rapallo acts as a sort of solvent for what in your very delightful letter to Florence you call writer's cramp. It was such a joy to see you after all these long and

---

one of the instigators of the address to Robert Ross. The others were Edmund Gosse, the Earl of Plymouth and Robert Clermont Witt.
[1] Max and Florence were in England from 1915 to December 1919, first with the Rothensteins at Far Oakridge in Gloucestershire and then in Well Walk, Hampstead. Reggie had stayed in Italy, and when Max's mother died he wrote from Florence on 27 March 1918:

My dearest Max,

I hear from a friend that your dear mother has died. The news deepens the gloom of the present time for me, and the happy days when I was a welcome member of your family circle—for which I can never be sufficiently grateful—seem more blotted out than ever. But the memory of them will always be good. I feel most deeply for you all and with you all.   Your loving friend   REG

awful years—here, in peace time, looking so young and well, and seeming so happy. And we are longing to see you again. I am glad you found your flat and your servitors in good trim. James,[1] I am sure, misses you. We lunched with him at the Savoia the other day. He was going to Genoa next day—doubtless in obedience to the call of some Genoese syren. But I expect he is back by this time, and we have written to ask him to lunch with *us*. He gave us a very good luncheon, with more *hors d'oeuvre* than I ever saw anywhere, and was in great form—fuller than ever of Mr Justice Vaughan Williams,[2] as it were, and of hydraulic pressure, and intensive culture, and how many germs there are on an oak-leaf. He talked much of the Reform Club—quite as though he didn't carry the whole place about with him, as he does, wherever he goes. For an Italianate Welshman, he is astoundingly English, don't you think? After luncheon he went up to his room and returned with a large book about insects that eat plants—an *immense* book, published by the Italian Government. This he lent to Florence. He also showed us his passport, with a photograph that I said was very good. He said *everybody* thought it good. I wonder if you saw it? Very eager and gay, very young, leaning slightly forward, very confident—the head and shoulders of one who *knows* himself a great favourite of the public. What was the name of the elder of the Sisters Arundale?[3] James's smile reminded me of hers. Afterwards we all went to tea with the Signora up yonder. There he was more silent—just the rapt young adorer—calf love. The Signora talked incessantly of you— thereby, I am afraid, making poor James feel very jealous, though he was too much a member of the Reform Club to let this be seen. She dilated on your great brilliancy in conversation, as did also Florence and I. She said "I know not to say in English the things that I do want to say. To Mister Turner I did want to say 'You are a charming chap!' "

I forgot to mention that in addition to all the other links that

[1] Max noted that he was a barrister, a member of the [Liberal] Eighty Club, a great connoisseur of wine and an impassioned Free Trader. He was almost certainly Gwilym Criston James, eldest son of C. H. James, M.P. for Merthyr Tydfil.
[2] Robert Vaughan Williams (1822–78) was a County Court Judge on the North Wales Circuit 1863–74.
[3] Sybil (b. 1879). She and her sister Grace were both well-known actresses.

bind us to James we have a picture-postcard of his house in Wales. He gave us one after luncheon. I am not quite sure how it ought to be framed. Personally I always like *passe-partout*. But James, one of the times he was up here with you, told me that the glass of a *passe-partout* prevents evaporation of moisture from the picture and is apt to be deleterious. So *that* won't do.

Today two ladies are coming to luncheon from a castle in Portofino—people introduced by Mrs Colefax.[1] Hide where one will, one still has to reckon with Mrs Colefax. " 'No escape!' said the wolf-man, laughing up into my face."[2] *No answer is required to this letter*. I will write again.   Your loving friend   MAX

18 May 1920   *Villino Chiaro*

My dearest Regie,

You are always much in my thoughts, as you know, and especially have you been there since the news of poor Frank's death.[3] I say "poor" rather because his life had become so miserable than because it was cut short. Even before his health failed, he wasn't ever, as I remember him, a happy man—though he had so much to make him so. *Too* much, I suppose. If he had been "poor" in the literal sense he would have had a better chance of really enjoying his life. At any rate, he had too much money, and had it when he was too young; and he wasn't able to stand up to it. Fate works in an odd way—generally giving scratches in proportion to her caresses; and the other way round. You are an example of her other-way-round system. You ought to have had lots of money at the outset—and would have been, in that case, so very much less cheerful than you have been, and so very much less beloved than you are by so many people. And now, it would seem, Fate has sheathed

[1] Sybil Halsey (d. 1950) married Arthur Colefax (d. 1936). He had been at Merton before Max, and in Max's day was a science don at Christ Church. He later became a barrister. Knighted 1920. Lady Colefax became one of the best known and most successful of London hostesses.
[2] Quotation untraced.
[3] Frank Lawson had died on 10 March, aged fifty-five. He left Reggie £20,000 and half the residue of his estate, which totalled £200,479. The other half went to Louise Prescott.

her claws altogether. Frank is out of his unhappiness forever. And you, just at the right sort of age, have just the sort of circumstances that will make you easy and "comfy" and make everybody *very* glad for your sake. You have always made so much, for other people, of the comparatively little that you had. And now—for you have reached the age when selfishness isn't a vice—I hope you will spend less money on kindnesses to other people, and more on yourself. I look forward to hearing that you have bought a curious and huge old *cinquecento* wardrobe for your flat and are filling it with suits made in New York.

I was glad, by the way, and rather amused, at hearing from old James that "in his flat he has *nothing* modern, in the way of furniture, and *nothing* that is not *really* good of its date." This was rather a new light. You said nothing about it to me. When did you begin to be this austere Florentine *dilettante?* Did the shade of Herbert Horne accompany you on your visits to the curio-shops, frowning and nudging, and uttering some faint echo of that hoarse raven laugh which meant "spurious"? Or did the living Loise[1] go with you instead? I can't imagine you going alone—you who are always so mistrustful of yourself and want such a lot of corroboration! I imagine you accompanied on those expeditions by *all* your friends. I see even Mr and Mrs Deerburg on the outskirts of the throng.[2] How *are* the dear Deerburgs?—or Dierenburgs?—I never can be sure of the name, though the lady herself I never am able to forget. You amazed me rather when you said that you dined with them nowadays every Sunday night. I suppose one gets inured. I dined with them only once. The dinner, I remember, was very good. But I felt, as I sat listening to my hostess's conversation, that I was

---

[1] Unidentified, but possibly Charles Loeser, wealthy and eccentric art-collector.

[2] Harry Dearbergh has been described as "a Phil May character, good-natured but grossly vulgar, who spoke with a Cockney accent and had made a fortune in straw hats." His second wife Lulie was an American with a vast repertory of ribald stories. She became a Roman Catholic and after Dearbergh's death married the Marchese Carlo Torrigiani, a Knight of Malta. After his death she lived on in Florence as a wealthy widow, entertaining sumptuously throughout the Second World War, regardless of battles and other difficulties. After her last luncheon-party she complained of a slight dizziness, lay down on a sofa, and died.

having a beautiful dinner in a cesspool. The well-trained English butler, noticing me grow paler and paler—and knowing, by his experience of other *débutants* at his mistress's table, what was going to happen—placed beside my plate a large and priceless majolica basin. The first time I was sick into it I apologised elaborately to Mrs Deerburg. She made very light of the matter. "You'll be worse," she said, "before you're better," and resumed the thread of her conversation.

Did Mr A.J.B. get hooked by them while he was in Florence? I was greatly tickled by your account of him and his pensive solitary session at the café.[1] I fancy his main feeling about Florence must have been "How wonderful to be here again, after all these years!" When he was eighteen years old he believed that he had certainly not more than three more years to live, and made all his arrangements accordingly. (Oscar Browning, in his book of reminiscences,[2] gives an account of "that fearful belief" on A.J.B's part.) And then, many years later, he found himself being somehow a militant Irish Secretary and feeling a little stronger and better, though still far from well and not at all long for this world. And later on he found himself being Prime Minister for ever so long and exasperating and dominating everybody over the Fiscal Question and feeling decidedly better.

And then came the crash when he lost his seat in Manchester and everybody thought his career was ended because the new Parliament, when he did get returned for another borough, wouldn't

[1] On 13 May Reggie had written to Florence Beerbohm:
"I saw a lovely sight here the other day which made me long for Max. Nothing less than Arthur Balfour—plump and all the grace gone, but big and well-looking—strolling up to the central café in the piazza and sitting down at a little table in the open air and having a drink all by himself, a thing no 'distinguished' people do here—only bohemians like myself. He had not been in Florence since he was seventeen and 'did' the galleries by himself, wisely leaving his secretary—Captain Baker—at home. At Viareggio they had a nasty experience, and had rifles wagged at them which might most easily have gone off, if only by accident. Not one of the party—A.J.B., secretary, servant and three English soldiers—could speak a word of Italian. Fancy a man like that making a motor-trip in these times without an Italian or interpreter. He wore tortoiseshell spectacles on the terrace of the café, in case Max should wish to make a caricature of the scene." See illustration opposite.
[2] *Memories of Sixty Years* (1910).

IL BALFOUR
FIRENZE
MAGGIO 1920
IL REGIE
I had the pleasure of knowing your brother Eustace
A not very Passionate Pilgrim
5
P.T.O.

listen to him. And presently the new Parliament was sitting at his feet. And then, years later, another crash, and Bonar Law took his place. And then, opportunely, the War; England being a maritime power, Balfour must be at the Admiralty; and then, nobody but Balfour could manage Foreign Affairs; and then, Balfour was the only man whom America would welcome. And now he's President or something of the League of Nations, and constantly improving his stroke in tennis, and is plump without being fat, and has a complexion like a blush-rose, and only one ambition is left to him, who started with no ambition at all and has yet achieved so much; only one ambition (barring the wish to improve still further at tennis), *viz*, to survive *everybody*. I think that perhaps it was the premature death of his old leader Randolph Churchill that first made him feel it was rather a score, as well as a surprise, to be alive. When his juniors, his disciples, began to go—famous athletes, like Alfred Lyttelton,[1] and hidalgos like George Wyndham—and when golden lads like Harry Cust like chimney-sweepers turned to dust, then it was that in the amiable but not very human bosom of A.J.B. there arose a desire to see us *all* laid to rest before his own last hour. I daresay that while he sat sipping his (I am sure) non-alcoholic drink in that Florentine café he was wondering how much longer, down yonder in Rome, that other and greater prodigy, Oscar Browning, was going to go on. I daresay he was paraphrasing a well-known sonnet by another Oscar:

> "But when I thought that in those walls out there
> Strong in senility the O.B. throve,
> I wept to see the land so very fair."[2]

All this sounds very cynical. But it isn't really so. I am convinced that A.J.B. is very cynical. Anyhow, he is a monster. To

[1] The Hon Alfred Lyttelton (1857–1913), eighth son of the fourth Lord Lyttelton, was a barrister (K.C.) and also Liberal-Unionist M.P. from 1895. Secretary of State for Colonies 1903–5. He was a first-class cricketer and for many years amateur tennis champion.
[2] Wilde's "Sonnet on Approaching Italy" ends:

> "But when I knew that far away at Rome
> In evil bonds a second Peter lay,
> I wept to see the land so very fair."

realise this, you have only to try to conceive that he is, in strict point of fact, an old gentleman. You *can't* conceive that of one who is so like a young lady. So there you are! He used in bygone days to seem rather like one of the dons at Girton; shy in a rather old-maidish way. But now (did I tell you I sat next to him at a men's dinner just before I came here in December?)—now he has sloughed whole decades; and the rose-pink flush on those rounded features that were once angular and pale, and a yet softer light in the eyes, and a yet greater timidity and *naiveté* in the manner, make one feel one isn't in the presence of a teacher, but of a recent pupil—a pupil who didn't do so well, either, but had a perfectly heavenly "time," at Girton, and would like to be back there, and is as yet rather bewildered by the fuss and glitter of the grown-up world in London, and is especially afraid of dinner-parties, with a man on either side paying compliments, and remembers with a pang of longing those awfully jolly "feasts" of potted meat and biscuits and jam and bananas in the other girls' studies, and—page 10!!! What a letter! And not a letter at all! I meant it to be a letter, but it went off the rails—miles away from the rails, and I can't get it back on to them now. It is a wreck. And so must you be if you have read it. I will write again when you have recovered, and will try to write a *letter* and not some wretched chunk of some sort of wretched essay.

Your loving MAX

P.S. Apropos of letters, I envy you your "wallowing" in Henry James.[1] I wrote to Hatchard's for them a fortnight ago, but they haven't yet arrived. Perhaps the postal strikers of Turin are wallowing in them. But I expect they will arrive at length. I long to read them. This craving is in despite of a nasty jar that I lately had. I tried again to read *The Awkward Age*, a book that utterly floored me some years ago. At that time I managed to read on as far as about the middle, where I broke down; and I was much ashamed of my breakdown. *This* time I wasn't able to get nearly as far as the middle, and I wasn't in the least ashamed of leaving off—nor even of laying the book down rather violently; nor even of some un-couth words that I uttered in the act of laying the book rather

[1] His letters, edited by Percy Lubbock, had been published in two volumes on 8 April 1920.

violently down.[1] As you know, the *A.A.* is by way of being the
earliest book in H.J's "later manner." And by that manner I have
always sworn. And I *will not* believe that *The Golden Bowl* and
The Wings of the Dove aren't H.J's greatest and richest achievement. But certainly the later manner *began* very inauspiciously.
And that beginning seems to me perhaps even worse than it was
because I happened, just after I had rejected it (almost as ebulliently
as though it had been Mrs Deerburg's conversation), to read *The
Adventures of Harry Richmond*.[2] It must be twenty-five years since
I had read those Adventures, and I had only the haziest memory of
them; and I feared they might be less golden than the haze made
them appear to me. And oh, lo! how much *more* golden they were
than I had remembered. *What* a book! *What* swiftness and beauty
and strength! It is the flight of a young golden eagle high across
seas and mountains—beholding which, one likens H.J. to a very
old mole burrowing very far down under a very poky back-garden
in South Kensington. I mean, one likens the author of the *A.A.* to
that mole. I won't hear a word against the rest of H.J's later manner. But I will willingly hear any number of words against G.M's
own later manner. For I turned from *Harry Richmond* to *Diana of
the Crossways*, a book which had also become dim to me. And oh,
the difference!—oh the tedious, crack-jaw, arid intellectual snob-
bery of *Diana*! Wonderful beauties here too—but coming only in
bursts, coming only in *escapes* from the book itself. Meredith ought
to have stuck to romance and let who would be clever. But of course
a man cannot be romantic in his later age. So the point is that Meredith ought to have died when he was young-ish. Anyhow, I am
quite sure it is by his young and young-ish work that he will be
remembered. *Diana* is as dead as a door-nail, and I tremble to think
what *The Amazing Marriage* and *Lord Ormont* must be as dead as![3]
Do read *Harry Richmond* again if you haven't read it in quite recent years. You might even read it aloud on Sunday evenings to Mr
and Mrs Deerburg. I can't imagine any one not being entranced by
it. And yet it made no stir in 1871. And a dozen years later what a

[1] This copy of *The Awkward Age*, rather the worse for its violent treatment, is now in the Houghton Library at Harvard.
[2] By George Meredith. First published 1871.
[3] Meredith's two last novels, published in 1895 and 1894.

stir there was for R. L. Stevenson's thin little prim little cardboard-and-tinsel attempts to do something in the manner of Sir Walter!![1] Apparently the public doesn't know what romance is when they see it. But they will humbly swallow any wretched pretence of it that may be guaranteed genuine by log-rolling Colvins and Langs![2] Colvin, by the way, must be rather a thorn in the side of A.J.B. He should have retired from the contest long ago. His persistence is unmannerly.

But who am I, on the fourteenth page of a letter, to twit anybody with persistence? And I have a hideous presentiment that there will be a fifteenth. But there won't!

Florence will be writing too. We are both very well. Dora and Curly Curtis[3] are coming to stay here in June—Curly will have a room somewhere near. I daresay the delay in your income will continue for some time, as lawyers are always so slow. And it is a pity to borrow money at interest. "I," says the mouse to the lion, "am good for £100 whenever you might care to have it."

10 July 1920   *Villino Chiaro*

Dearest Reg,

I was so very glad to have the delightful letter you sent me. And the photograph of Herbert in company with Charley Chaplin is also a joy for ever.[4] The two young chums together! I wonder who the supposed Herbert really was? He somehow hasn't a cinematic look about him. But then, so many people haven't. Why was poor

[1] Cf. "When Stevenson did not aim at realism, and was entirely oblivious of Sir Walter Scott, and was giving rein to his own riotous sense of fantasy, as in *The New Arabian Nights*, or *The Dynamiter*, or *The Wrong Box*, the jewelled elaboration of the manner becomes an integral part of the fun, and keeps us laughing the more irresistibly and the more loudly. These books are, I think, far and away his best—the most characteristic of himself, of his true and magical self." (From Max's Rede Lecture on Lytton Strachey, 1943. Reprinted in *Mainly on the Air*, 1957.)
[2] Andrew Lang (1844–1912), poet and litterateur, was, like Colvin, a friend of Stevenson. Max published his unfavourable impressions in "Two Glimpses of Andrew Lang" in *Life and Letters*, vol. 1, no. 1, June 1928.
[3] The daughter of some old friends of Dora and Max.
[4] Herbert Tree had died in 1917.

Herbert hit on? The fun is all the greater because for once they have got the name and title exactly right—no nonsense about Sir Tree or Lord Tree. Herbert couldn't have helped loving the thing, though I agree with you that he would have been slightly worried too.

I suppose I told you, when you were here, what a lot of niggling botheration I had had over the *book* about Herbert which I have edited—*not* edited, really, but just *collected*.[1] I thought, when I came over in December, the whole thing was ship-shape. But it wasn't. After I had corrected the galley-proofs out here, I found that many of my corrections did not get into the subsequent paginated proofs, partly because Maud had had her own set of galley-proofs; and also I found—but to cut a long story short: I had to skip back to London, in order to help Maud, and the Hutchinsons (whom one would have expected to be professionally capable), out of their difficulties and out of *my* difficulties. The journey there and back was easy enough, for I took nothing that would not go into a pill-box—or at least into a little sort of "attaché case" that Florence acquired recently: I simply *skimmed* across frontiers; and Maud had placed at my disposal one of her innumerable residences—a charming little flat in Adam Street—or rather, two large and noble rooms there (plus a bathroom and a sort of kitchen), full of eighteenth-century quietude and dignity and decency, so that I hardly had the horrible feeling of being in London at all, or at any rate only felt that I was living there in the good old days when London was habitable. While I was there I did finally straighten things out in such a way that the book won't appear with any idiotic misprints. The illustrations will come in appropriate places; and so on. The prefatory note won't have got printed as an appendix, and the title-page won't have been held over for the second edition.

I am having two copies sent to me here; one of which I will send on to you when it comes (I am not sure when the book is to be published: I left that to Hutchinson, of course. He thought it would be a good book for the *holiday* season—which I suppose means July or August). My own contribution, as I probably told

[1] *Herbert Beerbohm Tree: Some Memories of him and of his art collected by Max Beerbohm.* Published by Hutchinson in 1920.

you, is quite brief—about 5000 words, I fancy. Shaw's is about the same length. Maud's is much the longest of any of them. There's a good deal of "overlapping"—about Herbert's *vitality* and his indifference to money, and so on—but in a book of this kind this can't be helped. I would rather have had the book *much* shorter; but I didn't want to dictate to any one; and the book as it stands has anyway really *a great deal* in it that is excellent. Don't happen to mention to any one that I disclaim a certain amount of responsibility. This I do only into your own private ear. (Which sentence reminds me rather of Ernest Leverson, and of how I laughed the other day at your anecdote of him regretting the decay of classical education etc.)

I like to think of you surrounded once more with your own library; and also I like to think that you will, in spite of the burden of worldly wealth, write more books. I am perfectly sure that *The Respectful Memoirs* would be delicious. You, too, are fond of the idea of the book, and I am sure you would enjoy writing it. Personal enjoyment (however much mixed up with agony it may be, and must be) is the great thing in writing. Don't bother about what the public, so far as you can gather, wants. That is no use at all. It is the cart before the horse. Bother about what *you* want. Rejoice in *that*; and tear your hair over the difficulty of getting just *that*; and get it (as you certainly can); and then—who knows but that great "sales" shall be added unto you?

I haven't nearly so amusing a mind as you have, but I've always taken so much more pains over my writing than you have—or so *many* more pains, I should prefer to say, thus corroborating what I have just said about my painful carefulness. And thus it is that the public is beginning to regard me as really rather a wit. I hope you'll like my new book of essays. It will be out in October, I suppose.[1] Dutton wants to have it in America, and is rather angry that Knopf (a rival publisher) has got my *Seven Men*.[2] Dutton is the one who is

[1] *And Even Now*, published 7 December 1920. Reggie's copy was inscribed "For my dear Reg, hoping he won't object to things said on pp. 317–320." For these pages, and Reggie's reaction to them, see pp. 13–15.
[2] Dutton published *And Even Now* in America in 1921, but Knopf published all Max's subsequent books there. His edition of *Seven Men* (October 1920) contained six drawings and an appendix by Max, which did not appear in the English edition.

by way of doing the "definitive" edition. Heinemann showed me a letter from him that intensely amused me. Dutton began by saying how proud, etc., he was to have this privilege etc., and then burst forth: *"Please tell that splendid old lion, Max Beerbohm, that I"* [1] etc. etc. There you are! That's what comes of taking pains!

Best love from Florence and from me.

Your affectionate   WALTER SAVAGE LANDOR

22 December 1920   *Villino Chiaro*

My dearest Reg,

Ever so many best Christmas wishes and New Year wishes. I send two books—the long-overdue copy of the Herbert book and the just-available copy of my new essays. Bedside books. Dippable-into. The second of them just about as good as I could make it, if that's any recommendation. And the first with a lot of good in it. The first has been apparently a great "selling" success (and had "a fine press"). And I hope the second will do fairly well. I receive booksellers' catalogues naming queerly high prices for first editions of my previous books; so I suppose I am on the up-grade.

But nothing that I've read in recent times has given me half the pleasure I've had out of those two Disraeli volumes that you gave me.[2] Not mere pleasure, either; deep rich joy. Monypenny was a dullard, and Buckle is a greater and more illiterate dullard still, but what matter? The damp flat low-lying soil of Buckle exhales its dense grey mist of dullness only to be drunk up instantly by the Disraelian sun, on every page of the book. Buckle gives the facts, and even his comments on the facts can't for a moment spoil them. And it is absurd to wish, but one can't help wishing nevertheless,

[1] In the Preface (1921) to the Collected Edition of his works Max quoted this phrase as having been written by John Macrae of E.P. Dutton & Co, commenting: "That I was old I knew. That I was splendid and leonine was a revelation; dazzled by the light of which I made a feebler resistance than I should otherwise have made to the whole scheme."

[2] The last two volumes (v and vi) of Monypenny and Buckle's *Life of Disraeli*, which Reggie had sent Max on his birthday in August. The first four volumes had been published in 1910, 1912, 1914 and 1916.

that the book had been written by some fairly worthy person—Rosebery[1] in his prime, or Winston in leisure, or Mallock[2] perhaps. How lucky Gladstone was in falling to John Morley![3] A Buckle or a Monypenny would have blanketed Gladstone for ever. Gladstone's dullness *and theirs*, combined, would have been utterly fatal to the fact of Gladstone's nobility and grandeur. Nothing noble or grand about dear old Dizzy! Part of his charm is that one feels *no* respect for him. Intensely lovable, but entirely un-respectable. One even has the luxury of despising him. An old man ought to cease from playing the fool, surely? But this idea never occurred to D. Or rather, I have no doubt, it occurred to him often, but was always rejected. It is extraordinary to see how, up to the very last, after all that he had suffered and incredibly achieved, he himself remained a mountebank. There are some exquisite anecdotes in illustration of this feat; and I have turned down the corners of the pages where they come, in order that I may easily find them for you to revel in on this terrace which awaits your coming.

Dear old James was here the day before yesterday, and held out hopes that you would be coming about Jan 7th. How delightful! Old James seems very devoted to you. As are Florence and I to him. I do like a fruity, seasoned, Victorian man with *no* ideas, with *nothing* but sense and solidity and—information, I was going to say; but of that old James has of course rather *too* much: it is his only fault. I have a growing horror of "ideas." I am sure that ideas are exactly what is ruining the world we live in. If only the world could return to humdrum old Faith, and thereby to humdrum old Wisdom. But that can't be till all our present civilisation has collapsed and been forgotten. Alas! as George Street would say.

Meanwhile, I rejoice at knowing that your *conférence* was a huge success (as of course it was bound to be, with a *conférenceur* such as you—or is it *conférencier*?—my French grows less and less satisfactory as the years roll by, but I *will* go on singeing my wings, I know not why). Your loving MAX

[1] Lord Rosebery (see note, p. 164) published books on Pitt (1891), Napoleon (1900), Lord Randolph Churchill (1906) and Chatham (1910).
[2] William Hurrell Mallock (1849–1923), author of *The New Republic* (1877) and many other books.
[3] Morley's *Life of Gladstone* was first published in three volumes in 1903.

P.S. I forgot, in my last letter, to say how good I thought that silhouette of you. It isn't accurate, but somehow it has got a great deal of the character of you; and is therefore charming.[1]

P.P.S. I have had a great bout of caricaturing lately. I had thought my impulse for caricature was over. But something touched some spring in me, and I have done more than thirty cartoons, one after another, and I think they are good, and hope they'll be liked.

20 June 1921   *Villino Chiaro*

My dearest Reg,

It is a long time since I heard from you (and, to take the edge off the reproach, a longer time since you heard from me). In the course of which time I have been to England, and Florence has been to

[1] Here reproduced from the original at Merton.

America. She started from Genoa, on her long-promised visit to her brothers, just at the same time as I started with my sheaf of drawings. At this moment she is in Memphis—has been in New York, also in Pittsburgh—she has a brother in every city; but the Memphis brother is the extra-specially beloved one. I am not sure yet just when she will be home again. She will be back *some* time next month. I have been here just five weeks now, after a similar period in London.

Ah, *Londres!*—*parlons de cet endroit!*—or rather, don't let's! In the year that has elapsed since I saw it, it has sunk much lower. It doesn't look *dingy* any more, certainly. The house-fronts have been freshly painted. But oh the people in the streets! Oh Piccadilly on a May morning! I saw ladies and gentlemen in private houses. But only there. They *never* go out—except perhaps the ladies, un-attended, to earn something towards the rent, by night! In the day-time the streets are packed, thanks to the redistribution of what wealth England still has, with perfectly dreadful people—people who were perfectly charming in the old days when one didn't see them, when one had the pleasure of pitying them unseen somewhere in the slums and the sweating-shops, and of feeling how perfectly charming one was to be not forgetting them while one gadded about the brilliant metropolis. What are the names of the Five Towns? Burslem is the only one that I recall at the moment. Burslem will do. London has become Burslem.

From which it would appear that my reputation has at last reached the provinces; for my exhibition of caricatures[1] has had a really very great success—in the teeth of the coal strike, and of the casting down of the mighty, and of the exaltation of the perfectly dreadful lowly, and despite everything that was against anything but dismal failure. I came back home before the private view, etc. to avoid the embarrassments of the boom, which had already begun. But Brown and Phillips have of course sent me weekly re-ports. And I shall have a cheque for more than £1100, I calculate. The "proceeds," so far, "exceed" (as Hall Caine would have said—*would* say, by Jove, for he has cropped up again: the firm of Heine-mann is just bringing out a new book of his:[2] rather jolly!—quite

[1] Max's third exhibition at the Leicester Galleries (May–June 1921).
[2] *The Master of Man* (1921).

like old times!—but to resume) £1430—apart from "gate-money." And everybody has been most "keyind"—the Press collectively losing its head over me, and losing its heart to me, all except Clutton Brock of *The Times*, whom my new style vexed.[1]

I was much amused, by the way, to see that very few of the newspapers gave any prominence to the *Labour* drawings: not that they didn't love them, but simply that they had to dissemble their love. It's very odd, to one brought up in days of freedom, to find dear old England really in the grip of a great tyrannous power. The *Herald* (the Labour daily paper, you know) *did* mention two or three of the Labour drawings, and expressed pain and surprise—but only that such libels should emanate from a man of my genius, charm, penetration, refinement, and so on (which shows that if the worst comes to the worst, and the red flag *does* hereafter fly over Buckingham Palace, and I *am* in London at the moment of the great upheaval, I shall be given some kind of a job—101st private secretary to Overseer H. G. Wells, perhaps).

Which reminds me that H.G.W's two enormous scarlet volumes were here awaiting me on my return, at last.[2] Ever so many thanks, dear Reg. You *couldn't* have given me a present that I should have hated more. I know I "asked for it," as the saying is. You inquired what I should like. I, in my madness, said "H. G. Wells's *History of the World*." I am glad it was only a temporary aberration. I am perfectly sane at the moment of writing. And I have lent the two vols to Gordon Craig—and have implored him not to hurry over them. I want him to read them very slowly. I want him to let them

[1] The long review of Max's exhibition in *The Times* of 25 May was written not by Clutton-Brock but by A. B. Walkley, the dramatic critic, and signed with his initials. After complaining that the Labour drawings were too crude, and describing some of Max's subtler captions, he went on:

"These jokes will be obscure and probably trivial to the great crowd. They are not addressed to them; neither are they to the learned world. They are part of Max's 'figure in the carpet.' They will appeal only to the peculiar apolaustic scandal-loving, politely ferocious London tribe of belle-lettrists, and by these they will be keenly enjoyed. And they will be invaluable 'documents' for future historians of our literature."

[2] H. G. Wells's *The Outline of History*, having been serialised in twenty-four fortnightly parts (Nov 1919–Nov 1920), was published in two volumes in July and November 1920.

sink in, chapter by chapter, century by century, aeon by aeon. I want him to bring up his children on them—*very gradually*. I saw H.G.W. in London, and told him that you had ordered the book for me, and that I expected it had been sent by *petite vitesse*, and how much I was looking forward to it. Perhaps if he himself had *written* it by *petite vitesse*—if he had given, say, twenty years to the job (and surely twenty years for that kind of job would hardly—) —but this is pedantic and unpractical. A man who should say "I'll give twenty years to this" would immediately add "But I need two hundred," and give the job up. The glory is (for there *is* an awful glory) in the job having been *done*: the incredible job, done so neatly too—in a way, neatly—in a *very awful* cheap sciolistic polytechnic way, neatly. But why should I be telling you all this? ...

Thank you so very much for the Stevenson Cevennes book,[1] which reached me by *grande vitesse* long ago. I enjoyed it greatly. S. hadn't, when he wrote it, arrived at his what-a-good-boy-am-I-and-what-a-gallant-suffering-uncomplaining-Scotch-cordial-whimsical-yet-solemn-*best-of-boys*! manner; though even in that quite early volume there are, to the discerning therapeutical eye, visible the seeds of the deep-seated malady that was so soon to carry him off into Abraham Sidney Colvin's bosom for ever and ever.

How are the Dierburgs? But this question is the merest padding. I wanted a short sentence after such a long one. On the other hand, how is Trench?[2] I should really like news of him, for I do really like him. I had *some* news of him, the other day, from Mrs Hone, whom I lunched with at the Hone Villa.[3] She said he looked much stronger and better. And Miss Broster,[4] whom I liked also—how is she? Mrs Hone said she was very busy cataloguing H.T's library.

I have been doing some writing here, since I came back, which beguiles the time of waiting for my dear one's return from America.

[1] *Travels with a Donkey in the Cevennes* (1879), Robert Louis Stevenson's third book.
[2] Herbert Trench (1865–1923), poet and playwright, was now living at the Villa Viviani, Settignano, Florence.
[3] Unidentified.
[4] Dorothy Kathleen Broster (d. 1950), author of many popular historical novels.

Also a little drawing too. The Heinemann 750 edition of my books[1] has all been "subscribed in advance by the trade," and I gather that this is a speculative scheme on the trade's part: the trade will presently, or even at the moment of publication, demand more than the proper published price. You said in a letter that *you* were subscribing. But, if you have done so, do cancel your subscription. You have the original volumes. That is all you want. This edition is only for profiteers who have never read me at all (and don't *mean* to read me, either). This is all very well from the trade's point of view, I suppose; and it's in a way "gratifying" (Hall Caine, again) from mine. But on the whole this sort of success irritates me— seems to me not the *appropriate* sort of success for my rather exquisite talent. The appropriate sort I have always had, and have always liked. You remember my "solemn birthday thoughts" about Sargent and Meredith? This other sort pans out well from the money standpoint. And *that's* very nice of it. But still, it makes me slightly uncomfortable. And it and the terrific boom over my caricatures will inevitably tend to alienate the young, the budding Merediths and Sargents, whose enthusiasm in the past two years has touched and pleased me immensely. However, this is a crumpled rose-leaf; not a bed of thorns; and besides, I am a Stoic.

Have you read Lytton Strachey's *Queen Victoria?*[2] That I *am* a Stoic is proved by my having no jealousy of him at all, though his mind and his prose are so like mine and so exactly like what I should have loved mine to be. For sheer divine beauty of prose, and for clairvoyance of mind in dealing with past personages, and for wit, and for much else, nobody comes within a hundred miles of him. I was rather amazed and horrified that you did not seem to have quite realised what manner of book *Eminent Victorians* was. Pray tell me that you have been respectably bowled over by this other book.   Your loving friend   MAX

P.S. I do hope you have not been giving your *whole* time to reading John Morley? I do hope you have begun and are "well along with" that novel of which you told Florence and me the very delectable scenario. As you are, however, so awfully well up in John Morley,

[1] The Collected Edition of Max's works was published by Heinemann in ten volumes between February 1922 and June 1928.
[2] Published on 7 April 1921. *Eminent Victorians* had appeared in 1918.

let me rather say that I hope that, in the midst of the shadows which are settling down over the western world, a novel will shortly come out which, notwithstanding some grave aberrations, will make great spaces in Anglo-Florentine society very luminous.[1] Do say you do recognise this quotation. Otherwise you *aren't* up in J.M.!

29 March 1926   *Villino Chiaro*

My dearest Reg,

Florence was so delighted to have your letter, and I to have the "Low" drawings.[2] Next time do let your visit be longer. If you hadn't gone away so soon, you wouldn't have had to stand in the corridor all the way home! And every hour and moment of your presence here is a great joy.

I am sorry the phrase "Check, old chap" worried you. My intention was just the reverse. To any earnest chess-player it is always distressing, and even mortifying, to be checked. An opponent cannot prevent this feeling, but he *can* mitigate it a little by reference to deep and unalterable affection. Such at least was my idea. I am sorry it was erroneous, old chap. In future I will say "Check" *tout court*. Or rather I shall say "Check, *Tout Court*" at full length every time. Remember this. Don't say I didn't warn you.

Of all the "Lows" I think I like best the Lloyd George—a wondrous catching of an instantaneous and fleeting (but permanently typical) expression of face; and an exquisitely pretty use of lithographic chalk—not anywhere over-laboured at all. Conrad, too, could hardly be better, though there are traces of the use of photography in doing the head. Joynson-Hicks's[3] head perfect in accuracy and fun, and in contempt for pushful firms of solicitors, but the body over-laboured, and not belonging to the head. Ramsay MacDonald excellent: the self-made Scotsman revelling in himself

[1] Quotation untraced.
[2] Twelve caricatures by David Low were issued as loose insets to the *New Statesman* during 1926. They were published in a portfolio in 1927, and reprinted in *Lions and Lambs* (1928).
[3] William Joynson Hicks (1865–1932) was Conservative Home Secretary 1924–29 and his nickname Jix became a byword for reactionary stupidity. Created baronet 1919 and Viscount Brentford 1929.

and his purity and integrity and readiness and tenacity and all the rest of it. You were very right about the likeness of Low to Pellegrini. If Pellegrini had worked in colourless lithograph, these are just the results he would have got. And if Low took to water-colour —well, then, P. would once more be happily with us.

Love from us both.

Your affectionate   MAX

P.S. Best of all, *really*, I like the Arnold Bennett; because mine of A.B. are better.

Villino Chiaro

10 April 1926

Dearest Reg,

Thanks for very delightful letter. We miss you very much. Here are the Belloc verses.[1] So right of you to want them, for they are very certainly classic. I used to think the end of them was rather a mistake. But now I don't. The sudden break-away from irony into frank spleen and brutality is a fine stroke of art, I think now. . . .

I have attached a tab of paper to the copy of the verses. The side of the tab that is marked "O" is covered with glue. Moisten this very slightly with water and stick it down to a left-hand margin of one of the "Hate Poems"—and there you are, with a volume neatly amplified and enriched. I am nothing if not practical. . . .

Return soon. We keep open chess-box here.

Love from both.

Your affectionate   MAX

[1] On 31 March Reggie had written: "I wonder if it would be too much to ask Florence to copy out that poem of Belloc's about 'where bright young Wernher fell' (or something of that sort). I don't know where to find it and it haunts me. I want to copy it into *The Week-End Book* as an addition to great Hate Poems." The poem, entitled "Verses to a Lord who, in the House of Lords, said that those who opposed the South African adventure confused Soldiers with Money-Grubbers," appeared in Hilaire Belloc's *Verses* (1910).

Dearest Reg,

When I wrote, I had seen only that day's *Secolo*. The day before's had not been delivered here. And I had no notion that Mussolini had been wounded.[1] What a ghastly affair! I have only just learned about it from *The Times*. The *Secolo* that I had seen did not mention the wound. I suppose, from Mussolini's being able to make speeches and to travel, that the injury cannot be bad. I do hope he'll be all right. . . .

Do you take in *The Times Lit. Sup?* If so, and if you have kept last Thursday's number, I wonder if you would post it to me? Our copy has not been delivered.

Did you notice that the *D.T.* described my introduction to Will R's Iconography[2] as "animated and waggish." These adjectives are rather a relief from the usual ones that are applied to my works, and give me a sense of kinship with Frank Burnand[3]—and even with O.P.Q. Philander Smiff.[4]

                Love from us both.

                   Your affectionate MAX

P.S. I wonder if there would be "money" in a Standard Edition of Middle-Victorian Humorists? No. 1, O.P.Q. Philander Smiff.

Dearest Reg,

So delighted to have your letter—which, like all your letters, is so full of good things and also of things that one wanted to know.

---

[1] On 7 April in Rome Mussolini was slightly wounded in the nose by a revolver-shot fired by the Hon. Violet Gibson, daughter of the first Lord Ashbourne. She was deemed unfit to plead and was never brought to trial.

[2] *The Portrait Drawings of William Rothenstein 1889–1925. An Iconography* by John Rothenstein (1926).

[3] Francis Cowley Burnand (1836–1917), journalist and prolific writer of plays, burlesques and light literature, was editor of *Punch* 1862–1906. Knighted 1902.

[4] Pen-name of journalist Aglen A. Dowty (1847–c. 1902), who published *Smiff's History of England* (1876) and *A Comic History of France* (1888), as well as collaborating anonymously in verse-satires such as *The Coming K——* (1873).

I have not yet shaken off the after-effects of influenza—limpness and stupidity, etc.: but I am about to be in my ordinary form, I hope. Florence is now getting all right, though she was very much pulled down by all the awful pain she had suffered for several weeks, and the sleeplessness that resulted from the pain. What she had was a "whitlow" on the first finger of the right hand. This must have been started by a scratch of something poisonous. She wasn't at the time conscious of any scratch—only began to feel a slight pain and see a slight discoloration of the skin. A good local doctor, when the finger began to swell, lanced the thing. But this was not enough. We had a very good surgeon from Genoa, in collaboration with the doctor. There had to be a deeper lancing. Still not enough. The greater part of the finger-nail had to be removed. Great agony, of course (there was no time for use of anaesthetics as the operation had to be done at once, in order to prevent the spread of the poisoning). Florence was frightfully brave, as you can imagine, and very cheerful. But it was an awful time. Thank Heaven, the danger that she was in was averted by good surgery and a good constitution. She had, however, to lose the bone of the top phalange of the finger—the bone came out almost of its own accord. Her finger will consequently be shorter (but only slightly so). She is writing a short letter to you—perhaps with her right hand, perhaps with her left: she can write quite well with her left now.

We are both so sorry *you* haven't been feeling well either. The departure of poor dear X must have acted as a great tonic, however. And the arrival of not poor but (to us) dear Sybil must have been rather a tonic too.[1] I greatly sympathise with your desire only to see the people you *want* to see. In a city such limitation is very difficult—as I found in London. Bologna wasn't *really* a "Bunbury."[2] We wanted to go there in the autumn, but the weather was so hot that

[1] On 2 May Reggie had written from Florence:
"Lady Colefax stayed here some time, in a villino lent by the Berensons, with a very nice son Michael and—part of the time—old Sir Arthur whom you taught me to love. I wasn't well enough to see much of them but I enjoyed them. I really do like her."
[2] The imaginary invalid in the country, used as an excuse for evading engagements by Algernon Moncrieff in *The Importance of Being Earnest*. On May 2 Reggie had written: "I hear of you sometimes as being 'in Bologna' or going there, and wonder if Bologna is your Bunbury."

from day to day we stayed here. And then we stayed because of torrential rains. We got to Bologna in time for Christmas. The person who "was in Rome, quite well and jolly" was not *Will* but *Alice*[1] (who stayed at the Bristol for about three weeks on her way to visit Bettie, the second daughter, who won the Rome scholarship for sculpture in the S. Kensington school). Will himself seems to be getting quite strong again—working hard at his Parliamentary fresco etc.

Dear Dora arrived here a week ago—as sweet as ever, and much worldlier-minded than Florence or I. I haven't heard anything about Michael Arlen dedicating a book to me.[2] If he does so, I shall expect a "wide demand" for my own books to arise instantly on each side of the Atlantic. And God grant that I may keep my head! In the May number of the *Mercury* appears a story of mine that I told you about—"Felix Argallo and Walter Ledgett." It is entitled "Not That I Would Boast."[3] I think it's quite good. I will post the *Mercury* to you as soon as it reaches me. Don't read the story in your club (which probably takes in the *M*); for nothing that one reads off one's own premises ever *seems* good.

Love from us both,   Your ever affectionate   MAX

Dora sends her love too.

P.S. When X was here last and travelled hence to Florence, she wrote soon after her arrival in Florence, saying how kind and what splendid company you were being; and she mentioned the absence of Osbert Sitwell; "but," she said, "of course I have been seeing a

[1] Wife of Will Rothenstein.
[2] The dedication of Michael Arlen's novel *Young Men in Love* (1926) reads:

TO MAX

*I have searched for a phrase to put
beside your name, but I have not
found it, maybe there is not that
phrase, so let us leave it at—*

TO MAX

But the Max turned out to refer to Lord Beaverbrook.

[3] Reprinted in *A Variety of Things* (1928) and again, as "Felix Argallo and Walter Ledgett," in the 1950 edition of *Seven Men*.

Oct 2 1929

My dearest Dig. I remember we laughed here together when Ramsay MacDonald, on becoming Premier, uttered a tremendous paean to the memory of Keir Hardie — the "Don't Keir Hardie" of our boyhood, whom, because of his grave errors in costume, and the brass band which accompanied him in a wagonette when he went to take his seat in the H. of C., we never had thought of revering very much.

Well, R. MacD. has just been going one better than the previous eulogy. In fact, I'm not sure that he isn't slightly dotty.

Mr. Keir Hardie "arrayed in garments of great dignity, and endowed with almost superhuman purity and power."

The Times - Sept. 29

MR. MACDONALD'S TRIBUTE TO KEIR HARDIE.

The new Keir Hardie Institute at Glasgow, which is the only one of its kind in Scotland, was opened last night by Mr. MacDonald. There are committee rooms and a conference hall in the Memorial Institute, and a club which is run on temperance lines. Mr. MacDonald, who was given a hearty reception, said it sometimes filled him with a little bit of melancholy when he thought that to many in the Labour movement Keir Hardie was only a name. The generation that knew the man was steadily being turned out, and before many years would all have gone. Hardie would only be something like a myth in the imagination of the living. He would be arrayed in garments of great dignity, and with almost superhuman purity and power, which always happened when a great man had died and had become a historical figure. But whatever happened to Hardie, he would always remain as the first man in their great Labour movement.

We have just returned here after long wanderings. We were at Aeggi for about a month

(Oh, oh!)
(Laughter)
(renewed laughter.)

— Florence taking sulphur baths there, as last year, and ? feeling gradually better for the change of air. Afterwards up we went to Pongone, a tiny town on a mountains among

good deal of Lady Ida and other friends." This sentence somehow reminded me of something; but I could *not* think of *what*; and then suddenly I remembered what I was reminded of—George Robey— "And of course," swaying one foot to and fro, in a *negligé* manner, "I have been seeing a good deal of"—a pause, and a leer, and then a cut of his little walking-cane on one trouser—"Lady Ida"—roars of laughter from the audience, which G.R. rebukes by saying with slow stern emphasis, "*and other friends.*" I don't think the analogy is at all strained. Especially as X's later manner of dressing is so dreadfully like what G.R's manner of dressing has always been.

2 *October 1927*   *Villino Chiaro*

My dearest Reg,

I remember we laughed here together when Ramsay MacDonald, on becoming Premier, uttered a tremendous paean to the memory of Keir Hardie[1]—the "Don't Keir Hardie" of our boyhood, whom, because of his grave errors in costume, and the brass band which accompanied him in a wagonette when he went to take his seat in the H. of C., we never had thought of revering very much. Well, R. MacD. has just been going one better than the previous eulogy. In fact I'm not sure that he isn't slightly dotty.[2]

We have just returned here after long wanderings. We were at Acqui for about a month—Florence taking sulphur baths there, as last year, and I feeling gradually better for the change of air. Afterwards up we went to Ponzone, a tiny town on a mountain among many mountains. A lovely place. Have you ever heard of it? Nobody else seems to have. We were another month there; and it did us much good, and then we went down to Pavia, also to Voghera, for neither of which is there much to be said.

Have you seen Mrs Harter[3] lately in Florence? We met her in

[1] James Keir Hardie (1856–1915) was a Scottish miner who became Chairman of the parliamentary Labour Party. M.P. 1892–95 and 1900–15.
[2] See illustration opposite.
[3] Mrs Arthur Harter had a villa in Florence. She had been a great beauty, and had published poems and a novel (*A Love Conference*, 1922) under her maiden name, Ethel de Fonblanque. She ran an Italian Society in London, and was a friend of George Moore and R. B. Cunninghame Graham.

Acqui, and she was going on thence to her daughter's—or is it her?—villa. We liked her very much. She isn't exactly cosy, but she's very spirited, and nice to look at, and intelligent. We of course talked much about you and your brilliancy. Where have you been for the holidays? *Holidays* looks rather odd; after all, you aren't a schoolboy or a professional man. I only meant "Where have you been?" You never came here last spring. I hope you will *next* spring, or rather this winter. January is almost always a good time in point of weather here. And it would be a joy for us to see you and exchange thoughts on literature and politics and everything.

Have you read *Jew Süss*?[1] Tommy Lowinsky[2] sent it to me the other day. It's very remarkable, I think, very colossal; but it never seems to me great—though I believe everybody else thinks the world of it. I was reading just before it "Elizabeth" Russell's *Love*.[3] Nothing great about that, but it's deliciously *alive* from first to last, and I wished the vast *Süss* could have caught a spark or two from it.

But Memoirs and Diaries are my chief pleasure in the book-line nowadays. I have read Lady Paget's[4] for the first time; also, to skip back, Lady Holland's;[5] Lady P. a charming but rather dreadful lady; Lady H. dreadful without being charming; and neither of them with the slightest inkling that there is anything dreadful about her; each of them ladling the dreadfulness out to us with a calm, fixed, happy smile.

Have you been going through the *whole* of Dickens? Your tone about *Bleak House* seemed rather to imply that you were going to. Which reminds me that not long after you were here a rather nice Englishman—whose name I can't remember at the moment—came to see us, with a letter of introduction; a man amazingly like Hichens: same face, walk, voice, age, and everything; and not at all the sort of man you would have thought would care much about

[1] A novel by Lion Feuchtwanger. The English translation by Willa and Edwin Muir was published in November 1926.
[2] Thomas Esmond Lowinsky (1892–1947), painter and illustrator.
[3] Published 1925, by the author of *Elizabeth and her German Garden*.
[4] *In My Tower* by Walburga, Lady Paget (2 vols, 1924).
[5] Presumably *The Journal of Elizabeth Lady Holland (1791–1811)*, edited by the Earl of Ilchester (2 vols, 1908).

any books but Proust's and perhaps Henry James's. But as we paced the terrace together it transpired that he was a confirmed and even bigoted Dickensian. I rather hoped he might have read something of mine; but there was no pretence of that on his part; he frankly confessed that he never read *anything* but Dickens. He didn't speak much of Dickens. What he spoke of—in a high, twittering voice—was Dickens's *characters*. All of these he spoke of as though they were people who had actually lived—or were still actually alive. It was a most queer case of complete artistic illusion; and, as we paced together, I wasn't for an instant bored. Lady Dedlock somehow seemed to have wound herself around his heart even more closely than any of the others. "*Poor* Lady Dedlock!" he cried, throwing up his hands. "*Poor* Lady Dedlock!—sitting there night after night in that great gloomy room, with old Sir Leicester. And the sound of the rain on the long terrace outside!" At this point, to my great delight, he shivered. And then, with a look of horror, he spoke to me the name of Mr Tulkinghorn; whom he called "that hateful old man." And "I never," he said, "could understand why it was he *persecuted* that poor woman so, and went *on* persecuting her." "Well," I said, "I suppose it was just simply devilry." This theory seemed to impress him immensely, for he threw up his hands and said with extraordinary shrillness "*Devilry!*—Yes, *that's* what it was! Devilry!" And I think he went away with a great idea of my cleverness. If ever he comes out to Italy again, I shall put him on to you. You would delight in him, as I did. But, dearest Reg, he has occupied a great space of notepaper, and I spare you any more of my writing (the last sentence isn't grammar, but the sense is clear). Florence and I send you our love. Your always affectionate MAX

P.S. I now find that to read small print by electric light rather tires my eyes. So I am going to take the great plunge and experience the last curiosity and after night-fall wear glasses for small type.
P.P.S. Is Alfred Lambart[1] settled in Florence? If he is there, please

---

[1] Alfred Charlemagne Lambart (1861–1943), a kinsman of the Earl of Cavan, lived mostly abroad. He was twice married and was always very correctly dressed.

give him best messages from me. Has he adopted the Anglo-Florentine uniform? Tell him I hope he has refused to surrender his *panache*, and is exactly as of yore.[1]

14 October 1927   *Villino Chiaro*

My dearest Reg,

I felt, this morning, that I was living in the old coaching days—the days when *real* letters were written—and I was and am immensely grateful. Such a lot of things of all sorts, and all of welcome and precious sorts. I am delighted that you are going to write a new novel, and I long to hear about it. Perhaps you will still be in the thick of it when you come here—or shall you, at your old quick rate, have finished it? Poor old X, yes, do use all your ingenuity. It is sad that she hasn't been able, at her age, to settle down. If only she could be persuaded to occupy a comfortable armchair on a roped-off dais on the ground floor of what was once Stafford House and is now the London Museum! We only had a week or so of her here, last time she was in Italy, for the Sitwells were at Bagni di Lucca or somewhere and she rushed off, poor thing, on the chance of getting an invitation if she were nearer to them. It's a tragic survival. . . .

I do so agree about the movingness of the Jews at the Süss funeral. In the earlier part of the book there were four or five pages about the existence and persistence of Jews in the Holy Roman Empire; equally fine. The book ought to have been one twentieth of its size, and *all* about Jews. Gentiles seem to trip the author up. I haven't seen the Napoleon book.[2] It is most good of you to think of sending it to me. I like to think of you sitting and revelling at the *Théâtre Français*, night after night, in your element. It's a pity the Italian acting is so coarse and floppety. One would think they'd be such good actors, but assuredly they aren't. . . .

Craig is in Germany, and I do hope something lucrative will

---

[1] See illustration opposite.
[2] Emil Ludwig's biography, of which the English translation by Eden and Cedar Paul was published in 1927.

great idea of my cleverness. If ever he comes out
to Italy again, I shall put him on to you. You
would delight in him, as I did. But, dearest
Reg, he has occupied a great space of note-paper,
and I spare you any more of my writing
(the last sentence isn't grammar, but the sense is
clear). Florence and I send you our love.

Ever always affectionate Max

P.S. I now find that to read small print by
electric light rather tires my eyes. So I am
going to take the great plunge and experience
the last curiosity and after night-fall wear
glasses for small) type.

P.P.S. Is Alfred Lambert settled in
Florence? If he is there, please give him
best messages from me. Has he adopted
the Anglo-Florentine uniform? * Tell him
I hope he has refused to surrender his panache,
and is exactly as of yore.

REGGIE

A photograph taken by Carl van Vechten in Florence on 24 June 1935

come of it. Teddy *fils*[1] has been in England but has joined "Poppa" in the Fatherland.

Florence sends best love and so does your loving old friend

MAX

17 October [*1927*]   *Villino Chiaro*

Thanks for delightful letter. Most good of you to be sending *Napoleon*! *And*, yes, do send me *Some People*[2]—I mean, *lend* me *your* copy, which I will return exquisitely packed as soon as we've read it. H.N. has been "ever benevolent to my intention,"[3] and when the book was published I was delighted to learn from various press-cuttings that he showed traces of influence by me; and I am delighted that you confirm this notion; for of course H.N. is a very brilliant *and* sound person, and to have affected him even slightly is a waving feather in one's old cap. *En revanche*, I'll post to you his *Swinburne*, in the Men of Letters series—a thoroughly satisfactory summing-up.[4] Had *Gentlemen Prefer Blondes* already been published when you were here?[5] If so, of course I must have raved to you about it. Anyway, of course, you've read it since at *somebody's* recommendation. If you inconceivably *haven't*, tell me, and I'll send it—to *35*.[6] I, who never remember a number, and always have to ask Florence, was so proud of remembering *13*. This, I now remember, was William Nicholson's number in Pilgrim's Lane, twenty-five years ago. Hence the mistake. But perhaps the number was 42—and I daresay I have got the years wrong too.

Love from both   MAX

[1] Edward Anthony Craig (b. 1905), son of Gordon Craig. Writer, artist and film director as Edward Carrick.
[2] By Harold Nicolson, published 1927.
[3] Quotation untraced, but it was clearly an old joke, since in October 1909 Max wrote in Reggie's copy of *Yet Again*: "For Reg ever benevolent to my intention and by his permission, and with good reason—from his affectionate Max."
[4] First published 1926.
[5] Novel by Anita Loos (1925).
[6] Max had misdirected his last letter to 13 Viale Milton, Florence, instead of 35. On 1 April 1933 the number was changed to 45 by the Commune.

My dearest Reg,

Splendid news, this, of your coming next week. We do both look forward so to seeing you. Osbert[1] goes away on Friday; so I expect you won't be pursued hither by X. Rapallo is always supposed to be a good place for people who don't sleep well; and I greatly hope it will come up to the scratch in your case. I ought to have written long ago, telling how much I had admired and enjoyed the two beautiful books. Harold Nicolson has an exquisite, firm touch, hasn't he? I revelled in his pages—every one of them—and shall revel again. And the *Napoleon* is surely a great work, with the special virtue of being so un-German, so *swiftly-moving* all the way through, nothing anywhere over-elaborated. "What is Paris think-ing?"—the recurrence of that refrain gives one a great thrill every time; and it doesn't recur too frequently. How different from the very German Feuchtwanger, with *his* set of refrains that he goes on thrusting in stolidly a thousand times till one howls with boredom! What an awful creature, on the whole, Napoleon was! He had good qualities enough to make any ordinary man loveable. But they weren't nearly many enough to dulcify *him* and his overwhelming giganticity. And what an awful crew of scoundrels and wrong-uns surrounded him. Almost the only person who comes out well is Madame Mère—and her wisdom is so refreshing, wisdom being a quality that Napoleon had no trace of after his earlier years. "Mark my words," she appears to have been always saying, over the tea-cups, to her cronies, "that young man has bitten off more than he can chew" or "that young fellow will come a cropper one of these days." A solid and admirable and rest-giving figure in the midst of that wild vortex.

Dearest Reg, your arrival will be a great joy.

Your affectionate MAX

22 *February 1928* *Villino Chiaro*

My dearest Reg,

It only struck me when I was half-way up the hill that you might possibly *not* have found your bag lying in the hall. On my way

[1] Osbert Sitwell.

down the "drive" of the Bristol, a motor-car, which had been waiting beside the hotel omnibus, passed me, with a man and two
women in it; and this vehicle went up the hill after passing the gate
—possibly to Spezia, or Pisa, or heaven knows where. I wasn't
interested in its destination until—half-way home, as I have said—
it suddenly struck me that your bag might have been placed in that
alien car. I do hope this wasn't so? If so it was, what a bore and
nuisance for you! But of course the occupants of the car will by this
time have discovered the bag and sent it to the Bristol by railway,
and you will quickly receive it. All the same, I hope you found the
bag there. Florence and I miss you greatly, and are looking forward
already to your return to Rap, dear old friend.

Giles Dugdale[1] came here this afternoon and told us that George
Moore was to undergo a serious operation in a nursing-home. I
hope G.M. will be all right. But I am sure that Gosse, with his extraordinary flair in such cases, will have written an important letter to
him and have received an important reply, so that if the worst came
to the worst there would be *some* consolation for us all.[2] I enclose a
cutting from *The Times* that will interest you rather—so vividly
the Paris of the days that we didn't know and that Henry James did![3]

Your affectionate MAX

Monday, 21 July 1930   *The Athenaeum*

My dearest Reg,

Here I am, and here I shall be—not at "the Ath," but at 48
Upper Berkeley Street—till the end of the month. Constance, poor
dear, has to undergo an operation the day after to-morrow—infection of the gall-bladder. It isn't at all a dreadful operation, and

[1] Unidentified.
[2] The last letter printed in *The Letters of Robert Louis Stevenson to his
Family and Friends*, edited by Sidney Colvin in two volumes in 1899,
was one written by Stevenson, two days before his death, thanking Gosse
for the dedication of his book of poems *In Russet and Silver*. George
Moore was in a nursing home at 7 Portland Place from 14 February to
21 April but was too weak to undergo the operation. In the event, however, Gosse died in May 1928 and Moore lived till January 1933.
[3] A column from the issue of 20 February, which printed translations of
four recently discovered letters from Emile Zola to Edmond de Goncourt.

wouldn't be performed if her heart, and her constitution generally, weren't all right. The doctor and the surgeon are agreed that she is perfectly "operable," and that if the operation weren't performed she would have a recurrence of agonising pains. I will write to you again and tell you that all is going well, as soon as she is convalescent. I have told Florence that the operation will be performed on Friday, so that I shall be able to telegraph to her on Thursday that all is well, and thus relieve her mind before she is waiting for the news. And, for that matter, I'll wire to you also, knowing you also would be anxious. Con is very well "in herself" and in very good spirits—gay and amusing, as is her habit.

It is kind and delightful of you (Letter I) to put me down for the Norman Douglas book:[1] very many thanks: I do so look forward to having the book and reading it and (N.D. being N.D. and incapable of letting one down) revelling in it.

Kind and delightful of you, too (Letter II), to write to me about Edinburgh[2] (how awful!—I was just going to spell it Edinborough).

Edin*burgh* is a lovely city—and the University of it, having so sportingly hit on *me*, of all people, and warmly pressed me to its bosom, is a lovely University. "Its" is prosaic and ungracious. I should prefer to say "her"—or even "Her." "My most earnest prayers are with her to the uttermost and the last"—you remember Gladstone's death-bed message to "the God-fearing and God-sustaining University of Oxford."[3] Such places are female. Brav*a*, Edinburgh!

Your wish that Charles Boyd[4] had been alive to hail the occasion is my wish also. He instantly leapt back into my mind when I received the invitation from the Senatus Academicus. "Doctor Beerbohm," as you recall; and the fruity, well-wishing tone, and the clap on the back. I was one of three "Graduands" who had to make

[1] Probably *Paneros*, which was privately printed for subscribers by Orioli in Florence in 1930.
[2] Where Max had been made an Honorary Doctor of Laws on 3 July.
[3] Max quoted the whole of this message in his broadcast "A Small Boy Seeing Giants" on 26 July 1936 (printed in *Mainly on the Air*).
[4] Charles Walter Boyd (1869–1919), Scottish journalist and critic. One of W. E. Henley's "young men" on the *National Observer*. Secretary of the Rhodes Trust 1904–8.

a speech at the dinner on the night before the Graduation; and it seemed natural that I should talk of Charles and his "Doctor Beer-bohm," and, as Charles had been well-known to many of the diners, the speech went very well—especially because it followed a huge long speech by the Procurator (or Controller or something) of the United Protestant Churches of Switzerland (a charming but over-hugely-long man) and a spirited but very lengthy speech by Lowell, of Harvard.[1]

I thought of you at the Graduation on the following day, knowing you would have been pleased. I had a great "reception." Edinburgh being so remote from London, and I so remote from the young, I hadn't expected anything of the sort. But there it was. Huge academic "theatre," with about 2000 people in it, mostly aged twenty or so. More or less loud applause for each of the seventeen scarlet-gowned Graduands as he stood forward to the dais, to receive his allocution from the Dean of the Faculty, and then mount the dais and be capped and hooded. But *rounds of cheers* only for two venerable dons of the University, for one venerable man of Edinburgh, and for the venerable Sir Thomas Barlow[2]—and for the (hang it all, not quite so) venerable me! And thus I was much touched and moved, and was conscious of a quivering of the upper-lip behind the moustache, when I was ushered to my place on the dais, amidst all that noise.

This is all very egoistic. So I won't mention that a charming man, Arthur Bendir, head of a firm of bookmakers in Old Burlington Street, is paying me £600 for six caricatures of racing celebrities. Yet the fact remains that he is doing so. People spoil me![3]

Your loving friend MAX LL.D

[1] Abbott Lawrence Lowell (1856–1943), President of Harvard University 1909–33.

[2] First Baronet (1845–1945). President of the Royal College of Physicians 1910–15.

[3] These six caricatures (of the King of Spain, General C. R. de Crespigny, Mr James de Rothschild, the Duke of Richmond, Sir Hugo Hirst and Mr Ralph Lynn) were reproduced in colour in a racing calendar by Messrs Ladbroke & Co in 1931.

Ever dearest Reg,

How long since we have done aught but telegraph! And the fault has been mine, of course; for my unwillingness to write letters (which I know will be "literary" and would-be-remarkable) has grown more and more pronounced with the passing years. But you know that you are constantly in my thoughts, and are always the dearest to me of all my friends.[1] You held out hopes that you would be coming to Rap. But you never came. I hope you have been having a happy time and good health in the midst of this troubled universe. How odd it seems that we once lived in a time when the world was quite gay and careless, and its ways smooth—and there was nothing for one to worry about but one's own affairs! What a lot we shall have to talk over when we meet, dear Reg! I hope that will be soon.

Florence sends her fondest love. She is going to act again—this time at the Old Vic, playing Aase, the mother of Peer Gynt. It isn't much of a part, but I imagine she will make great beauty out of it. We are starting for England now—as the rehearsals begin within a few days—and we shall be in England for eight weeks. I don't quite know where we shall stay. But the Athenaeum would "find" me; and I should so love to hear from you. I hope all will go well in the crisis.[2] I think it likely that there won't be any really serious trouble between the countries of our respective birth and adoption. You, living in a city, are a much better judge than I. If you have any doubts as to the immediate future, you will of course, won't you? hasten forthwith to some land where it won't be unpleasant for English people. If things didn't turn out well, it would worry me to think of you being here. Albert Burney[3] was here recently,

[1] Reggie answered on 1 September: "To be so placed in the category of your friends is to have been a success in life and made it worth living, and far indeed beyond my deserts."

[2] Mussolini was preparing his invasion of Abyssinia, which began in October, and the British Mediterranean Fleet had been considerably reinforced.

[3] Albert Bernard Burney (who changed his name from Birnbaum in 1914) was born in 1871 and went up to Merton with Max in 1890. The view from Max's rooms in Mob Quad was ruined by Butterfield's Grove Building of 1864, and in 1930 Burney contributed a large sum of money

and the talk hinged continually on you and your wit and your lovely character. He is a great dear. Chesterton was also here lately —*enormous* as compared with what he was; but delightful. But it is absurd to touch the fringe of news, after all this time! Word of mouth is what's wanted. Let us have it soon. Meanwhile, here is the devotion of   MAX

7 September 1935   *41 Tavistock Square, W.C. 1*

Very dearest Reg,

I hadn't been able to go to the Ath (or rather the United S. Club, which is putting us up while we are being repaired) during the past three days; and it was a very great joy to find *three* envelopes in your handwriting. The U.S. is not a particularly emotional club, and I hope none of the members saw signs of how deeply moved I was by the three beautiful letters. Thank you very much, dearest Reg. And incidentally excuse this strangely dismal note-paper.

Florence is out, rehearsing at the Old Vic, and this is the only paper I can find. I of course understand well your wish to be with your beloved and loving servants at this juncture. They must be sad and anxious at their son's departure to Africa;[1] and so must you. Please give them my best messages. If there is trouble—*real* trouble, I mean—between Italy and England, I fear you are right in thinking that even the most popular English residents (such as you) won't have a charming time; and if that turns out to be so, I hope you will go away *soon*, before the uncharmingness progresses and becomes in any way dangerous. Do consult all your most knowledgeable friends. Would there (I shudder at the thought) be

---

towards its deButterfielding. The top storey and a number of ornaments were removed, and the whole refaced with Cotswold stone. Max registered his delight in "A Sight that Gladdened Me" (*Oxford*, vol. i, No. 2, Winter 1934), which ended:

"The prompter, and generous abettor, was an old friend; a coaeval of mine at Merton and my earliest friend there. . . . The years and the seas have parted Albert Burney and me. But across them I send him my love and deep respect."

Burney responded warmly, and their friendship was renewed.

[1] As a conscript in the Italian army.

any possible idea of internments of British and French and other foreign subjects? I cling to the belief that ultimately there *won't* be any recourse to "sanctions" of any kind. England, as you say, is genuinely keen on the idea of the League of Nations, "not *merely* self-interested" (though of course, as you say, the Italians will never believe this). But I think she won't—in spite of the Labour Party etc—be so madly silly and wrong-headed as to make herself and France and Italy weak in the face of sinister Germany. How Germany must be hugging herself with delight at the idea that this folly *may* come to pass! I am sorry, and I expect you are sorry too, for the Abyssinians, but, after all, they are black and barbarous. And their fate is nothing as compared with that of England, Italy, etc.

But let us turn to lighter things. Before leaving home, I went through a lot of old letters, keeping the interesting ones (many from *you*, of course), and among them was one that I kept though it wasn't in itself an interesting one. It was written by a young Oxford man, asking if I would come and give an address to a little club that had been formed to study Architecture, Sculpture and Painting. And the signature was that of him whose eyelashes cut no ice in spite of Mrs Keppel's[1] great approval of them.[2] He seemed to have no premonition of future failure.

It is a charming idea of yours about the Pocket Volumes of my "works." But I rather think my essays are best in their original settings; the early ones with the other early ones, and so on. But I'll think it over. Thank you, meanwhile, for the idea. I think of trying to write a sort of autobiography, and have brought over with me much of the material that might be useful—in case the worst should come to the worst between England and Italy. Also, things of sentimental interest, etc. If you do leave Italy, I think you had better deposit similar things of your own with some Italian friend, don't

[1] Alicia Frederica, daughter of Admiral Sir William Edmonstone, Bart, married (1891) Lt.-Col the Hon. George Keppel (1865–1947), third son of the seventh Earl of Albemarle, and became a great beauty, hostess, and friend of King Edward VII. The Keppels had a villa at Bellosguardo, above Florence, where Reggie had met them. Mrs Keppel died in 1947.
[2] On 1 September Reggie had written, discussing the international situation: "I fear Anthony Eden's long eyelashes (which Mrs Keppel doats upon) don't cut much ice." The original of Eden's letter to Max (dated 20 March 1922) is at Merton.

you? I also took winter clothes. How good of you to think of helping me in that respect!

And how like you to think of giving us a radio!! But we have one. We have lent it to some Italian friends during our absence; and I quite envy them it. It has been a great delight and interest. The B.B.C. is a wonderful triumph of variety and soundness, isn't it? Did you hear G.B.S. and the Girl with the Golden Voice?[1] It was very well done—G.B.S's acting quite capital. But he's no good in a "talk": much too loud and quick—too platformy and grimly determined to be a vigorous hefty youth. G. K. Chesterton *very* good, don't you think? The right technique. A friend in one's room, pensively and quietly monologising. The best voice I've heard is D. S. MacColl's. Next to his the King's. I like Gracie Fields's also. I have only heard one of the "What is the Law?" series. It was exquisite. Almost to be mentioned in the same breath with your reproduction of two English clergymen conversing in an Italian railway-carriage. I wish I had heard Eric.[2] I thought the Vicar of Bray's[3] voice in the balcony scene rather hard and dull. I have a deep regard for the Announcers. They seem to be a lesson to us all—morally, intellectually, and in every way.

The Observers—or Reporters—what *does* one call the men who describe the Derby and Grand National and so on?—are rather rough, inferior fellows, and have such bad coughs. I like very much the female Italian Announcers, with their liquid notes. Did you hear of the young Englishman who, in London, fell wildly in love with the Genoese Announcer, by reason of her voice? Every time he listened to her he felt more and more sure that she must be the most beautiful woman in all the world. He packed a couple of suit-cases

[1] On 23 June 1935 Miss Jane Cain was chosen as the first operator to record the time of day for the telephone and was dubbed The Girl With the Golden Voice. On 17 August she broadcast from a radio exhibition at Olympia a conversation with Bernard Shaw, who spoke from the post office at Malvern, where his play, *The Simpleton of the Unexpected Isles*, had received its first English production on 29 July. Miss Cain believes that the script of the broadcast was written by Shaw.
[2] Eric Parker, whose broadcast on his garden Reggie had praised. It was printed in the *Listener* on 28 August 1935.
[3] On 1 September Reggie had written of the Pope: "Although I am not quite sure that he is the Vicar of Christ, I am quite sure that he is the Vicar of Bray."

and travelled to Genoa. He was determined to marry her. He hurried
to the broadcasting station of Genoa. He explained his resolve. He
was treated with sympathy and cordiality, and was shown into a
small waiting-room. He waited in throbbing rapture. Presently the
door opened. She came in—and she *was* the most beautiful
woman in all the world. Don't you think that's touching and
charming?

Florence was immensely pleased by your beautiful reference to
her acting.

Our fond love to you, dearest Reg, and all our thoughts. Let
me know that this reaches you safely.

Your devoted MAX

30 September 1935   *41 Tavistock Square*

Very dearest Reg,

Florence was so immensely pleased and touched—and so was I—
by your telegram for the first night.[1] Her performance is of the
utmost loveliness, and has made a deep impression. I do wish you
were here to see it. You would love it so. Devlin, a young Oxford
man, aged twenty-four, is very fine as Peer Gynt, and the whole
production is a good one. But Florence outstands.

I don't *think*, in spite of various bad signs, that anything really
serious or dangerous will be done by England. But if it seems to
you likely that such things should be done—why then it would be
very good indeed of you to mention to your influential and kind
friends the case of Florence and me; to say that we have lived in
Rapallo since 1910[2] (except during the European war, when we
were in England); that Italy is our home; that we have no residence
elsewhere; that we are highly respectable; that my books are good—
and my drawings; etc. etc.

By the way, we have *two* little houses now: the Villino and the
"Casetta." Do you remember the peasant's cottage next door (on
the side remote from the Boitanos)? The old man who lived there

[1] The revival of Ibsen's *Peer Gynt* opened at the Old Vic on 23 September, with William Devlin as Peer and Florence as Aase his mother.
[2] Max accidentally wrote 1925, clearly thinking of the twenty-five years
he had lived there.

died some time ago, and the cottage and garden might have been built over, destroying our view; insomuch that we had to buy. The Casetta is now a pleasant and civilised habitation, and we spend a lot of time there.

Living in Santa Margherita is a certain Colonel Pio. He and his wife and his two sons are great friends of ours. He isn't, I think, an active member of the Fascist party, but he had a very distinguished war record, and after the war was sent out to America on a diplomatic mission. He would be the person to communicate with. I am sure he would be delighted to help in the matter. His address is: La Carolina, Santa Margherita, Ligure. I am writing to him to tell him of your kindness—and of the kindness likely to be shown by your friends, should the necessity arise. Meanwhile, I do hope that your money in Italy will be all right. I am worried for you about it. Let me know more. I hope your servants' son will have good health and safety. His parting message was indeed delightful.[1]

London looks appallingly commercial, and so do the inhabitants. But it's nice to see old friends. I think Lady Oxford's epithet "lonely" did not mean "unique."[2] I think she had a vague recollection that once when I was in London I was given a choice of three dates for lunching with her and didn't avail myself. On a subsequent visit, however, when Florence was with me, we did lunch with her; and I really liked her: she had greatly softened. We met her at a party the other night; and she is softer still—quite a dear. She said, "I know you both hate parties. But do come and lunch, and I'll ask *no one but Elizabeth*."[3] Whereat my heart sank very low; for Elizabeth is still just as she was. However—dearest Reg, I will write again—a less dull letter, I do hope. All thoughts and love from us both.   Your devoted   MAX

[1] It read "VADO—VINCO—TORNO" (I GO—I CONQUER—I RETURN).
[2] On 2 September Reggie had written from Lausanne:
    "I have just read in the *Daily Mail* an article by Lady Oxford in which she refers to a dinner with G.B.S. at which the only other guest she could remember was Mr Max Beerbohm, a lonely man and an exquisite writer. Why lonely? Does she mean no bridge and cocktail parties?"
[3] Lady Oxford's daughter (1897–1945). She married (1919) Prince Antoine Bibesco and published a number of novels and other books under her married name.

Ever dearest Reg,

We had been hoping for that message—and here it is, and we are so glad and so looking forward. That day at Bex[1] was very memorable, and now there are to be other days of that kind. It was very good of you to send me those books, all of which I devoured with delight—the Crotchets especially, of course. With what a little difference would Crotchet be a really great novelist![2] And if he *were* one, I'm not sure that I should enjoy his books so much. The great novelists aren't apt to be such good narrators as he; they have to be bothering about interpretations of life, instead of just carrying one along. I like to be briskly, professionally shouldered by Crotchet and carried along. By the way, I hadn't, at the Trois Couronnes,[3] realised that it was there that Henry James met Daisy Miller. I have been reading that story again, with pangs of longing for the dear delicate un-panic-stricken world of sixty years ago.

Till next week—Monday?

Your loving friend   MAX

Dearest of Reges,

It is great good news that you will be here so soon, and great is the joy of Florence and me. The weather today is very good, and looks, *unberufen*, as if it were going to go on abounding in that vein for you. Florence telephoned to the Bristol; and you can certainly have a room with a balcony seaward; but there doesn't seem to be a room with a bathroom attached. The bathroom, we are assured, would be quite *near*, however. I hope that will do? It will be lovely to see you. I hope we shan't all three be exhausted by interchange of news, ideas, etc. But there will certainly be a great

[1] A medicinal-springs village in Switzerland, twenty-five miles from Lausanne. Reggie had visited Lausanne each summer for the past ten years.

[2] Robert Hichens was originally a music-student and in his early days as a journalist had written under the name of Crotchet a weekly article called "Crotchets and Quavers" for the *Gentlewoman*. Max always called him by this nickname.   [3] At Vevey, near Lausanne.

deal to be said. I expect you are very glad about the turn-for-the-better between England and Italy. I am much relieved at seeing now only the back-view of the graceful and well-meaning but deleterious Anthony, and so glad to know that he is "content to await the verdict of history"[1] and let things be conducted meanwhile by persons less picturesque. Of course the Labour Party will work up whatever it can of agitation; but I don't think they'll get much backing in the country: the general feeling will be one of relief—and hope.

D'Annunzio's death[2] has somewhat moved me; for Florence and I and Armando Lanni and Dorothy Lanni were hearing so much about him so lately from Mme Baccara, the comrade of his later years, a most charming woman. Vittoriale is quite near to Drugolo,[3] and one day we had tea with Mme Baccara there and saw—not the poet himself, of course, for he had been seeing no one in recent times—but a vast succession of the fabulously strange little rooms of the abode into which daylight never penetrated; all very beautiful, but beyond the dreams of *A Rebours*[4] and incompatible with great adventureship in the sky and elsewhere. I received from the unseen host a souvenir which pleased me much. You will like it.

And now, dearest Reg, *a domani—dopo domani—quando?*[5]

Your affectionate MAX

[1] From a speech made by Anthony Eden to his constituents at Leamington on 26 February 1938, six days after he had resigned as Foreign Secretary owing to a disagreement with the Prime Minister, Neville Chamberlain, about the handling of the Italian situation.
[2] Gabriele D'Annunzio, poet, playwright, novelist, soldier, airman, revolutionary patriot, and for fifteen months Dictator of Fiume, died on 1 March 1938, aged seventy-four. Since his retreat from Fiume in 1920 he had lived in retirement with Luisa Baccara, a Venetian singer, in a fantastic assembly of buildings high above Lake Garda called *Vittoriale Degli Italiani* (the Shrine of Italian Victories). The forecastle of a discarded battleship was hoisted 1000 feet and set down in the garden; one room contained the aeroplane in which the poet had flown over Vienna during the war; countless others were filled with relics and works of art, books, and a coffin in which D'Annunzio occasionally slept.
[3] The house of the Conte and Contessa Lanni.
[4] Novel by J. K. Huysmans (1848–1907), first published in 1884. Its hero, Des Esseintes, attempts to cure his own *ennui* by indulging in exotic surroundings, scents and pleasures.
[5] Till tomorrow—the day after tomorrow—when?

Friday [Postmark 18 November 1938]   62 Inverness Terrace, W.2
Dearest of Regies,

We were so very glad to hear from you that you were feeling well. Of course the strain of the operation and the cure cannot *entirely* wear away in a short time, and you must take care of yourself and not get tired.[1] When you were with us at Rap, you seemed so wonderfully better and stronger than I could have hoped, but you mustn't tire yourself. And don't let yourself be depressed and distressed about Europe! Things are, as I'm sure you'll agree with me, considerably better now as between England and Italy—thanks to our very admirable Chamberlain. I have no patience at all with the Bloomsbury donkeys who go on snarling at him because he thought an European war would be a slight mistake and was worth averting.

Except that you would be annoyed by them too, I wish you were in London with us—though the fogs have begun in a way that recalls the worst excesses of the time when there was but little electricity. I was much saddened by the news that your beautiful little dog had died. The only comfort in the death of a dog is that to *lose* him, and never find him, and not know where, with what sort of people, he is, is infinitely worse. I am very glad that the dear creature has a successor—who I am sure is devoted to you. Those lovely handkerchiefs that you gave me are the envy of all beholders, and make me feel very grand. I rather look forward to having a cold in the head, so that I can flaunt them even more than I do. Ever so many thanks. Florence has had an attack of lumbago, I'm sorry to say; but it is now almost gone. I myself have had a varicose vein in one leg—which was rather inconveniencing, producing a sort of rash on the calf and having to be kept bandaged. But now all is almost well. We have been "asked out" a good deal by old friends and new; and I enjoy such festivities at the time, but I don't keenly look forward to them, and feel rather tired after them—though not always so. But then, I never was, by nature, much of a gad-about. Perhaps I ought always to be in the country. We shall be returning to Rap soonish, I expect; but not, I think, before Christmas. We shall stay to spend that with Con and Agnes. They and Dora are in very good spirits—though, like me, not young and dashing. I say

[1] In December 1937 in Florence Reggie had undergone an operation for cancer of the tongue, from which he never fully recovered.

"good spirits," but of course the death of dear Viola is a great sorrow.[1] Florence and I went to see her several times in the University Hospital. She had never properly rallied from the very bad attack of pleurisy which she had at her home in Broxbourne. It seems that her heart had been weak ever since an attack of influenza that she had when she was quite young. She died quite peacefully. One will miss her wondrous vitality and gaiety and kindness.

I wonder if you have read a little critical biography of Ouida? I will send it to you on the chance that you haven't. It's the best book about Ouida, far and away. Its author is a Miss Yvonne ffrench, of whom I know nothing. I was so glad that you rejoiced in the Winston book.[2] People complain that he's so like Macaulay. Personally, I think it's a merit. London has lost, since I was away, many of the few beautiful aspects that she still had, and I am very angry, not having forgotten the example of Barry Pain. The Rothermere and Beaverbrook press are sillier and vulgarer than ever. With Bayswater I am pleased: the inhabitants all look so clean and fresh and respectable and happy: a great contrast from the fauna in and around Tavistock Square, where we lived throughout our last visit.[3]

Well, dearest Reg, forgive a dull letter because, with all its dulness, it does carry to you our devoted love.

Your affectionate old   M A X

[*Reggie died in Florence on 7 December 1938, and shortly afterwards Max wrote to their mutual friend Sydney Schiff:*
I had known him so long; he was the earliest of my great friends, and remained always the greatest—and will always remain so. . . . I think his life had been on the whole a happy one, full of interest and fun. Of course he had been too sensitive an observer and feeler of things to be genuinely and uninterruptedly happy in such a world as this. But he had had a good share of happiness. And now he is beyond reach of the other thing, and is at peace, dear fellow.]

[1] Viola Tree died on 15 November 1938, aged fifty-four.
[2] *Great Contemporaries* (1937).
[3] See Max's essay "From Bloomsbury to Bayswater," published in *World Review*, August 1940, with two illustrations by Max, and reprinted in *Mainly on the Air*.

APPENDIX A

OSCAR WILDE

By

[MAX BEERBOHM masquerading as]

AN AMERICAN[1]

Last winter I was standing at the entrance of the most charming of
all Paris restaurants, the Maison Dorée, waiting for a friend who had
asked me to sup with him that night. As he had not come, I amused
myself by watching the people of the night, as they passed by me on
the pavement, their faces illumined for an instant by the pale glare
of the electric light over the doorway.

One of the men who passed up the steps into the vestibule was
wrapped from head to foot in a fur coat of great size, the collar of
which, turned up against the cold, revealed only a pair of curious
grey eyes, shaded by the brim of an opera hat. In his hand he carried
a little ivory cane with tassels, and the smoke of the cigarette which
he had just thrown away still circled round him. The glimpse that
I had caught of his eyes annoyed me—I could not imagine where I
had seen them before. I had a vague notion that it was during a
visit which I had paid to Europe many years ago. My mind troubled
itself to remember more, but could remember nothing.

As I stood wondering, my friend arrived and we passed at once
into the supper-room, where one of the many little crimson-lighted
tables had been reserved for us. At the next table to ours there sat,
with a party of young Frenchmen, the man whose appearance had
so puzzled me.

"Who is that?" I whispered to my host.

[1] So far as is known, this was Max's first published article.

"The fat man?" he replied. "Oh, don't you know? It's Oscar Wilde."

Oscar Wilde! And all at once I remembered that years ago, in the rooms of an Oxford undergraduate, I had been introduced to a young man who was called Wilde and whose curious grey eyes had impressed me at the time; then I had forgotten all about him, had never associated his name with that of the man of whom I afterwards read, in the American papers, that his manners and his theories of art had struck a fresh note in English Society.

Since the days of his youth, however, Oscar Wilde has changed curiously in all but his calm, sphinx-like expression, and the strange, half-fatuous, but wholly charming smile which plays from time to time upon his lips. He had been, as I remembered him, in face and figure most thin, with sallow complexion and long rough hair falling down upon shoulders bowed beneath the weight of premature affectation. His clothes had been ill-cut, ill-brushed, hanging in loose folds, and his manners offensively tinged with the languor of superiority. The man upon whom I now looked, and whose acquaintance I was soon to make, was not only immensely tall, but in proportion fat—fat not after the manner of ordinary men, but rather as some huge overgrown schoolboy, short-waisted, and seeming to carry his size in the vast *contour* of his shoulders. His hair, comparatively short, was brought in smooth curves over his temples, giving a slightly effeminate appearance to the huge oval of his face. But it was in his dress that the most notable change had taken place. The collars he wore, turned back at the points in enormous *revers*, the bunch of Parma violets in his buttonhole, the plentiful satin of his dress coat, as well as the curiously-set green stones on his breast, and the many little gold chains which insinuated themselves from one pocket to another over his portly person, proclaimed in unison a dandy of the type most elaborate and voluptuous. There is, indeed, something amusing in the thought that Oscar Wilde, who began life in an attempt to introduce into London the long flowing neckerchief and velvet knee-breeches of his first cult, has ended by accepting with exaggeration the sumptuary laws of Philistinism herself. A Bohemian friend, resenting this change, which he ascribed, perhaps rightly, to the gradual turning of the great man from the purely literary set of his early days to the smart circles in which he now moves, is said to have sent the following triolet to Oscar, who greatly enjoyed it:

He has cut off his hair
    And his collars are high,
To Bohemia's despair
He has cut off his hair;
But in Grosvenor Square
    They are strict—which is why
He has cut off his hair
    And his collars are high.

But whatever may be said of Oscar's appearance, whether we think, as he himself once insisted in my presence, that he is "most exquisitely overdressed," or whether we agree with the irreverent person who said he looked "like a man who had something to do with Neapolitan ices," we cannot but acknowledge that his face and figure are those of a distinguished personality, that they bespeak someone of intellectual charm, and are excellently in accord with the strange, exotic reputation which is his.

In Society he is adored by ladies and envied by men, not only for the incomparable wit of his conversation—he is infinitely the best talker in London—but also for the great charm and grace of manner with which he is able to imbue his slightest remark. The deferential smile with which he listens to other people, the bow of pleasure with which he notes anything in the conversation which is not dull or common-place, the wave of his hand which emphasises his own playful theories, are all of them quite fascinating in their way. I have heard people complain that the instant Oscar Wilde enters a room, everything must go to the wall; that he stands on the hearthrug and monopolises the conversation, using continuous speech as a means of avoiding repartee. Alone with his admiring cohort of young men this may be so—has not Mr Wilde himself described them as "exquisite Æolian harps that play in the breeze of his matchless talk"?—but in a room full of ladies at teatime, or in the smoking-room of a country house, I have always found in the short time that I have known him that he is as charming a listener as he is a talker.

Nobody is ever offended by the rude things which Mr Oscar Wilde says; yet he is often severe. On one occasion I remember Mr

Lewis Morris was complaining of what he called a conspiracy of silence against his poems. "How I wish, my dear Morris," said Oscar, "we could induce you to join that conspiracy." Another time, at the Savile Club, a certain well-known money-lender, who, since he has been received in society, spares no pains to conceal his Hebrew extraction, was inveighing against the Jews for having, as he put it, worked their way into every trade and profession, and assimilated themselves to Christianity for their own purposes. "Upon my word," he cried, with a strong nasal accent, "I hardly know nowadays what a Jew is!" "A Jew," murmured Oscar, "is one who speaks through the nose and makes others pay through it."

But the Master (as his disciples call him) is not usually so cruel as that; his humour is more often of an impersonal kind, as when he was called upon one evening to arbitrate between a novelist and a writer for newspapers who had grown rather warm over the relative positions of journalism and literature: "I really don't know that there is much difference between the two things," he said, languidly; "the one is unreadable and the other is not read; that is all, I fancy."

Once, in a certain country-house, Mr Asquith, the popular lawyer who has recently sold all and become Home Secretary, was chaffing him about an article which he had written in one of the magazines, proving that Socialism was, after all, the only manner in which Individualism could be established in fact; scattered about the article were certain sentences of a didactic nature, printed for emphasis' sake in italics. "And pray," said Mr Asquith in rather a browbeating way, "what on earth induced you to print those sentences in italics? their meaning was quite obscure. They didn't seem to me to have any particular importance." "Exactly," replied Oscar with a condescending smile; "when I read over the proofs I found certain sentences which struck me as rather stupid and unimportant, and I thought that if they were italicised they would, at any rate, pass muster. Your lawyer's mind was right as usual, my dear Asquith."

Many people in Society, seeing Mr Wilde every day in the Park, meeting him out at dinner night after night, and at some Club in the small hours of every morning, are apt to forget that he is also a distinguished man of letters. They, like Oscar, laugh at Oscar's jokes and think Oscar rather a humbug. If you were to ask them what they thought of Oscar's writings, they would probably reply that they hadn't ever seen any of them. And for this the author is himself largely responsible. He is not only indolent by nature, writing seldom and never save when the fancy seizes him, but he invariably smiles as at some piece of folly whenever his books are mentioned in his presence; although vanity is one of the most salient and not the least charming of his qualities. I remember meeting him in Paris a few days after I had been introduced to him, when he told me he had been breakfasting that morning with M. Zola. "Do you know," he said, "whenever that man writes a book he always takes his subjects directly from life? If he is going to write about dreadful people in hovels he goes and lives in a hovel himself for months in case he shouldn't be accurate. It is strange. Take *me* for example. I have conceived the idea for the most exquisite tale that was ever written. The period is the eighteenth century. It would require a morning's reading at the British Museum. Therefore," he sighed, "it will never be written."

Mr Wilde is indolent and so his writings are few; he has a most fastidious literary taste and so he has produced nothing which is not in its way perfect. Yet what a born writer he is! He is so versatile that he has hardly ever attempted two things of a like kind. He is a writer of poetry, and he is a writer of plays; a critic of books, and of paintings, a philosopher, an essayist and a teller of fairy tales; two or three of the few well-written short stories in this language are by him; he has introduced a new form of novel, has lectured upon art and has even touched politics with a light hand. He has passed through as many phases as Proteus, yet never surrendered one tittle of his personality. In every new venture he has always been equally a scholar, a poet, and a wit, "an amateur of beautiful things and a *dilettante* of things delightful." In future, I am told, Mr Wilde intends to devote himself rather to dramatic than to literary work. I hope this is not so. It is infinitely nicer to read such writings as his silently from between the exquisite covers which always enclose his books and convey to the reader even a faint reflection of their author's identity, than to hear them loudly filtered through the lips of "supers" with an admirable elocution and perfect lack of intelligence. Mr Wilde is far too charming for self-effacement.

If he had lived in the days of Socrates he would surely have been impeached on a charge not only of "making the worse cause appear the better"—for paradox as a method is never acceptable to the many—but also of "corrupting the youth"; he would have been condemned, and would have drunk the hemlock under protest, and one of the corrupt—perhaps Mr John Gray—would have written another *Phaedo* in his memory. Indeed, the harm that Mr Wilde has done within a certain radius is incalculable. For the love of beauty for its own sake, which has absorbed his whole system and inspired everything he has written, is a very rare thing indeed. It is inborn and cannot ever be communicated. And thus the young men who have tried to reproduce not only the manner of "the Master" but his spirit also have, for the most part, failed absurdly. Partly from vanity, partly from pure good humour, and partly, perhaps, because he does not realise quite the unique quality of his own genius, Mr Wilde has always encouraged them, hoping to found what he describes as a cult for the beautiful. He has attempted a vain thing. The chief claim of his disciples to be called artists is that they are not aesthetes; they have no truer desire for beauty—who shall blame them?—than any other young men; they are fascinated by Mr Wilde—who shall rebuke them?—but they will never produce the faintest echo of his power. Sitting eternally at the feet of Gamaliel, they have learned nothing but the taste of boot-polish.

Those faithful servants of Demos, the critics, ever ready to palliate the stupidity of their employer, tell us that Mr Oscar Wilde is "a young man of great natural ability, who has hitherto frittered away his undoubted talents" in the production of foolish and artificial work, and that his frivolity and insincerity are such as to place him beneath the serious notice of the public. A more foolish criticism can hardly be conceived. Apart from the truth that the excellence of a work lies not in the possession of any ulterior motive or original conviction of its author, but in the aspect of the work itself, to say that Mr Wilde is not in earnest is manifestly false. No writer has pleaded with greater zeal and consistency for the preference of Æsthetics to Ethics, or preached more fervidly that the road to Happiness lies behind the broad gates of Beauty. No writer is more enamoured of purpose than he. That people have not flocked into the desert to hear him; that there are more things in his philosophy than ever will be dreamt of in heaven and earth, cannot surely be so justly made a ground of reproach against him as against those who have not the force of intellect to comprehend his sayings as ideas nor the force of character to obey them as precepts. But the rewards of literary virtue are, in this country, for the most part posthumous, and it is not until, after Mr Wilde's death, someone has taken the subject in hand and published a biography—*Wilde: His Life and Work* would be a popular title—that the English people will realise the banality of their present attitude towards him.

After all, the chief weapon of the critics, the brazen serpent by which all literary excrescence shall be cured, is the charge of plagiarism. We have heard the grumble that the idea of an inanimate complicated by an animate personality developed in the story of *Dorian Gray* has been done before; we have steeled our nerves against Mr Whistler's shrill fury at the notion of his friend, "the amiable, irresponsible, esurient Oscar," having pilfered from the famous "10 o'clock" lecture, we have even been told with much tabulation that many of his paradoxes are borrowed from a Chinese philosopher. All this is very likely true, but I cannot see that it matters. So long as the writer has assimilated all his material in a right way and presents it to us attractively, we have no cause to complain. *Les lettres, c'est l'esprit des autres*, and we must not at the end of this century be over-particular. That which is good in literature let us accept "with no questions asked."

But Oscar Wilde himself has written that "to be some one is of greater importance than to do anything," and it is not by his works alone that we must judge him, but by the personality of which his works are a part. That he has genius is, I think, beyond dispute. According to some, genius is the infinite capacity for taking pains; to others, it is to be judged less by its achievement than by its essence. Some say its chief attribute is a kind of ecstasy, twin with insanity, others that it is merely the possession of perfect facility in one direction. But all are agreed that the man of genius must be typical and exemplary, perfect of his kind.

And a more complete figure than Oscar Wilde has not been known since the days of Byron. It is true that he is not, like Byron, a great elemental force. Rather is he a combination of many elements. In his passion for all that is gorgeous in life or stately or mystic he is

Eastern; in his love of gaiety and movement he is a Greek, and a Greek also in his reverence of all that in Art is chaste and simple; his humour is entirely Irish; his literary attitude is nothing but Parisian; there are traces of a German influence here and there in his mode of criticism, and there is much in him (though he may not know it) that is American.

So eclectic a creature is he, that there is in him a little of every time save that into which he was born, a little of every nation save that in which he lives. And binding all these threads into one fabric is something which cannot be described, a spirit which makes him a perfect type and a personality without flaw.

[*Anglo-American Times*, 25 March 1893]

APPENDIX B

For many years the contents of *The Orient* have been written by one hand. That hand is now stilled. Sister Dora had never had robust health, and recently she fractured her arm by a fall. The effects of this accident were too much for her frail body. It seemed to the doctors possible that she might to some extent recover, and live on. But it was destined that she should, after much suffering, borne bravely and patiently, die, in her sleep, on the night of August 13th, and in the seventy-fourth year of her age. She was buried in the City of London Cemetery, Ilford, in a plot of ground that belongs to the Priory.

Mother Cicely has kindly asked me to write something in memory of this Sister—who was a beloved sister of mine. And I take a sad pleasure in obeying her wish.

I cannot remember a time when Dora, who was my senior by five years—she, with her eldest sister Agnes, who now mourns her with me—was not a source of dear delight. She was, it seems to me as I look back, a far more spirited child than I, brighter and more adventurous: something even of a tomboy. I was fairly fond of swinging rather slowly on a trapeze in the nursery; but Dora swung always far and fast, and moreover performed alarming acrobatic feats whilst swinging—regardless of protests from our nurse. I remember also that in a summer holiday, when we were at Malvern, she enlisted me in a sort of Robin Hood system of life. We wore green tunics (made by our nurse) and velveteen caps, and each of us had a horn slung across one shoulder, and carried a bow, and went about shooting into the air assiduously. I was glad the arrows had blunt tips, but am not so sure that Dora was. Two or three years later her free spirit happened upon another phase. "The Aesthetic Movement" had begun, and Dora accepted with ardour the Preraphaelite influence, with the Kate Greenaway influence thrown in. She gravitated to sage-green and terra-cotta and "greenery-yallery" hues, and puffed sleeves and short waists and (I think) sandalled shoes. I liked the effect very much, but I was Philistine enough to laugh when, one morning, as she and I were looking at the window of a music-shop in the Pantiles of Tunbridge Wells, she devoutly said, "What a graceful instrument an harp is!" And Dora, though she did rather like that "an," joined whole-heartedly in the laughter. She wouldn't have been Dora if she hadn't.

Her sense of artistic beauty, a sense that was innate in her, as in Agnes, and was so vital a part of her life, was intensified by a governess, Miss Stone, a gifted woman who had travelled much in Italy, and was an ardent student and interpreter of "the Old Masters." But the altruistic element in Dora, her desire to serve, first emerged in the summer of 1882, when the Beerbohm family was installed for a couple of months in a charming old Elizabethan house at Thurnham. A little boy in the village, the son of very poor parents, suffered an accident that was likely to cripple him for life. Dora, then aged fourteen, had often heard (as who had not?) that the Baroness Burdett-Coutts was a very rich and very good lady. Dora, without saying anything to anybody, sat down and wrote to the Baroness. Some days later, when she was walking in the garden, a gentleman appeared at the gate, and the following dialogue ensued: "Can you tell me if Miss Dora Beerbohm lives here?"—"Yes, she does"—"Well, I have come to see her. I have come from Lady Burdett-Coutts. Would you go and tell her?"—"I am Miss Dora Beerbohm. I thought you would come." And the little boy was medically treated for two years or so, and became quite well and strong.

I think it was when she was fifteen years old that Dora felt, and wrote in her diary, that she wanted to become a Sister of Mercy, and a year or so later that she came to hear of St Saviour's Priory, and went to see it, and resolved that it was there that she would some day be a Sister. My parents were not of the kind that would have tried to dissuade her from such a resolution, if it persisted. I daresay they thought it was evanescent. Dora "came out" in due course, and was, on the surface, a normally worldly young person, and enjoyed the usual gaieties. But within her the resolution persisted strongly; and at some time in 1893 she became a Postulant. In the following year she entered her novitiate, and in May 1896 was professed.

On the day when she left home to become a Postulant, I, accompanying her in a hansom to the Priory, rather supposed and feared that I was saying good-bye for always to the Dora that I had known. I imagined that Sisters of Mercy were a solemn race apart. A callow delusion, of course. Knowledgeable people agree that these Sisters are an ever young race.

In about 1908 Dora's health waned, and the doctors said that she could hardly live long unless she spent some years abroad in a sunnier climate. Two good angels, Mrs and Miss Curtis, great friends of hers, took her away (with, of course, the full approval of another good angel, Mother Kate) and, entirely for her sake, lived on the Continent for five years. They tended her with the utmost care and loving solicitude all the time, in appropriate parts of France, Switzerland, Italy, until at last Dora was able to return, cured, to the Priory.

Twice only in that period did the two good angels allow her out of their sight. In 1910 I had married and gone to live in Italy; and they knew that in my wife's care Dora could take no harm, and entrusted her to us for an interval of two or three weeks. In the later years Dora always spent her annual holiday (usually in the spring) with us. My sister Agnes would come with her; and Miss Curtis would be there for part of the time to make it all the happier for us. How Dora did love Italy! I would not say that in her affection it was a good second to the Priory. England itself was that good second; Italy a good third. Dante was, I think, her favourite of all writers. Her taste in literature was very wide. *War and Peace* she read three or four times (in some French translation of that enormous masterpiece). She said she found it "so very cosy"—a remark typical of her whimsical way of mind. Her favourite things in English Literature were, I think, of the slighter and more "exquisite" kind. She had a keenly sensitive appreciation of the *texture* of writing. To well-balanced cadences, to felicities of expression, she responsively thrilled. She herself had a beautiful gift for writing —as is testified by so many pages of *The Orient*. But—all the more because her taste in writing was so fastidious—she dreaded, four times a year, the approach of the moment when she must begin to write; and when she had completed her task she always felt, as she said, "ten years younger."

Literature apart, her knowledge of life, and of all that was going on in the world, was so remarkable as to be almost puzzling: it seemed to spring from intuition. There was nothing she didn't know of the latest fashions in politics, in social life, in all kinds of life; and on all these points she had a quiet, sane little opinion of her own, gently Tory, and profoundly English.

But such matters, doubtless, were but a small thing in the glow of her inner, her spiritual existence. In the few weeks that passed between her last illness and her death, her mind was as clear as ever. She insisted on knowing all the news of the war. Though it was mostly bad news, and worse news, she was perfectly confident of victory for her darling England, and would have liked to see it. But she was entirely glad that she should die soon, if it were God's will. And so it was willed. [*The Orient*, October 1940]

APPENDIX C

CELEBRITIES AT HOME

No. MCLXXIII. Mr Max Beerbohm at No 48 Upper Berkeley Street

"I do all my work at a card-table," remarks Mr Max Beerbohm, as he welcomes you to a seat beside a green-baize-covered board, upon which manuscripts and caricatures, in various stages of incompleteness, jostle one another in most admired disorder. "You see, it gives a kind of illusion of conviviality to my proceedings, and so does something to mitigate the distress of writing—that 'agony of creation' by which every conscientious writer is afflicted." The card-table which fulfils this useful if abnormal function occupies the central position in the cosy studio-study which forms what may be called the working department of Mr Beerbohm's pleasant chambers in Upper Berkeley Street, a quiet backwater just sufficiently remote, both for peace and convenience, from the whirlpool of traffic that roars and eddies about the contiguous region of the Marble Arch. Among the mingled products of its owner's versatile talent which litter the table you catch glimpses of one or two sketches which attract attention as singularly happy examples of the fantastic humour which has come to be associated with the signature of "Max"—notably a ludicrous fancy-portrait of Mr Bernard Shaw, grown sleek and portly under the beneficent influences of domesticity, and an equally droll and good-humoured libel upon a prominent dramatic critic not unknown to readers of this journal.

But it is impossible to be long in this citadel of caricature without observing that its pervading "note" is one of admiration for the genius of Carlo Pellegrini—in your host's opinion, as in that of most competent judges, by far the best caricaturist who has lived within our time. The brilliant and lamented "Ape," in fact, may be described as the presiding spirit of Mr Beerbohm's sanctum, the whole of one wall being allotted to a series of his famous *Vanity Fair* cartoons; while at the opposite end of the room, on each side of the fireplace, hang a pair of original cartoon-drawings of larger size, in which the forms of Mr Henry Chaplin and the late Mr Christopher Sykes respectively are bodied forth, with the characteristic blend of fidelity and suggestive humour, by the same inimitable hand. Here, too, is a speaking likeness of Pellegrini himself, in his habit as he lived, drawn for the caricaturist and inscribed "*A lui*" by the master-hand of Degas. A memorial of an artist of another school, who died all too soon for his fame, is the portrait of Aubrey Beardsley—taken during his last unavailing quest of health in southern latitudes—which is not the least cherished of Mr Beerbohm's possessions. Above the bookshelves, which "speak volumes" for the catholicity of your host's literary tastes, you notice a pair of charming last-century prints of his Oxford college, Merton; and elsewhere room is found for an amusing allegorical pen-and-ink memento of his Carthusian days. Hard by is an artistic curiosity of a very different character, in the shape of a huge metal "sign" which once adorned an old shop in a Surrey village, and which displays the full-length counterfeit presentment of the once famous harlequin Will Tarleton, in all the pantomime bravery of tights and spangles, the picture being executed with an amount of technical skill which speaks more than well for the ability brought by the artist to his unambitious task. You realise that Mr Beerbohm's taste in art is as eclectic as in literature as you pass from this product of undistinguished talent to the fine original Landseer drawing of a recumbent lion, from that to Mr Steer's pretty "Dieppe" sketch, and thence to a large and somewhat sombre canvas on which Mr Will Rothenstein shows Mr Beerbohm in the midst of a group including Mr Walter Sickert, Mr D. S. MacColl, Mr Charles Furse, and other artists. With regard to his books he will assure you, with unwinking gravity, that he has no sympathy whatever with the vice of the bibliophile, and always cuts books with his thumb; further, that his collection contains no volume of the slightest value, any such that might at any time be found on his shelves being the property of confiding friends which he has duly forgotten to return. On the subject of dogs he is more reverent, and his sentiment is evidently appreciated as it deserves by the graceful Pomeranian "Niki," who, it is clear, is fully compensated by his master's devotion for his somewhat violent transition from the quiet of his Florentine birth-place to his home "amid London's central roar," despite the fact that he was narrowly saved from a tragic end on the very day that he came into his present owner's possession.

Looking back upon his five years' experience as a Charterhouse boy, Mr Beerbohm is moved to wonder that people should profess to regret their schooldays, and to conventionally recall them as the happiest period of their life. Personally, he found the exigencies of his school routine an almost unsupportable burden, though he is careful to insist, with abstract enthusiasm, that Charterhouse is a most excellent school. In these days of his emancipated manhood, he can imagine few more exquisite pleasures than to return to the scene of his former scholastic servitude and watch boys of a later generation bearing the same yoke and doing the same things at the same remorselessly unvarying hours, with the triumphant sensations of a quondam victim who has escaped for ever from the toils. At Oxford, he will tell you, he found life wholly congenial, and enjoyed himself thoroughly—a fact which he attributes to his strict fidelity to the conviction that the undergraduate, like the nation, is happy who has no history. By way of putting this theory into operation, he carefully refrained from anything in the nature of definite action—including the taking of his degree—during the four years of his university career. Being congenitally free from athletic proclivities, a circumstance for which he gives the credit to his Dutch–German–Lithuanian ancestry, he neither rowed nor played cricket; nor did he "orate" at the Union or join the O.U.D.S., or do anything else that involved an undesirable activity, mental or physical. As for his day, "one breakfasted, and smoked a cigarette or two, and there was a lecture that one had to attend, and then one played some kind of a game, and then—well, the day was pretty well over."

It was in the intervals of these exacting occupations that he made his early essays in literary composition—a form of labour which he will confidentially assure you he regards as of all varieties perhaps the most thoroughly tiresome and objectionable. Having succeeded in making the critics angry by means of a "Defence of Cosmetics" in the receptive pages of the *Yellow Book*, he found, later on, a more popular platform for the exposition of his quaint philosophy in the columns of the *Daily Mail*. Since that remote period—now some two or three years ago—Mr Beerbohm has been able to publish his *Works*, and *More*, and he is now engaged in illustrating the art of unconventional dramatic criticism for the weekly instruction of the readers of the *Saturday Review*. His theory of the whole duty of the public writer is that he should say exactly what he has to say in the way that suits him best; that he should take his own time about it; and, above all, that he should be unfailingly careful to "give himself airs." If he abides by these simple rules, he need write but little—"the less the better"—and is assured of obtaining a recognised position and those satisfactory terms at which he naturally values his literary products. The most fatal mistakes he can make are to underrate himself and to cheapen his work by doing much of it. As for dramatic criticism, Mr Beerbohm is inclined to regard it, on the whole, as a rather depressing exercise, but finds by experience that its tedium may be considerably mitigated by the easy expedient of gliding from the matter in hand as soon as it becomes wearisome into the discussion of some more or less irrelevant subject. He confesses that he has no enthusiasm for the theatre; the only theatre he ever took quite seriously was a cardboard affair given to him on his fifth birthday. Nor has he ever wished to be an actor. Since the ill-starred evening when he hopelessly ruined a domestic charade by entering in the character of a Turkish slave and salaaming with misdirected vigour in the wrong place he has felt convinced that his half-brother has absorbed all the theatrical genius of his family.

When you desire to elicit the views of "Max" as to his remarkable work as a caricaturist you are confronted with the initial difficulty that he flatly refuses to regard this branch of his versatile achievement as "work" at all. He does these things, you learn, because it comes naturally to him to do them, and he disclaims any technical ability as a draughtsman with a frankness that would satisfy his most exacting critic. But his theoretical philosophy is no less dogmatic on this subject than on others, and he holds that it is the business of the caricaturist to caricature—in other words, to seize mercilessly upon the points of the subject's features, expression, and general appearance which lend themselves to burlesque, and to emphasise them for all they are worth, with a frank disregard for the feelings of the victim or the remonstrances of his friends. To do this, of course, is to invite hatred and court resentment; and the most pitiless caricaturist since Pellegrini cheerfully recognises that the art is of necessity an unpopular one, and that to attack a man with the weapon of ridicule in the most vulnerable points of his anatomy is not to catch the nearest way of securing the goodwill of himself, his family, and his admirers. This, however, and nothing less, is caricature, as "Max" understands it; and no one who has studied the brilliantly fantastic works of his irrepressible pencil will accuse him of lacking the courage of his opinions. For he does not even hesitate to include brother *littérateurs*, and even brother dramatic-critics, in his Chamber of Horrors—although his little play, *The Happy Hypocrite*, is to be produced at the Royalty Theatre within a few days.

[*The World*, 5 December 1900]

APPENDIX D

THE MAISON LEFÈVRE[1]

By Max Beerbohm

My memory often travels back to it fondly. I spent there some of the happiest days of my youth.

It stands—I hope I need not say "stood"—exactly opposite to one court-yard of the Hôtel de Ville, Dieppe. It belonged to old Madame Lefèvre, and in days past, when the Emperor and Empress used to come sometimes to Dieppe and stay in the Hôtel de Ville, it had been used as a lodging-house for some seven or eight of the equerries and other courtiers for whom there was no room in the great building over the way. Here it was that these distinguished, these whiskered and more or less frivolous gentlemen, had slept and eaten. And they had eaten well, for Madame Lefèvre was a very good cook. Their approval had given to the little house a cachet which it still had in the first year of this century.

It was in the August of that year that I first sojourned there. I had been recommended to do so by Walter Sickert, who loved the place. Whistler, his early master, had loved it too, but in none of the Augusts that I was destined to spend there did Whistler re-appear. This was perhaps a good thing, for the *maître* was no longer *cher*, having become very violent against Walter, and having even called him, for no good reason whatsoever, Judas. The only fracas that I ever witnessed *chez* Lefèvre occurred during my very first luncheon there. At one of the seven or eight tables was seated an elderly Frenchman in company with a very pretty young lady. I was told that she was a Russian dancer, known in several capitals as La Bunskaya. In through the open door from the sunny street came

[1] This undated, and so far as is known unpublished, essay is printed, by kind permission, from the original manuscript in the University of Texas.

a man bearing a milliner's hat-box. La Bunskaya had, it seemed, ordered a hat. But neither she nor her companion was willing to pay for it on delivery. There was some such altercation as might have arisen between Whistler and Walter. The flushed bringer of the hat hissed out something detrimental to the repute of La Bunskaya, and instantly all the other men in the room were on their feet, shouting "*A la porte, Monsieur!*" I myself was shouting as loudly as though I had known the lady all my life. And amidst a deafening din the envoy of the shop withdrew in deep embarrassment, but not without the hat.

My mention of such a name as La Bunskaya might lead you to suppose that Lefèvre's was an expensive establishment. It was not so. It was, in spite of the aforesaid cachet, far from being so. Otherwise I couldn't have stayed there. I think that for staying there one paid nine francs a day, "*tout compris*"—"*tout*" except wine. And this one exception made very little difference to one's weekly bill. For *vin rouge ordinaire*, of which I drank always a bottle at luncheon and another at dinner, cost next to nothing in those blissfully cheap days. I am afraid that my capacity for absorbing light wine without apparent ill-effects rather amazed and troubled the two Frenchmen who, year after year, sat at the same round table with me and with Sickert and with Reginald Turner, dearest of all my friends.

Monsieur Kratz was one of those two. He was also *conseiller* of the Cour de Cassation, and as charming an old gentleman as can be imagined. He dressed rather like a tramp, but to see him enter the dining-room was a good lesson in deportment. It was with an exquisitely rhythmic movement that he swayed his spare body and bent his shapely bald head in all directions, so that no one at any table did not receive his benign old smile. He wafted one much further back than the days of Louis Napoleon. He took one as far as those of the Roi Soleil. "*Dans ma jeunesse*" was a phrase with which he usually prefaced anything that he had to say in the course of a meal; and instantly one seemed to see him in a periwig. But he was no disapprover of the modern world—the modern world as it was then. Or at any rate he was too polite to disparage it. I wonder if his good manners would preserve their goodness now?

The other Frenchman had also great charm. He was Camille Prévost, the famous *maître d'escrime*. At the time of which I write, he was in his middle years, and though he did not "dress the part,' and always wore a black tail-coat and white duck trousers, looked exactly like an Arab chieftain. He was acknowledged to be the greatest living exponent of the *haute école* in fencing. It was said that a miss by Prévost was better than a hit by any other man. He had once lived for six months in England, and spoke English with as pure a classicism as he showed in manipulation of the rapier. I have not had news of him in recent years. I hope he is alive and well—and perhaps in England, where his heart would be less stricken than elsewhere.

I wish I were young again and were at this moment sitting there at that round table with him and old Kratz, and Sickert and Reggie Turner, in that unthreatened world, that world of ease and good talk and laughter.

INDEX

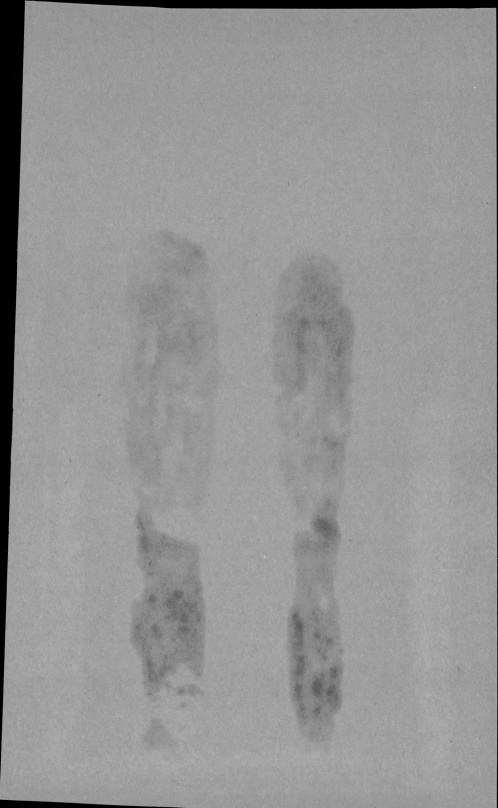

DATE DUE	